TREATISE

ON

SERVICE EXPLOSIVES.

1907.

The Naval & Military Press Ltd

Published by

The Naval & Military Press Ltd
Unit 5 Riverside, Brambleside
Bellbrook Industrial Estate
Uckfield, East Sussex
TN22 1QQ England

Tel: +44 (0)1825 749494

www.naval-military-press.com
www.nmarchive.com

In reprinting in facsimile from the original, any imperfections are inevitably reproduced and the quality may fall short of modern type and cartographic standards.

CONTENTS.

		PAGE
INTRODUCTION		1

Part I.—GUNPOWDER.

CHAPTER.		
I.	Introductory—Constitution and Action of Explosive Substances	7
II.	Manufacture of Gunpowder	19
III.	Examination and Proof of Gunpowder	32
IV.	Products of Fired Powders and Changes taking place on Explosion	40
V.	History of Gunpowder	47
VI.	Explosive Compounds	54

Part II.—GUNCOTTON.

	History, Chemical and Physical Properties of Guncotton	57
VII.	Manufacture of Guncotton, Ordinary or Old Process	69
VIII.	Manufacture of Nitro-Glycerine	80
IX.	History, Properties, etc., of Smokeless Powders and Cordite. Manufacture of Cordite	95

	Part III.—MISCELLANEOUS EXPLOSIVES.	107
	Appendices	121
	Addendum	152

APPENDICES.

APPENDIX		PAGE
I.	Gravimetric Density Table	121
II.	Work done by Gunpowder	122
III.	Manufacture of Powder	123
IV.	Conditions of acceptance of Powder	124
V.	Conditions of acceptance of Cordite	125
VI.	Guns for which Cordite is intended	126
VII.	Explosives Act, 1875—Heat Test	128
VIII.	Exudation Blasting Gelatine	136
IX.	Stability	137
X.	Addenda	152
	I. Heat Tests, various	152
	II. Silvered Vessel Test	155

LIST OF PLATES.

PLATE		OPP. PAGE
I.	Burning Charcoal	10
II.	Sulphur Refining	12
III.	Saltpetre Refining	15
IV.	Incorporating Mill	20
V.	Breaking down Machine	21
VI.	Hydraulic Press	22
VII.	Granulator	23
VIII.	Glazing Barrels	25
IX.	Finishing Reel	26
X.	,, ,,	28
XI.	Prismatic Powder Machine	29
XII.	Cam Machine	30
XIII. XIV. }	Cotton Waste Machine	69
XV.	Beating Engine	71
XVI.	Poacher	72
XVII.	Cotton-Hydraulic Press	73
XVIII.	Nathan & Thompson Apparatus	75
XIX.	Nitro-Glycerine Factory	80
XX.	Cordite Incorporation	84
XXI.	Washing Tank	85
XXII.	(Figs. 1a and 2a) New Nitrating Process	89-90
XXIII.	Incorporating Mill Cordite	102
XXIV.	Reeling Gear Cordite	104
XXV.	,, ,, ,,	106
XXVI.	Press Rifle Cordite	106

INTRODUCTION.

A considerable number of substances are known which under certain conditions "*explode*."

An explosion is some sudden or rapid disturbance or disruption of matter. It may arise from several causes.

In an explosive action there is (firstly) always some change of volume. Perhaps a steam boiler explosion illustrates this. A quantity of highly heated and confined water flashes rapidly into extremely bulky steam. Secondly, some heat change—rise in temperature—causing a rapid expansion of some material. Thirdly, some molecular change due to potential or latent energy becoming converted into actual energy of motion. This may be without final change of volume of the materials.

The substances in actual use as explosives may be classified in various ways, but possibly the most useful is into those employed as gunpowders or for projecting something to a distance—propellants, and into blasting explosives or detonators.

A propellant is an explosive such that its rate of explosion can, to some extent, be regulated within certain time limits. Its action must be of such duration that the inertia of the projectile is overcome. It then produces a gradual or regular effect and something, with which it is in suitable contact, can be projected in some definite manner.

A *detonator* or detonating substance is one that on its explosion produces a disturbance of exceedingly short time duration. It may be extremely violent, but as a rule, owing to the short duration of the effect in time, materials in its proximity are not projected so much as they may be disintegrated or powdered, or even undergo molecular disruption; the time being far too short for the inertia of the neighbouring matter as a mass to be overcome.

It is doubtful if any one substance can be called a perfect detonator or perfect propellant. Some things can be made to act as one or the other—more or less completely—by slight alterations of method of excitation.

The terms "high" and "low" explosive are sometimes employed in the sense of detonator or propellant respectively.*

In some cases the products of this combustion are gases. During the process heat is produced and much of this heat energy is expended on these gaseous products causing them to expand very considerably. The most commonly occurring combustibles contain carbon and hydrogen both of which in

---

* In most cases to-day, explosive action is due to a rapid combustion In the ordinary act of "combustion" some substances are combining chemically with oxygen.

burning produce gaseous products—carbon mon- or di- oxide (CO or CO_2) and water or steam (H_2O). Sulphur also produces a gaseous product—sulphur dioxide (SO_2).

The rate at and area over which the combustion is taking place often determines whether the action is simply burning or explosion. Many instances of this will occur. Petroleum* burns quietly when drawn up into a lampwick and there vapourised and burnt on the spot. But if petroleum (or any similar oil) be vapourised and the vapour mixed with air or oxygen and the mixture, or some part of it heated to a particular definite temperature combination will take place throughout the whole volume practically at once and an explosion results. This passage from ordinary quiet burning to explosion is better seen in the case of a powder like coal dust or flour. A little heap of dust of either of these substances is somewhat difficult to ignite or start burning. But if either of them be well diffused as dust in the air of a room and an electric spark or a flame applied at one point a "dust" explosion can be obtained; the combustion spreading from particle to particle with great rapidity. In this sort of explosion the oxygen of the air is the supporter of combustion and is surrounding each particle, handy to commence action when the requisite initiative, viz., a certain necessary igniting temperature, is produced in any part of the mixture. When the combustion once starts between one dust particle and its surrounding air the heat produced is (generally) more than enough to transplant the action throughout the mass.

When 1 gramme of hydrogen burns with oxygen to produce 9 grammes of steam sufficient heat is produced to warm 34,000 grammes of water from $0°$ to $1°$ C. One gramme of carbon, similarly burning to form carbon-dioxide (CO_2), produces heat sufficient to warm 8,080 grammes of water $1°$ C.

These quantities are generally spoken of as Calories. One gramme weight of water heated $1°$ C. being the unit.

Now suppose the 1 gramme of hydrogen to occupy 11 litres volume and the 8 grammes of oxygen to occupy 5·5 litres at $0°$ C. They combine and 34,000 units of heat are expended on the 9 grammes of product. Supposing the steam to have the same specific heat as water the temperature should be $34,000/9 = 3,777°$ C. But the specific heat of steam is about half that of water so that this temperature figure must be almost doubled.

It is probable that the specific heat of steam increases very much with the temperature.

Assuming, for an example only, that the temperature is $7,000°$ C. what effect would this have on the volume of the steam? When one volume of, any, gas at $0°$ C. is heated to $273°$ C. it becomes two volumes if there be room for it to expand. If the gas be in a closed vessel so that it cannot expand or escape and be then heated from $0°$ to $273°$ C. it will

---

* Liquids do not burn as such, they must first be vapourised.

exert an additional atmosphere pressure on the walls of the containing vessel. So that if heated in a closed vessel to 7,000° C. the pressure produced would be about 25 atmospheres or 375 lbs. on the square inch. The 16·5 litres of mixed gases produce 11 litres of steam which should be expanded (roughly speaking) to 280 litres.

A mixture of hydrogen and oxygen, or air, explodes very violently. It is a rapid action, but not sufficiently so to be called a detonation, although much force is exerted as will be understood from the foregoing.

Carbon is a solid, as charcoal, of about the same specific gravity as water; as coke or gas carbon or graphite the specific gravity rises to 2·5, 2·8, and as diamond to above 3.

When completely burnt in oxygen the reaction is shown by $C + O_2 = CO_2$, which means that 12 parts of carbon unite with 32 parts of oxygen. Assuming these parts to be grammes then 12 grammes of carbon may be taken to represent (for convenience) a gramme-atom of carbon, and the 32 of oxygen represent a gramme molecule (O_2), and the expression CO_2 a gramme-molecule, or 44 grammes weight of carbon-dioxide. This quantity occupies as gas at 0° C. a volume of 22·4 litres.*†

As 1 gramme of carbon produces 8,080 units of heat in combustion to CO_2, a gramme atom produces, in round numbers, 97,000 units. Supposing again that all the heat of this combustion to be expended on the 44 grammes of product and that its specific heat was unity, like water, the temperature should be, roughly, 2,200° C.; but the specific heat of CO_2 is one-fifth or one-quarter, probably, that of water, so that the temperature should be much higher, say 8,000° C.‡ The 22·4 litres of oxygen, therefore, should give about 650 litres of CO_2, or 29 atmospheres pressure.

In practical explosives atmospheric oxygen is not depended upon as the combustion supporter. Oxygen can exist in combination with other elements in (for our purpose) two states, in one of which it has done some work at the moment of combination, as in the two instances (water and carbon dioxide) just given, and produced some heat. The compounds thus resulting are in a state called "Exothermic."

In another set of compounds a considerable amount of energy, in some form or manner, must be expended to force oxygen into combination. These compounds are distinguished as Endothermic. These are not absolute but relative states.

An oxygen compound of the "exothermic" class is of no use in an explosive. It is a very difficult matter indeed in the cases of some exothermic compounds to drive oxygen from them, and in many almost impossible.

---

* The 32 grammes of oxygen also occupy the same volume, and generally the molecular formulæ and molecular weights in grammes of all gaseous substances represent the same volume of 22·4 litres.
† This point is useful to note.
‡ These temperatures cannot be directly measured.

On the other hand endothermic oxygen compounds can with more or less ease part with a portion or the whole of their oxygen. In many compounds the oxygen may be considered as being in a solid, or liquid condition. On the resolution or decomposition of the compounds the oxygen assumes its usual gaseous state or forms gaseous compounds.

The number of known endothermic substances is not large. Very few occur naturally; most are the products of more or less complex chemical operations.

Calcium, magnesium, potassium, and sodium nitrates are naturally occurring endothermic compounds. They doubtless result from the effect of electric discharges in atmospheric air whereby oxides of nitrogen, and finally nitrates are produced. The two last-mentioned compounds are practically the source or starting materials from which most of our explosive compounds are made. They are represented by the formulæ KNO_3 and $NaNO_3$, which really mean that in 101 parts of KNO_3 39 are potassium, 48 oxygen, and 14 nitrogen, and in 85 $NaNO_3$, 23 are sodium, 48 oxygen, and 14 nitrogen, by weight. In both cases, five-sixths of this large quantity of oxygen is available for external work, such as the combustion of carbon, sulphur or a metal. In fact, if either of these substances be heated pretty strongly decomposition finally ensues in the manner shown by the equation, $4KNO_3 = {}^2K_2O + {}^2N_2 + {}^5O_2$.

The meaning of this equation is that from 202 parts of solid potassium nitrate 108 are gaseous. The volume of this weight of nitrogen and oxygen, and the change of volume on the decomposition of the nitrate are indicated by the equation.

The specific gravity of saltpetre is (about) 2, that is, 200 grammes occupy a trifle under 100 c.c. volume. The 28 grammes of nitrogen occupy at 0° C. 22·4 litres, and 80 grammes of oxygen occupy 56 litres. Neglecting the potassium oxide, K_2O, the change of volume is from 100 to 78.200.

In ordinary gunpowder and other explosives the source of oxygen is saltpetre. The combustibles are charcoal (which contains carbon, hydrogen, and oxygen), cellulose (also carbon, hydrogen and oxygen), &c. The carbon is the main constituent in these substances, and the final products are carbon-dioxide, water and some carbon-monoxide. Sulphur produces a gas—sulphur-dioxide—and then some solids, sulphates or sulphides.

The volume of gases is determined, almost entirely, by the quantity of saltpetre. Steam occupies the same volume as its contained hydrogen, and the carbon oxides have the same volume as their contained oxygen.

During the explosion of gunpowders the greater part of the heat of combustion of the carbon and hydrogen is expended on the gaseous products causing them to expand, or increase their volume in accordance with the law of expansion.*

---

* Gases expand regularly 1/273 of their volume at 0° C. for every 1° C. they are heated, $\therefore$ when heated from 0° to 273° a given volume will be doubled, or if in a closed space the gas pressure in that space will be doubled.

As the foregoing indicates, most explosives are independent of external atmospheric oxygen for their action.

Combustion in oxygen, and its attendant heat production, is not the only cause of an explosion or reason for a compound or mixture to be "explosive."

The production of larger volumes of gases—or the formation of any gas—is not necessary.

Several substances, notably glass, can by suitable treatment be rendered explosive.

The long-tailed glass bulbs called Ruperts drops, and the tubes known as Bologna phials are examples. These articles are made by rapidly chilling glass from the melting temperature. They are considerably harder than the same glass cooled slowly. On being scratched to a certain depth with some hard and sharp substance this chilled glass will crack and fly about with considerable force. The Ruperts drops generally produce a coarse powder the particles of which are not sharp edged like pounded glass.

The probable cause of their somewhat violent bursting when filed or the tail broken is that the glass is in a state of internal strain owing to the material occupying at the ordinary temperature the same, or nearly the same, volume it occupied when melted. Glass on melting expands or occupies a larger volume than when solid under ordinary conditions. If a drop of red hot melted glass be chilled so that a rigid outer skin is formed the next interior layers will solidify in turn and adhere to the skin. This process will proceed until all is solid. But the outer skin retains the size of the melted and expanded material. As the interior portion solidifies there is contraction, and finally there is not enough material to fill the space, so vacuus spaces, which appear like gas bubbles, are left. There is therefore a state of tension between the outer skin and the interior portions. On breaking the skin at any part this tension, or spring, is released, and the whole drop flies into powder, the glass regaining its normal volume.

A number of compounds are of this type. They do not contain oxygen. There is no combustion possible, and they give off very little or no gas. The explosion of Ruperts drops is due to molecular strain, and something identical or very like this state exists in certain compounds. For instance, some compounds of acetylene decompose by friction or heating with great violence, but produce no measurable quantity of gases. They simply fall in pieces, that is into their elementary components, and at the same time some of the energy which was rendered potential at the moment of formation becomes active.

The explosion of a boiler is not quite of this class, but it is not a case of combustion. When water and steam are confined in a vessel and kept at a higher temperature than the boiling point of water, there is a strain and pressure on the sides of the vessel. If this be suddenly released by a part of the vessel giving way there is a sudden production of steam from the superheated water. Water passes into steam at 100° C. If water be heated in a closed vessel to 200° C the boiling point of the water is raised, and heat which would have produced steam at atmospheric pressure is stored up in the water. At 200° C the pressure in the vessel is more than the ordinary atmospheric pressure. If the pressure fall to atmospheric (that is, 15 lbs. per square inch) all the heat represented by the temperature above 100° is immediately used up in producing steam. Nitrogen forms some interesting compounds with chlorine and with hydrogen which explode in a most violent manner either by heating or by friction. These explosions are the result of resolution of the compounds into their elements.

CHAPTER I.

Gunpowder.

Gunpowder (proper) is a mechanical mixture of three substances, charcoal—a material consisting for the most part of the element carbon, along with small quantities of oxygen and hydrogen and mineral matters,—sulphur—a pure elementary substance—and saltpetre or nitre = potassium nitrate.

The two latter of these are absolutely definite substances, but charcoal is not so definite. Its composition may vary considerably, depending upon its source and mode of preparation.

Charcoal.

Many kinds of plant, or animal, product, such as wood, straw, cotton, sugar, bones, wool, and even so-called mineral substances as coal, petroleum, &c., when heated to some moderately high temperature in such manner that air has little or no access during the heating, give off gases and vapours, and there remains a more or less black substance which may be either charcoal or coke. This black and non-volatile residue consists for the most part of the element carbon, but unless the temperature employed is very high, oxygen, hydrogen, and nitrogen will be retained, probably in some form of chemical union, and in all the examples mentioned, except perhaps the sugar, there will also be some mineral matters or ash as it would have been called had these materials been burned away in a plentiful supply of air. Of the above natural products sugar is the only one capable of being obtained in a perfectly pure state by a simple physical process, namely, that of dissolving and recrystallising from water. If this substance be heated, as above, for a long time to an extremely high temperature, a residue of nearly pure carbon can be obtained, but by this prolonged and extreme heating it becomes comparatively hard and dense.

In the process of charring, some of these substances will retain the shape, but not the size, of the original material (wood, straw, cotton, bones); others will melt, or at any rate change entirely their outward shape (coal, wool, sugar).

Charcoal to be suitable for gunpowder must have certain properties. Pure carbon would not answer for the purpose, whatever the source (and there are no convenient sources available), on account of its comparative slowness in burning.

Charcoal as the chief combustible constituent of gunpowder should burn freely; leave little or no mineral residue or ash, and be sufficiently friable to be ground up to a non-gritty powder.

These properties are secured, more or less perfectly, by selecting woods from plants of comparatively quick growth, open or light texture, and low ash or mineral content.

The plants generally employed in England are dogwood (*Rhamnus frangula*); willow (*salix alba*); and alder (*betula alnus*). These form trees of very moderate size, and are more properly classed as underwoods.

Alder and willow charcoals are generally used for all ordinary powders for field and heavy guns; dogwood charcoal being generally preferred for small-arm powders, both here and abroad.

There is considerable difference between dogwood charcoal and that from alder and willow. Powder made with it seems to burn more violently, even when all the conditions of making are the same.

It is difficult to account for this behaviour entirely on chemical grounds. Physical difference of structure very probably has an effect. The main substance of these woods is cellulose, and some related compounds, and the action of heat in the charring process must be much the same for all. During this charring steam, methane, acetone, acetic acid, and many other liquid substances, a little carbon-dioxide, and more carbon-monoxide, are given off. The composition of cellulose may be represented by the chemical expression $n(C_6H_{10}O_5)$. Its decomposition by brutally heating to redness in a retort cannot be expressed by any rational chemical equation. Many actions are superposed in such a case. The temperature at which the charcoal is made has a very decided influence on the speed of taking fire, and therefore on the explosiveness. The lower the temperature of the charring process the more hydrogen and oxygen are left in the charcoal, which is also softer and more easily ignited. It usually gives a quicker burning powder, higher velocity, but puts more strain or pressure on the gun.

Charcoal made at very high temperatures is denser and harder, and gives a slow-acting powder and low-muzzle velocity (other things being equal of course in both cases).

Cotton wool is very nearly pure cellulose ($C_6H_{10}O_5$). When gently heated, to not more than 250° C, water is given off and the residue becomes a light brown very friable substance. The mechanism of the process has not yet been carefully followed; it may possibly be represented by

$$C_6H_{10}O_5 - H_2O = C_6H_8O_4 \text{ and } 2(C_6H_8O_4) - H_2O = C_{12}H_{14}O_7$$

or some action of this type.

Charcoal made from varieties of straw at very low temperatures for brown powders gives very low pressures and high muzzle velocity, which seems at first to contradict the above statements about low temperature and high temperature-made charcoals.

Some of these charcoals for brown powders are really little more than baked cellulose, and an important fact must be taken into account in comparing these substances with charcoal proper.

Cellulose is the main constituent of wood, paper, cotton, linen, &c. The common idea is that all these substances may be set on fire or ignited, but it is not quite correct. When a piece of paper is brought into contact with a flame it apparently ignites, but really the heat of the flame has first to decompose the paper in immediate contact, charring it, and producing inflammable gases and vapours which burn with a flame, the heat of which continues the charring process on the neighbouring part of the paper, and so on. Undoubtedly this process has to be undergone, during the burning of the charge in the guns by the material called "slack-burnt" charcoal—charbon rouge—and the straw charcoal for brown powders. Consequently these brown powders are comparatively slow burning, produce low gun-pressures and yet high velocities. (The high velocities produced is, however, more a matter of greater total volume of gaseous products than in the case of black powders.)

The following table of results of experiments carried out some time ago at Waltham Abbey shows the composition of charcoals from alder and willow when heated for different times and at different temperatures. (Unfortunately the actual temperatures are not given; a low heat is however, about 450° C., and the very high heat about 900° to 1,000° C.):—

	No. 1. 7 hours low heat.	No. 2. 4 hours greater heat.	No. 3. 3 hours at very high heat.	No. 4. 3½ hours at heat intermediate between 2 and 3.
Carbon	78·23	82·23	87·55	85·57
Hydrogen	3·67	3·31	2·91	3·02
Oxygen and trace of nitrogen	16·96	13·19	8·29	10·09
Ash	1·41	1·27	1·25	1·32

The most important point about this table of results is its showing the diminution of oxygen and hydrogen at the highest temperatures of charring. (Nothing with certainty is known of the "form" in which this large amount of oxygen and hydrogen is held in the charcoal). Woods generally contain from 48 to 50 per cent. carbon, about 6 per cent. hydrogen, and 42 to 45 per cent. oxygen and nitrogen; the nitrogen seldom amounting to more than 1 per cent. The rate or speed of charring has a great effect on the yield of charcoal. Slowly heating giving a larger yield than rapid rise of temperature.*

* According to Violette 100 parts of a certain wood (faulbaum) gave:—

°C.	Charcoal.	Carbon.	Hydrogen.	Oxygen.
250	49·57	65·58	4·8	28·9
350	29·66	76·6	4·13	18·44
1,020	18·75	81·97	2·29	14·14
1,500	17·31	94·56	0·739	3·84

Charcoal Making from Wood.

The wood is generally cut in the spring, and is stripped of its bark very thoroughly. This point is important since the bark is very different in ash contents to the wood. As a rule wood is kept for three years, dogwood in thatched stacks and willow and alder piled by cords in the open so that they are weathered; losing moisture, shrinking somewhat and also changing a little in texture.

The wood, cut into 3 feet lengths, is packed into cylindrical iron cases called "slips," see Plate I., which are 3 feet 6 inches long and 2 feet 4 inches diameter. Sometimes the wood must be split up to ensure moderate uniformity in size and therefore uniformity in the charcoal. The lid is fastened on and two openings are left in the base of the slip, each about 4 inches in diameter. The slips are then placed in horizontal cylinders or retorts (Fig. I). The retorts, which have openings at the far ends to correspond with those in the slips, are closed air-tight by iron doors.

The furnaces are arranged so that the retorts are uniformly heated by the flame and that the heat may be regulated during the charring operation; this occupies with dogwood, about four hours for Blank F.G., and eight hours for R.F.G.[2] gunpowders; with alder and willow, the time of burning varies from three-and-a-half to six hours, according to the nature of the powder for which it is required; the time, moreover, would in each case be somewhat increased if the wood were beyond the average size. The gases and volatilised tar from the wood, pass out through the openings in the slip into pipes communicating with the furnace, in which they are burnt; thus saving some amount of fuel.

When the wood has been sufficiently charred, which is known by the violet colour of the flame from the burning gas, indicating the formation of carbon monoxide, the slip is withdrawn by means of tackle, placed in a large iron case or cooler (Fig. C), covered with a close-fitting lid, and allowed to remain until all the fire is cold, which takes about four hours; the charcoal is then emptied into smaller coolers, and sent into store.

The charcoal is carefully picked over by hand, to ascertain that it all is properly and evenly burnt, and that no rivets from the slips have broken off. It is then kept for about a week in store, before being ground, to lessen the danger of spontaneous combustion, to which charcoal is very liable when ground directly after burning; this arises from the very rapid absorption and condensation of oxygen from the air by the finely powdered substance. Freshly burnt charcoal will absorb many hundred times its volume of gases. It is exceedingly porous, and offers a large surface for the condensation or adhesion of gases.

Well-burnt charcoal is jet black in colour; its fracture should show a clear, velvet-like surface; it should be light and sonorous when dropped on a hard surface, and so soft as not to scratch polished copper. Slack-burnt charcoal, that is, charcoal

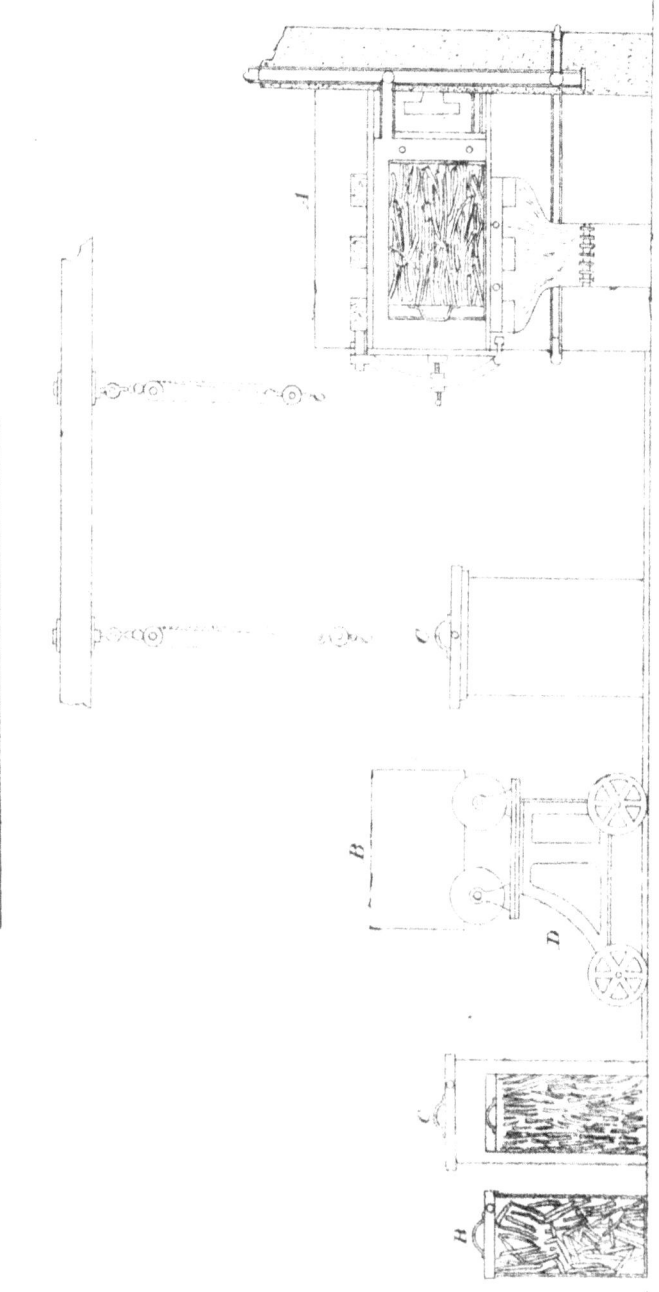

PLATE 1.

APPARATUS FOR BURNING CHARCOAL.

A. Retort showing pipes for conducting gases to the furnace.
B. Ship for holding wood.   C. Cooler.   D. Carriage for Ship.

prepared at a very low temperature, is at once known by its reddish-brown colour, especially when ground. This colour is distinctly perceptible in R.F.G.² up to the glazing process. Charcoal burnt at a very high temperature is known by its hardness, metallic ring, and greater density.

During the storing of charcoal it is exceedingly probable that some, at least, of the oxygen of the air absorbed becomes converted, by slow action, into carbon dioxide. A little moisture is also absorbed, either from the air or produced likewise by slow combination of some of the hydrogen.

The charcoal mill is built on the same plan as an ordinary coffee mill. It is 4 feet 6 inches diameter at the top. The powdered charcoal is sifted on a reel or cylinder. This reel is 8 feet 6 inches long and 3 feet diameter set at a slope of about 4°, and is covered with a 32-mesh copper-wire gauze.

The reel revolves about 38 times a minute. It is enclosed in a case to prevent, of course, the fine charcoal powder flying about.*

All the charcoal not fine enough to pass through the meshes travels to the end of the reel and falls into a box and is re-ground. The powder passing the meshes falls into the reel case. After the day's work the charcoal powder is placed in iron coolers and removed to the ground charcoal store. This store is built of iron and stands isolated from other buildings as freshly ground charcoal is liable to spontaneous combustion owing to absorbtion of atmospheric oxygen. It is more dangerous now than before grinding for every little particle of charcoal dust has a decided layer of air surrounding it.

In 1847 Violette described a method of preparation of charcoal by heating wood in super-heated steam. Steam at about 15 lbs. pressure passes over the wood, effecting a partial charring and at the same time removing the volatile decomposition products. The charcoal produced is sometimes called charbon rouge. The amount of oxygen and hydrogen contained in charcoal made by the super-heated steam process is considerably higher than with the ordinary slip heated black charcoal.

Sulphur.

Sulphur is found as a natural product in several forms—as free sulphur and combined with other substances. Only free or native sulphur can be used as an ingredient of gunpowder.

At Waltham Abbey the sulphur used is imported from Sicily, it contains a small quantity of foreign matters—generally less than 5 per cent.—from which it is freed by distillation.

Sulphur melts at 115° C., and on heating above this point undergoes some remarkable physical changes, and finally at about 440° C. boils, giving off a brown vapour, which in contact with air generally ignites. The product of its burning

---

* Fine powder of charcoal is well adapted to make a "dust explosion."

is sulphur dioxide (SO_2), which dissolves somewhat freely in water and slowly takes up more oxygen forming sulphuric acid.

Sulphur is a very brittle substance. On cooling down after melting it rapidly crystallizes. When the vapour from boiling sulphur comes into contact with a cold surface some will condense into a fine powder, which has somewhat different properties to the ordinary crystalline form. This also happens when the sulphur vapour escapes into a cold room or space. This powder is known as "flowers of sulphur" (or flour of sulphur). It is probably an allotropic modification.

Sulphur Refining.—The refining apparatus (*see* Pl. II) is very simple. A large iron melting pot, or retort, A, is set in brickwork, about 3 feet above the floor, with a furnace underneath; this retort has a heavy movable lid, which is luted into the pot with clay, and in the lid is a 4-inch opening, closed by an iron conical plug that can be removed at pleasure. From the melting pot two pipes, at right angles to one another, lead, one (15-inch) to a large circular dome, C, and the other (5-inch) to an iron receiving pot, B, placed below the level of the melting pot. The 5-inch pipe has an iron casing or jacket, D, round it, through which cold water is allowed to circulate. The communication of these pipes with the melting pot can be shut off or opened as occasion requires, by means of valves worked from without. A lead pipe passes from the lid of the receiving pot into a small wooden chamber lined with lead, in which any vapour still remaining uncondensed may be deposited, as in the dome.

The grough sulphur is broken into small pieces, and about 7 cwt. of it is placed in the melting pot, and subjected to the action of the furnace. The plug-hole in the lid and the pipe leading to the dome are now left open, but the pipe leading to the receiving pot is closed: after about two hours a pale yellow vapour rises, the plug is now put in and the vapour allowed to pass into the dome, where it *sublimes*, or condenses on the sides and floor in the form of a fine powder, known as "flowers of sulphur"; a small pipe leads from the bottom of the dome on the opposite side into a tub filled with water; the air escapes by this pipe, and the sulphurous or sulphuric acid is taken up by the water. In about three hours from the commencement, the vapour becomes a deep brown colour, the pipe communicating with the dome is then shut, and that into the receiving pot opened, and at the same time cold water from a tank above is allowed to circulate through the jacket covering the pipe of the receiver; the vapour entering is condensed in the pipe, and runs into the receiving pot below in the form of a clear yellow fluid. When nearly all has passed over into the receiving pot, which can be known by the jacket getting cold, the pipe communicating with the receiving pot is again closed, and the fluid sulphur left about an hour to get sufficiently cool (120° C., not below 220° F.) to ladle out into the moulds (wooden tubes saturated with water to keep the sulphur out of the cracks);

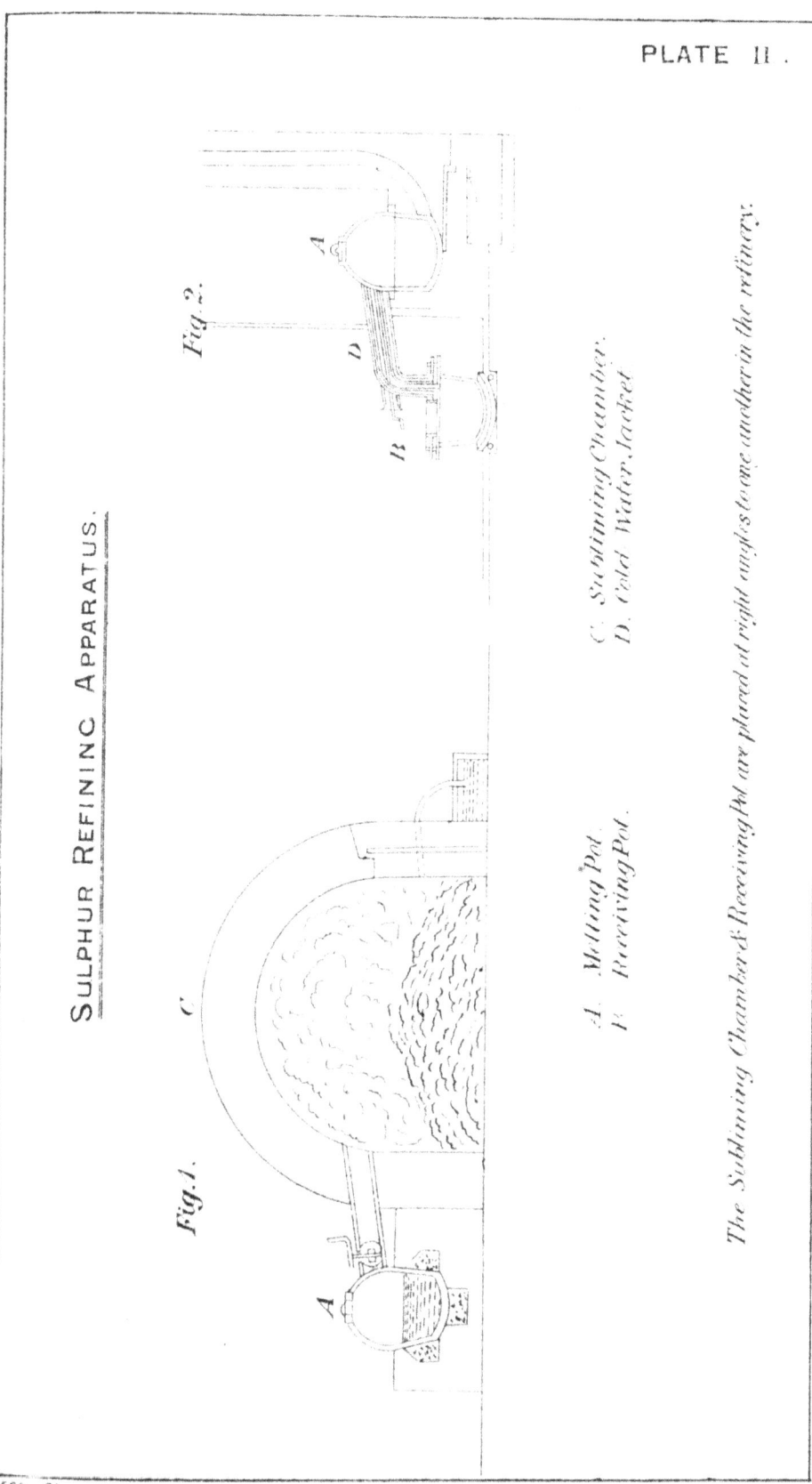

at the same time the furnace doors are thrown back, and the communication with the dome reopened, so that the rest of the vapour may pass into it; the mechanical impurities all remain at the bottom of the melting pot, which is cleaned out once a week.

The flowers of sulphur thus obtained, being unfit for the manufacture of gunpowder, are treated as grough sulphur.

The crystalline sulphur, after being allowed to cool in the moulds, is broken up and put into barrels ready to be ground.

Refined sulphur may be tested as follows:—

(1) Burn a small weighed quantity in a porcelain or platinum dish, when the amount of the residue should not exceed ·15 per cent.

(2) Boil a little with water, and test with blue litmus paper, which it should at most only very feebly redden.

The large pieces of sulphur from the refining operation are ground under iron edge runners. As sulphur is exceedingly brittle, this operation does not take long. After grinding it is passed through a reel of 36-mesh wire gauze similar to the charcoal sifter, and stored in bins until required.

Nitre or Saltpetre.

Nitre, potassium nitrate, saltpetre = (KNO_3).

This substance is a natural product of the oxidation of nitrogenous organic matters in the soil, and is also one of the final products of the action of electric discharges in the atmosphere.

At one time large quantities were imported from India (and tropical regions), where it can be obtained by washing out surface soil in which this and other nitrates have concentrated owing to the above mentioned oxidation of organic matters. In some places on the Continent of Europe nitre is produced artificially by a process imitating the natural process taking place more rapidly in warmer regions in ordinary surface soil.

All kinds of animal refuse is mixed with soil, old mortar, brushwood, &c., and piled in heaps under sheds where it is protected from rain by a roof, but obtains abundant ventilation from the open side, and these heaps are just *moistened* with stable drainage, &c. Certain microbes start work and convert the animal substances, which contain nitrogen in combination with hydrogen and carbon into nitrites, of calcium and other bases present, and these absorb oxygen again from the atmosphere and become nitrates.

At the same time, some of the carbon and hydrogen of these organic substances becomes oxidized, and considerable heat may be developed, so that these heaps require a little attention in the way of keeping the temperature within certain limits. The action taking place is similar to that going on in heaps of ordinary stable manure. A considerable amount of carbon dioxide escapes from these heaps, but when in proper action there is scarcely any appreciable odour observable even on the lee side.

At the end of the summer season these heaps and the drainage from them are washed out with water, the liquor filtered, and treated with the requisite quantity of potassium carbonate. Calcium and magnesium carbonates are precipitated, and potassium nitrate left in solution. After settling, the clear liquor is then evaporated and yields an impure nitre, which can then be purified or refined by recrystallization from hot water.

Immense quantities of sodium nitrate are obtained from Chili. This nitrate is quite unsuitable for the manufacture of gunpowders on account of its deliquescent nature. It absorbs water very rapidly from moist air. On an ordinary damp English day, a pound of Chili saltpetre will become wet and partly liquified in the course of a few hours' exposure. It is, however, very largely employed, as a manure, for the manufacture of nitric acid, and also by a very simple and elegant reaction for the production of potassium nitrate.

In a certain geological formation in Germany (Stassfurt), occur large deposits of a mineral consisting essentially of potassium and magnesium chlorides ($KCl + MgCl_2$). This mineral is systematically washed or lixiviated, and very large quantities of the potassium salt (KCl) obtained. (A good deal of this is also used as a manure under the name of Kainite.) Potassium chloride and sodium nitrate are very soluble salts even in cold water. When solutions of these salts are mixed there is a tendency for the metals to change places, and at a high temperature in concentrated solutions an almost complete reaction, as expressed by the equation

$$KCl + NaNO_3 = NaCl + KNO_3 \text{ takes place.}$$

Without entering into details the operation is conducted by making very strong hot solutions of equivalent quantities of the two salts and boiling the mixture. The temperature of this saturated boiling solution is considerably higher than that of boiling water. The common salt, NaCl, formed is not nearly so soluble in hot water as the nitre, KNO_3, consequently it crystallizes out or precipitates to a great extent during the boiling The hot solution is filtered off and on cooling to about 40° C. most of the nitre, KNO_3, crystallizes out. It is, of course, not pure at this stage, but is the basis of the commercial nitre, and the substitute to a very great extent of the Indian nitre (so-called).

The "earth" (Caliche) from which Chili saltpetre is extracted contains iodine (which is extracted and forms part of the Chili saltpetre industry). Small quantities of the iodine remain in the Chili saltpetre, probably in the form of sodium iodate, $NaIO_3$. During the conversion process some of this may change over into potassium chlorate (or sodium chlorate), the solubility of which is little different of that of potassium nitrate. It is therefore difficult to remove during the refining or recrystallizing process. Chlorates are particularly dangerous substances when in admixture with sulphur, or organic substances of any kind. Such mixtures can be exploded by very gentle friction or pressure. No doubt many explosions in recent years in gunpowder works can be referred to the presence of small quantities of chlorate being contained in the nitrate used,

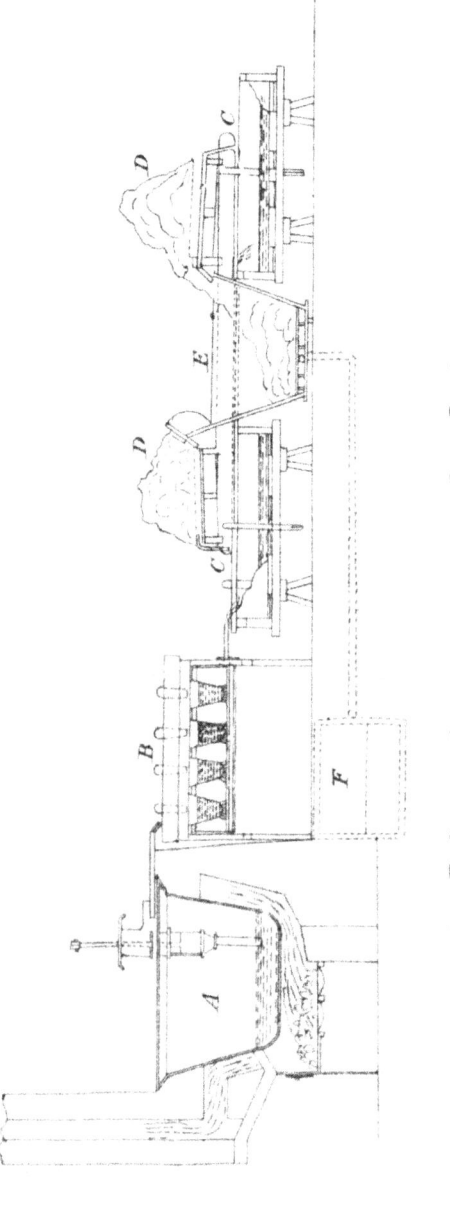

PLATE III

APPARATUS FOR REFINING SALTPETRE.

A. Refining Copper.
B. Filtering Stand.
C. Coolers or Crystallizing Pans.
D. Drainers.
E. Washing Vat.
F. Liquour Tank.

Saltpetre melts at 352°C. (Carnelly). Its specific gravity at 15° C. = 2.09. The crystals do not contain water, and are, when pure, not deliquescent. 100 parts water at 0° dissolve 13, at 20° C. 31, at 30° 44, at 50° 86, at 70° 139, at 90° 206, at 100° 247 parts of saltpetre. At 116° the solution is saturated, and then contains 335 parts of the salt to 100 water.

Refining Saltpetre.—The saltpetre used at Waltham Abbey is exclusively that imported from India. The refining process is based upon the fact that saltpetre is far more soluble in hot than cold water, while the chief saline impurities found in grough nitre are almost equally soluble in either. Water at 100° C. 212° F. holds about *seven* times as much saltpetre in solution as water at 70° F. (at 20° C. = 31 at 100° C. = 247) (NaCl at 0° = 35·5; at 100° 39·6) (KCl at 0° = 28·5; at 100° 57). If, therefore, a saturated solution of grough saltpetre be made at a temperature of 212° F., as the solution cools to 70° F., six-sevenths of the nitre contained in it will be deposited in the form of crystals—which can easily be removed—whereas the chlorides of sodium and potassium, or other foreign salts, will still remain in the liquor.

Solution.—The refining coppers (Pl. 3, Fig. A), which are capable of holding 500 gallons each, are fitted with false iron bottoms to prevent the saltpetre adhering to the coppers, and perforated with holes to enable the sand and mechanical impurities to fall through. The coppers are each charged with about 280 gallons of the washings of the purified saltpetre, and in all some 40 cwt. of saltpetre, partly grough, say 25 cwt., partly crystals from reduced liquors, 5 cwt.; partly crystals left in crystallizing cisterns, 5 cwt., and about 5 cwt. in the washing water. These details vary according to circumstances.

In about two hours after the fires have been lighted the greater part of the saltpetre in the refining copper will be dissolved, and the solution begin to boil; the temperature will now be about 230° F., and the specific gravity of the solution about 1·49. Just before boiling, the thick scum formed on the surface is carefully skimmed off, and the false bottoms are pulled out: while boiling, cold water is from time to time thrown in to induce the scum to rise to the top, and it is removed as long as it forms. The boiling continues for half-an-hour, or until the scum ceases to rise: the coppers are then filled up with cold water, and the solution is again made to boil briskly for a few minutes, when the furnace doors are opened and the fires allowed to cool down.

Filtering.—In about two hours more the solution will have fallen to the proper temperature, 220° F. (specific gravity 1·53), for pumping out. A hand-pump is then lowered into the copper, and the solution pumped out into the wooden "supply troughs" (*see* Fig. B), each of which is provided with six holes, having filtering bags of dowlas suspended underneath, and fitted with plugs so that the holes can be stopped in case of the bags becoming clogged; the solution filters into a long enclosed trough below, which conducts it to the crystallizing cisterns at a temperature of from 180° to 190° F.

Crystallizing.—The copper crystallizing cisterns, or "coolers" (*see* Fig. C), are each 12 feet by 7 feet, and about 11 inches deep, the solution between 5 and 6 inches deep in the pan. The liquid is kept in agitation by workmen with long-handled wooden hoes, and as it cools, fine crystals fall to the bottom of the cistern. If not kept in agitation, large crystals would form, which would enclose liquid containing impurities. The crystals are from time to time drawn up to the side of the cistern, and by means of perforated copper shovels, thrown upon the inclined draining frames (Fig. D), from which the liquor drains off, and the crystals, having almost the appearance of snow, and technically called "flour," are then raked into the washing vat. After the temperature falls below 90° F., the solution in the crystallizing cistern is not stirred, nor are the crystals removed, as it is not worth the labour, the crystals being then deposited so slowly. It is left to cool, when large crystals will form, which are treated as grough nitre.

Washing.—The washing vats (Fig. E) are placed between each pair of coolers and drainers; they are about 6 feet long, 4 feet wide, and 3 feet 6 inches deep, and are fitted with a false bottom of wood pierced with holes; there is a plug-hole in front below the false bottom.

The vat being full of saltpetre, the plug is withdrawn, and the crystals are washed by sprinkling about 70 gallons of water over each vat by means of a rose. The saltpetre is then left to drain for half-an-hour and the liquor which passes through, runs into an underground tank. The plugs are now inserted and enough water is permitted to run into the vats to cover the saltpetre; this *second* water is allowed to stand half-an-hour when the plugs are again withdrawn, and it also runs into the tank, the crystals being allowed to drain for another half hour. A *third* and final washing is then given by sprinkling about 100 gallons of water over each vat, the plug-holes remaining open as at the first washing. It is desirable that distilled water should, when procurable, be used for these washings in order to avoid the impurities which are contained in the best ordinary water. The water from the three washings flows into the same tank, and is used in the refining coppers for dissolving the next charge of grough saltpetre. Whatever quantity remains in the tank after the coppers are filled, is pumped into the evaporating pots. The saltpetre in the vats is now allowed to drain all night, and in the morning it is removed (with the exception of about 6 inches from the bottom, which contains a large amount of moisture) to the store bins, where it remains until required for use. After about three days in store it is ready for the manufacture of powder, and contains from 3 to 5 per cent. of moisture, according to the season; the exact amount of water is ascertained and allowed for. From each copper of 40 cwt. of grough nitre, about 25 cwt. of refined saltpetre is obtained.

Testing the Saltpetre.—A solution of the saltpetre should now be tested as follows:—

(1) With blue and red litmus paper for acids or alkalis.

(2) With a few drops of a solution of silver nitrate for the presence of chlorides: a milky appearance indicates the formation of chloride of silver, and hence the presence of some chloride. (Many chlorides are deliquescent and none of them are supporters of combustion.)

(3) With a solution of chloride or nitrate of barium for the presence of sulphates, which would be shown by a white precipitate of barium sulphate.

(4) All salpetres should be tested for chlorates by first heating to redness in a platinum or silver dish, dissolving out the residue with water, acidifying with nitric acid and adding silver nitrate. A white precipitate now will, if the saltpetre showed no reaction with silver nitrate in the first instance, indicate some chlorate which has been destroyed by the heating leaving chloride. This test must be done quantitatively, a weighed amount, about 5 grams, of the saltpetre being taken.

On the following morning, the solution which was left in the crystallizing cisterns at 90° F. having become cold, the mother liquor is run off into the evaporating pot, and the large crystals which have formed are set to drain. These are afterwards placed in the refining coppers with a fresh boiling.

Evaporating the Mother Liquor, &c.—The process of *evaporation* separates the greater part of the soluble impurities—chlorides and sulphates—the separation depending upon the high solubility of saltpetre in *boiling* water. As the water evaporates, the nitre is still held in solution, while the foreign salts, being much less soluble at that temperature than the saltpetre, are separated, and fall to the bottom of the copper.

The evaporating pots contain about 300 gallons each. The liquor to be evaporated consists of the mother liquor from the crystallizing cisterns, the mother liquor from the saltpetre crystallized in small pans (hereafter described), such of the "washings" as are not needed for the refining coppers, and other impure solutions. The liquor is kept briskly boiling, and is occasionally stirred to prevent the salts caking at the bottom. When the liquor is reduced to about one-fourth of its original bulk, the fires are allowed to go out, and about nine hours from the lighting of the fires, the solution, just simmering, is ready for filtering. It is filtered in the manner already described, and run into small circular copper crystallizing pans, containing about 17 gallons each, and left all night. When cold the mother liquor is run off and sent back to the evaporating pot. The crystals formed in the pans are drained and sent to the refining coppers as grough nitre.

Thus a constant process is going on of "petre" (saltpetre) to the refining coppers, and of mother liquor to the evaporating pots. The residue, after being treated with hot water to dissolve out as much saltpetre as possible, is put aside for a *second* boiling in liquor already saturated with impurities, after which it is transferred to the waste salt store for sale. It finally consists chiefly of the chlorides of sodium and potassium, with some sulphates.

Bag Washing.—The jute bags, in which the saltpetre is imported, are first scraped as free from it as possible, and then set aside in stacks in order to have the considerable amount of nitre retained in their coarse fibres extracted by boiling, after which the bags are dried and sold. This is done during the summer months.

Extracting Saltpetre from Damaged Powder.—The large percentage of saltpetre contained in condemned gunpowder (Class VI), and also in the *sweepings* from the factory, is extracted by boiling with water in coppers holding about 400 gallons each, and filtering the solution, first through coarse canvas, and a second time through dowlas. The liquor containing the saltpetre is then evaporated down, filtered, and crystallized in pans, as before. The mixture of charcoal and sulphur left in both sets of filters is boiled a second time before being thrown away. About 94 per cent. of the saltpetre contained in powder can be recovered by extraction, against the value of which must be set the cost of labour, fuel, &c.

The refined saltpetre required at the Royal Laboratory, at Woolwich, is dried at Waltham Abbey in a hot chamber, at a temperature of about 220° F., gradually raised and lowered; it is then ground at once. Saltpetre intended to be stored for any length of time is also dried and ground.

The recovered saltpetre can also be used for the manufacture of nitric acid.

CHAPTER II.

MANUFACTURE OF GUNPOWDER.

For the purposes of describing the manufacture, gunpowder may be divided into three classes—

        A.—Granulated.
        B.—Cut.
        C.—Moulded.

Manufacture of Class A Powders.

In this class are included every description of gunpowder which is *granulated* in machines consisting of pairs of rollers connected by vibrating screens of copper wire, and which consequently is composed of irregularly-shaped grains of different sizes. This class includes all fine grain powders, as well as those for use, speaking generally, with field guns and guns of position.

The following are the successive processes of the manufacture of granulated powders, but there are slight variations in the case of some of the descriptions, which will be noticed in due course.

Processes of Manufacture.

1. Weighing and mixing the ingredients.
2. Incorporating, or milling.
3. Breaking down the mill-cake.
4. Pressing.
5. Granulating.
6. Dusting. (Fine grain powders only.)
7. Glazing.
8. Stoving, or drying.
9. Finishing.
10. Blending.

The first three of the above processes are precisely similar for all three classes of gunpowder.

1. *Mixing the Ingredients.*

Weighing.—The ingredients being brought into the mixing house, are very accurately weighed out, in separate scales, in mill charges, in their proper proportions to 100 lb., with an extra amount of saltpetre to compensate for the moisture it contains. All Class A and Class B powders have the normal composition of 75 saltpetre, 15 charcoal, and 10 sulphur. R.F.G.^{2}, Blank F.G., and Q.F. shell F.G. powders are made of dogwood charcoal, S.P., R.L.G.^{4}, R.L.G.^{2}, Blank L.G. and shell P., of alder and willow. The largest charge authorised for the incorporating mill is 80 lb.

Mixing.—The charge is now placed in the mixing machine, which consists of a cylindrical gun-metal or copper drum, about 2 feet 9 inches in diameter, and 1 foot 6 inches wide, with an axle passing through its centre, on which there are eight rows of gun-metal "flyers," or fork-shaped arms; the machinery is so arranged that the flyers and drum revolve in opposite directions; the drum making about 40 and the flyers 120 revolutions per minute. The ingredients are mixed for about five minutes; the machine then empties itself into a box, and the composition is passed through an 8-mesh copper-wire hand sieve over a hopper, in order to catch any splinter of wood, small copper nail, or other foreign substance which may have got into the saltpetre during the process of refining; it then runs into a bag placed below the hopper, and is tied up ready for the incorporating mill. In this state it is called a "green" charge.

2. *Incorporating or Milling.*

Incorporating Mill (*see* Pl. IV).—The incorporating mill consists of a circular iron or stone bed, about 7 feet in diameter, fixed very firmly in the floor of the building, on which the iron or stone cylindrical edge runners revolve; the old pattern beds and runners are of stone, the later ones of iron. The stone runners are 5 feet 10 inches in diameter, and from 14 to 18 inches in width; the iron runners are $6\frac{1}{4}$ feet in diameter, and 15 inches wide; stone runs upon stone, iron upon iron. The runners have a common axle, resting in gun-metal bouches in a solid cross-head attached to a vertical shaft, which, passing through a bearing in the centre of the bed, is in gear with the machinery, which is above the bed in the old water mills, and beneath it in cast-iron tanks in the steam mills. The stone runners weigh about 3 tons, and make about $7\frac{1}{2}$ revolutions in a minute; the iron about 4 tons, and make 8 revolutions per minute.

The bed has a sloping rim on the outside, called the "curb," and on the inside, an edge formed by the "cheese," or bearing through which the vertical shaft passes. The runners are *not* equidistant from the centre of the shaft; one works the part of the charge nearest the centre of the bed, the other the outer part, but their paths overlap; two "ploughs" of wood covered with leather, attached to the cross-head by arms or brackets, one working next the vertical shaft, the other next to the rim, throw the composition under the runners, as it works away from them.

PLATE IV.

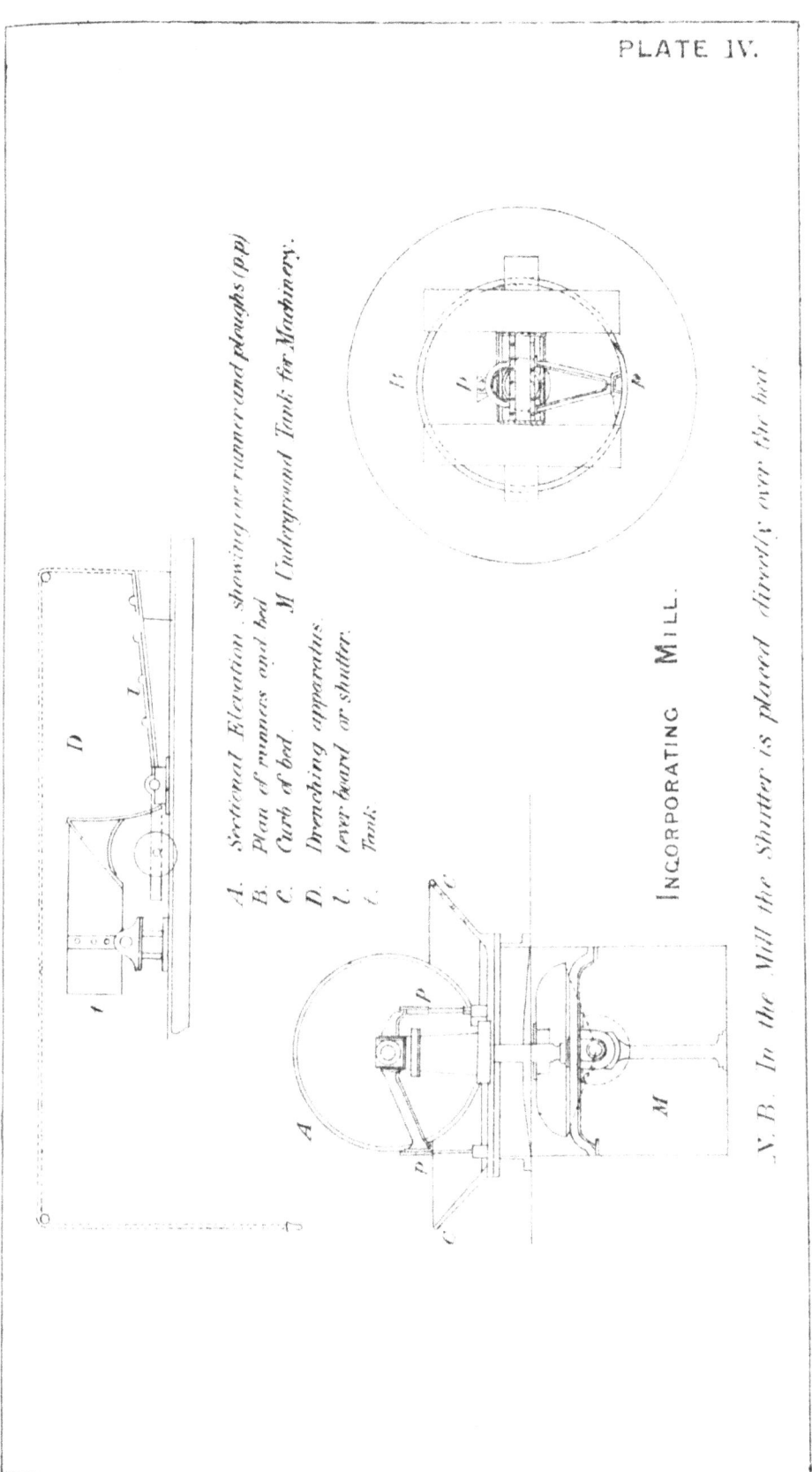

A. Sectional Elevation, showing one runner and ploughs (P.P)
B. Plan of runners and bed.   M. Underground Tank for Machinery.
C. Curb of bed.
D. Drenching apparatus.
l. lever-board or shutter.
t. Tank.

INCORPORATING MILL.

N.B. In the Mill the Shutter is placed directly over the bed

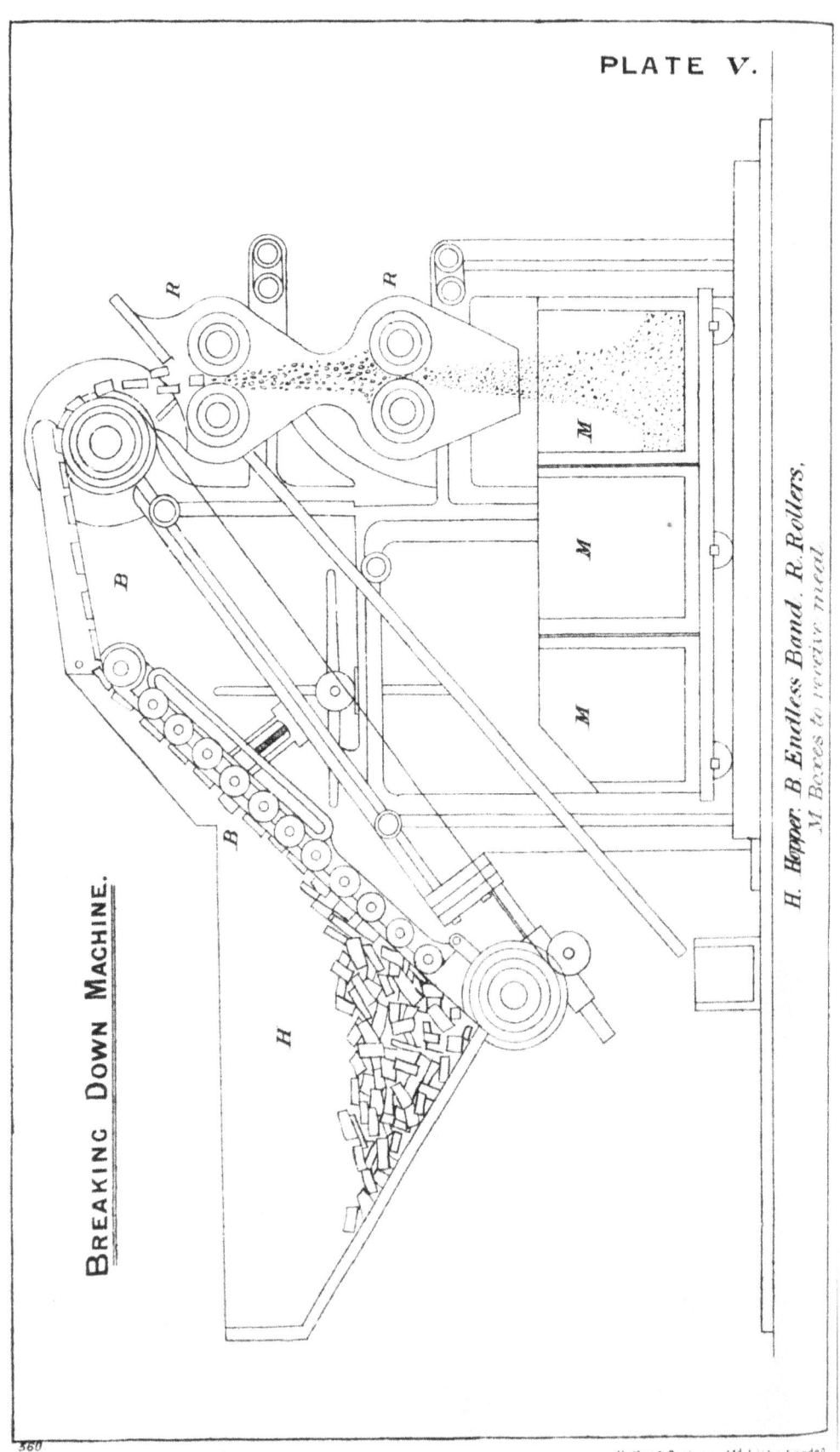

The green charge is brought in its bag, and put on the bed of the mill, being spread evenly by means of a wooden rake; it is then "liquored," or moistened with distilled water, and is worked for 4 hours under iron runners for fine grain powders, but R.F.G.^{2} powder is incorporated about 8 hours under iron runners. The *granulated* cannon powders now made (R.L.G.^{2} and R.L.G.^{4}) are incorporated for 3 hours under iron runners, an additional half-hour being allowed if worked under stone runners. All "dust" and "re-work" charges are milled for 40 minutes.

Amount of "Liquor."—The charge when placed on the bed of the mill contains about 2 pints of water (the moisture of the saltpetre), and a further quantity of from 2 to 6 or 7 pints of distilled water is added from time to time, according to the nature of the powder and the state of the atmosphere, in order to facilitate the incorporation, and prevent the charge from flying about as dust. If too wet, the runners would pick up the composition from the bed. During the time of working the millman enters the mill occasionally, takes a wooden "shover," and pushes the outside of the charge into the middle of the path of the runners, so that every portion may be regularly incorporated.

Action of the Runners.—The action of the runners is a combination of rolling and twisting, and has, on a large scale, somewhat the effect of a pestle and mortar, crushing, rubbing, and mixing, thus giving the charge a most intimate union.

Drenching Apparatus.—Each mill has a flat wooden leverboard, or "shutter," directly over its bed, in gear with a tank of water, and so arranged that when the shutter is in the least degree raised on its pivot by an explosion, the tank is upset into the bed, and the charge "drowned;" a horizontal shaft connects all the shutters in a group of mills, so that the explosion of one mill drowns all the remainder. The tanks can also be pulled over by hand.

When the charge, which in this state is called "mill-cake," is ready to be taken off the bed, it should be uniform in appearance, not having any specks of either saltpetre or sulphur visible to the eye, and of a greyish or brownish colour, according to the charcoal used.

It is of the greatest importance that the incorporation should be carefully attended to by experienced men, as much of the goodness and uniformity of the powder depends upon this process being properly carried out.

The mill-cake is carefully tested every day in order to ascertain whether it contains the proper amount of moisture, which ranges from $1\frac{1}{2}$ to 3 °/$_\circ$ for fine grain powders, and 3 to 6 °/$_\circ$ for the larger descriptions of gunpowder.

3. *Breaking down the Mill-Cake.*

Breaking Down (*see* Pl. V).—The mill-cake, on being taken off the bed of the mill, is placed in wooden barrels, removed to small magazines, and thence to the breaking-down machine, which is somewhat similar in principle to the granulating machine, but of simpler construction.

The object of this process is to reduce the mill-cake to meal, in order that it may be in a convenient form for loading into the press-box, and also in a state which will admit of its being pressed into a homogeneous mass. The machine consists of a strong gun-metal framework, in which are fixed two pairs of gun-metal rollers, which revolve towards each other, one roller of each pair working in sliding bearings, connected with a weighted lever (pressure about 56 lb.), so that, in the event of any hard substance getting in by accident, the rollers would open and allow it to pass through, thereby preventing the dangerous friction which would otherwise ensue.

A hopper, capable of holding 500 lb., is fixed at one end of the machine, and an endless feeding band of web or canvas, 2 feet 6 inches wide, and having strips of leather sewn across at distances of about 4 inches, passes over one roller at the bottom of the hopper, and another at the top of the machine. When set in motion, the band conveys the cake from the hopper to the highest point of the machine; it then falls between the first pair of rollers, which are grooved, and from thence through the second pair—which are plain, and situated directly below—passing in the form of meal into wooden boxes placed upon a carriage under the machine. This meal is now ready for the press, and is taken to an expense magazine until required for use. The mill-cake for all descriptions of gunpowder is broken down in the same manner.

4. *Pressing.*

Press-box (*see* Pl. VI).—A very strong oak box, with gun-metal frame, 2 feet 6 inches square, and 2 feet 9 inches deep, is divided vertically into two parts by a partition, and so constructed that three of the sides can turn back on hinges, or form a compact rigid box when screwed firmly together. Being laid sideways, the top temporarily closed by means of a board, and the uppermost *side* alone open, a number of copper or gun-metal plates, 14 inches by 30 inches, are placed vertically into this box, and kept apart at a distance depending on the description of powder required, by two gun-metal racks with corresponding grooves, which can be removed when no longer required.

About 800 lb. of meal is put into the press-box while the plates are in a vertical position: when the box is full the racks are withdrawn, the plates being only separated by the meal between them; the *present* upper side is firmly screwed down with short gun-metal screws, and the box turned over, so that the plates are now horizontal, and the temporary lid taken off; then, by means of a travelling crane, moving on a rail overhead, and having two claws which hook on to trunnions fixed on the sides of the box, the latter is lifted, pushed easily

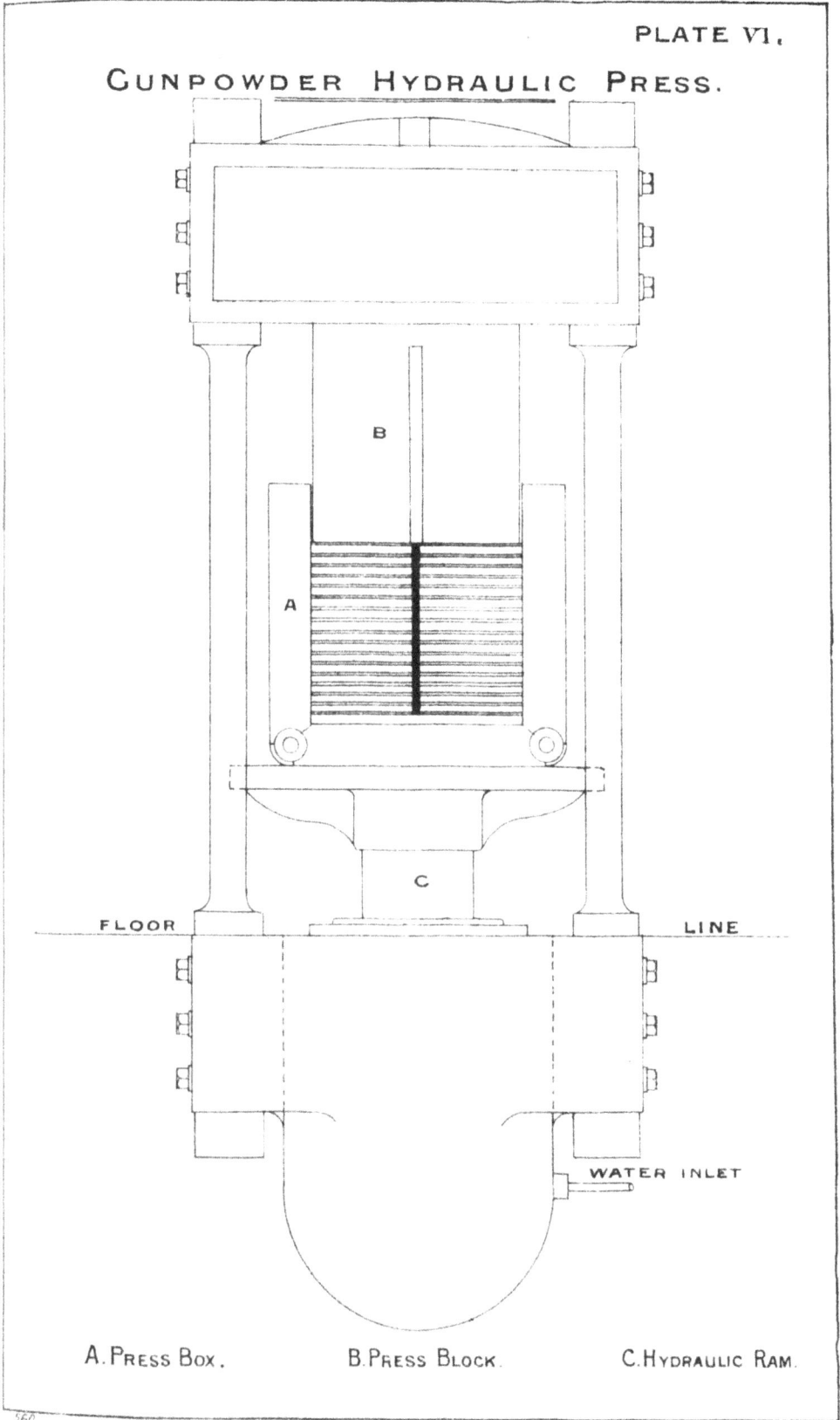

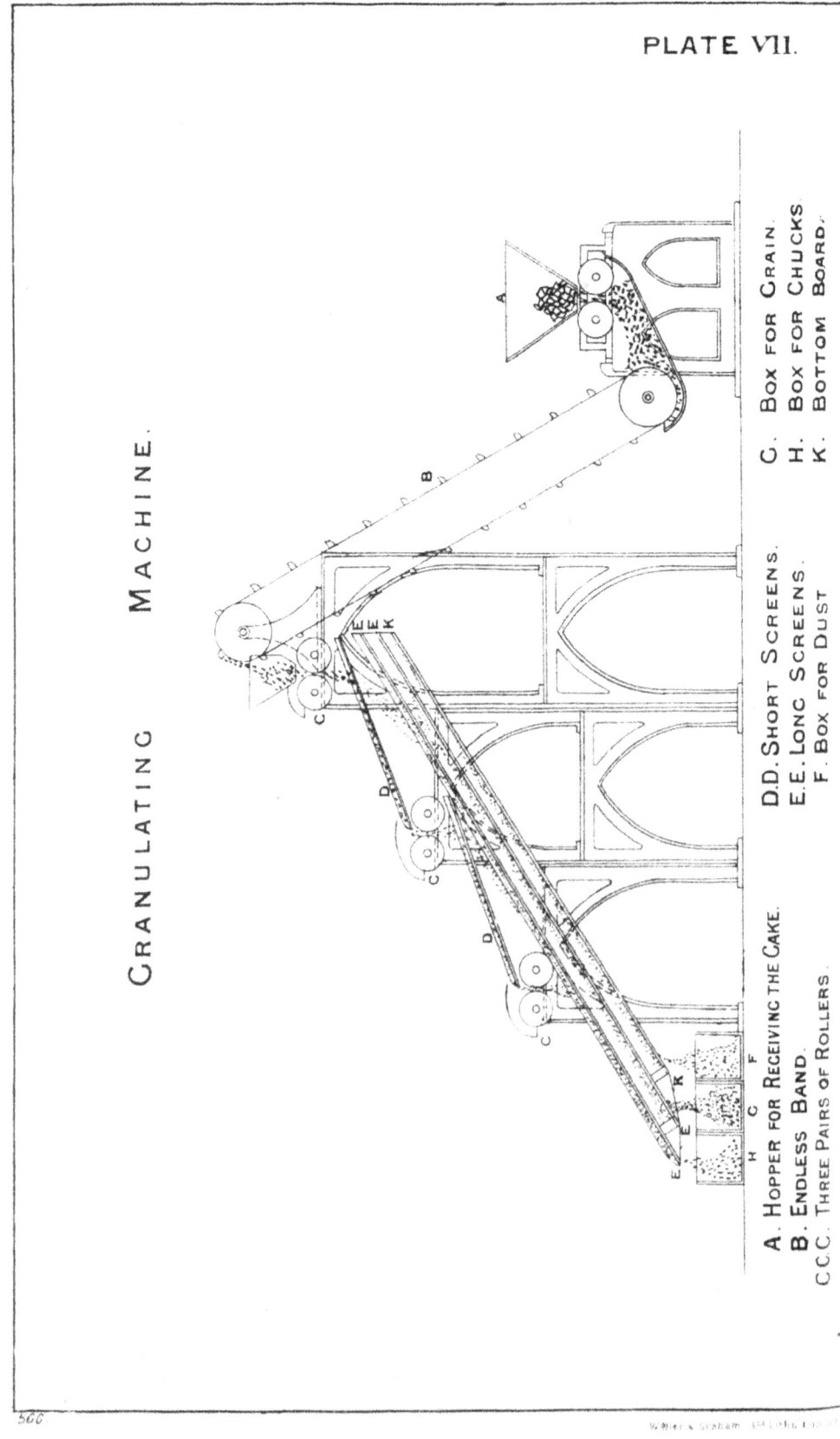

along, and deposited on the table of the ram under the *fixed* press-block. The pumps, which work the hydraulic press in a separate house, are now set in motion by a water-wheel (or by hand if necessary), and the box is raised until the required amount of compression has been attained, according to the density to be given to the powder. For this purpose the block is allowed to enter the box *a certain distance*, which is measured by means of a metal scale fixed on the block.

The above mode of regulating the pressure is found to give more reliable results than trusting to the indicator-gauge of the hydraulic ram, for the reason that the elasticity, or *resistance to pressure*, of the meal varies considerably with the amount of moisture present in it and the state of the atmosphere. To get uniform density, it is necessary to compress *equal quantities* of meal containing *equal amounts of moisture, at the same rate*, into *the same space*. In practice, however, the moisture in the meal will vary slightly, whatever care be taken, and even if the mill-cake were always taken off the bed perfectly uniform in this respect, the hygrometric state of the atmosphere would cause a difference by the time it came to the press. Moreover, it is found that atmospheric conditions have an influence upon the manner in which powder-meal can be compressed, even apart from the actual percentage of moisture contained in it, so that the exact distance the press-block is allowed to enter the block has to be varied with the season, and even according to the prevailing state of the weather.

After the required amount of compression has been given, which is known to the men in the pump-room by the edge of the box releasing a spring catch and ringing a bell, the box is allowed to remain under the press for a few minutes; a valve is then opened to permit of the free passage of the water from the cylinder, and the ram and press-box descend. The box is run from beneath the press by means of the travelling crane, and again turned over on its side to be unloaded.

The three movable sides being unscrewed and thrown back, the press-cake, which now consists of layers about half an inch thick for all *granulated* powders, is broken into pieces, and put in barrels.

In most gunpowder factories press-cake is produced by pressing the meal between loose piles of copper plates; the less dense portions of the cake at the edges being cut off.

5. *Granulating.*

Granulating Machine (*see* Pl. VII).—The granulating machine consists of a strong gun-metal framework holding three pairs of gun-metal rollers, C, arranged *in échelon*, the second pair being in front of and in a plane below the first, and so on. When making fine-grain powders in the machine with three pairs of rollers, the bottom pair is without teeth, the finest pair of toothed ($\frac{1}{4}$-inch) rollers are next above the plain ones; the teeth of the upper pair are half an inch apart. The rollers work in sliding bearings, with counter-weights, of the same kind as those of the breaking-down machine, so that the rollers may open to allow any hard substance to pass through, and prevent undue friction.

At one end of the machine is a wooden hopper, A, filled with press-cake, which constantly supplies an endless band, B, similar to that in the breaking-down machine, through a pair of rollers with coarse teeth; when the press-cake arrives at the highest point of the band, it falls over and is received between the first pair of rollers. Underneath each pair of rollers, except the bottom, is a short wire screen, D, connecting it with the top of the next lower pair.

When making fine-grain powders, for example, these short screens are covered with 10-mesh copper-wire cloth; all the powder which is not broken sufficiently small to pass through the *first* screen is carried by it to the second pair of rollers, and in like manner that which is not broken small enough by the *second* pair of rollers is carried to the *third* pair by the *second* screen. In addition to these *short* screens there are two *long* screens, E E, the top one covered with 10-mesh and the under one with 20-mesh copper-wire cloth, which are set at an angle *below the whole* of the rollers, and about three inches apart. All the screens, long and short, are fixed in a separate wooden frame, which is suspended on lance-wood springs; by means of a polygonal friction wheel, or pinion, this frame is made to vibrate quickly, when the machine is in motion, so as to cause the grain to pass through, or to travel on to the end of the screens, to be delivered between the next pair of rollers, or into the boxes at the bottom. That grain which is broken small enough to pass through the 10-mesh short screen leading from one pair of rollers to the next, will fall on to, and of course pass through the 10-mesh long screen, which runs from the top of the machine to the bottom; then that which is retained on the 20-mesh is R.F.G.^{2} powder. It falls into boxes, G, which are moved forward as they are filled, fresh ones taking their places, while the pieces which do not pass the 10-mesh screens, called "chucks," fall off at the lower end into separate boxes, H, and are again placed in the hopper to be re-granulated; that which is fine enough to pass through the 20-mesh screen falls on the bottom board, K, of the frame, and is conducted into a box, F; this is called "dust," and is sent back to the incorporating mill in 60-lb. charges to be run for 40 minutes. In making any other powder the wire-cloth covering of the screens must be changed, according to the limits of size required.

The same machine is used for granulating, R.L.G.^{2} and R.L.G.^{4}, the mesh of the copper wire gauze forming the screens being of suitable size.

All grain from the granulating machine is called *foul grain*.

6. "*Dusting.*"

Blank F.G., Q.F. Shell F.G. and R.F.G.^{2}.—These *dogwood* powders have a much greater proportion of dust in them

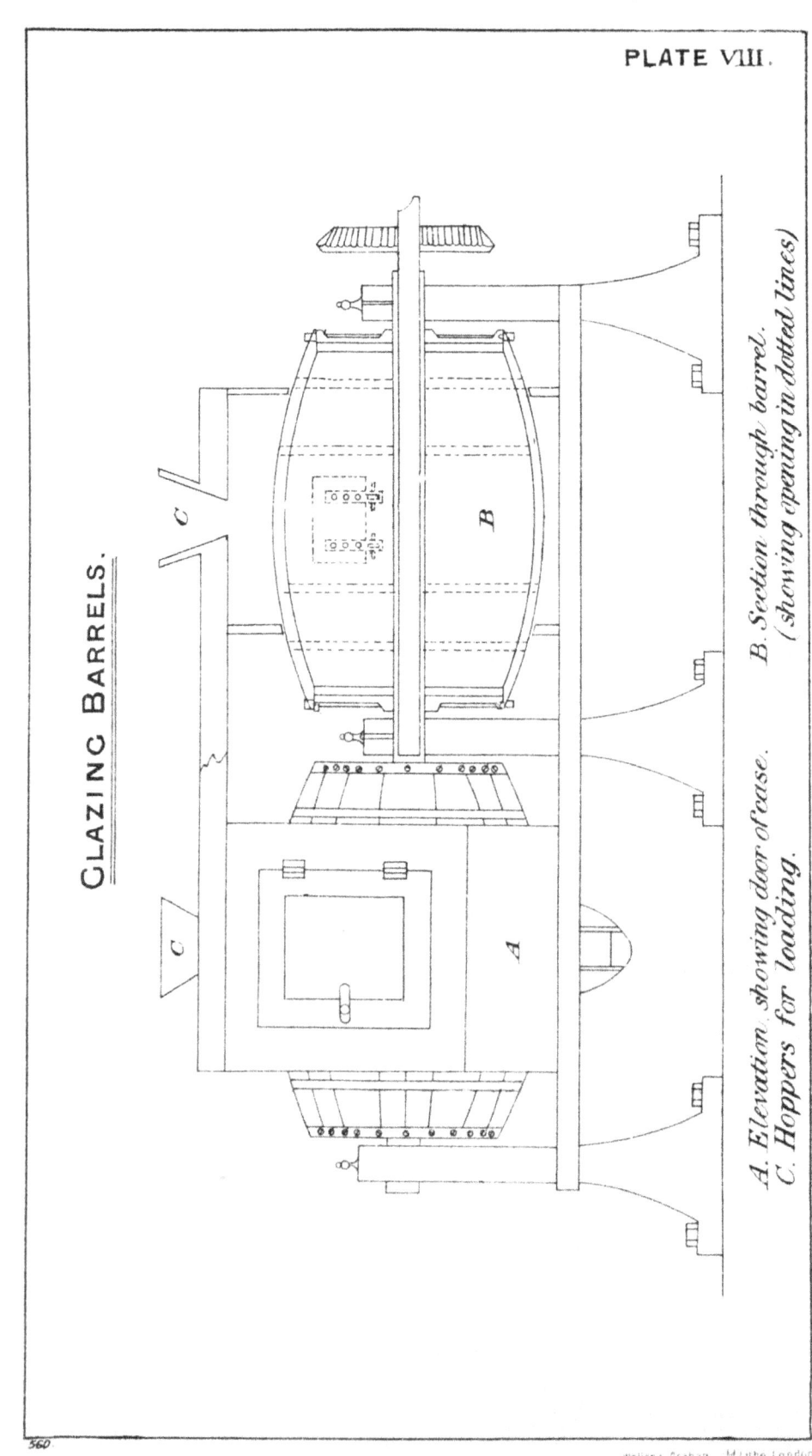

when they leave the granulating machine than the large cannon powders; it is necessary on this account to use a dusting reel, called a *slope reel*, on account of its being set at an angle of about 4°. It consists of a cylindrical frame about 7 feet 10 inches long, and 1 foot 5 inches in diameter, open at both ends and covered with 20-mesh copper-wire cloth for R.F.G.^{2} and 36-mesh for the blank and shell powders; it makes about 40 revolutions in a minute. A continuous stream of powder, fed by a hopper at the upper end, passes through while the reel revolves, and falls out at the lower end into barrels. The slope reel is enclosed in a case to catch the dust, which is sent back to the incorporating mill to be reworked.

7. "*Glazing.*"

Blank F.G., Q.F. Shell F.G., and R.F.G.^{2}.—These powders, after passing through the slope reel, are put into glazing barrels (*see* Pl. VIII), 5 feet in length by 2½ feet in diameter, which revolve about 34 times in a minute. About 500 lb. are put into each drum, and run, the blank and shell powders for five hours, R.F.G.^{2} for 8 to 10 hours; a fine black glaze is imparted, merely by the friction and the heat evolved by the motion. The powder is then unloaded into barrels, passed again through another slope-reel covered with 20-mesh wire-cloth for R.F.G.^{2}, and 36-mesh for the blank and shell powders, and afterwards sifted on an 11-mesh sieve, which retains any large pieces and allows the powder to pass into barrels. It is then ready for drying.

R.L.G.^{2} and R.L.G.^{4}.—These powders are glazed for two to three hours in the same glazing barrels, with about an ounce of graphite per 100 lb.

The drums are arranged in the glazing house in sets of four, and are enclosed in a wooden case with hoppers, to facilitate loading and unloading. A glazing consists of about 20 barrels of 100 lb. each.

8. "*Stoving*" or *Drying.*

All kinds of gunpowder are stoved in the same manner. A "stove" or drying room, heated by steam pipes, is fitted with open framework shelves one above another, to 7 or 8 tiers in height, the steam pipes being underneath. Wooden frames with canvas bottoms, about 3 feet long, 1 foot 6 inches wide, and 2½ inches deep, each holding about 20 lb. of powder, are placed on these shelves. About 5 tons are dried at one time.

The length of time and the temperature vary according to the nature of the gunpowder and the amount of moisture it contains. Blank F.G. and Q.F. Shell F.G. require one hour at 100° F., while R.F.G.^{2} takes two hours at the same temperature; R.L.G.^{2} and R.L.G.^{4} require from two to four hours at 100° F. The temperature is raised and lowered gradually.

The ceiling and roof are fitted with ventilators, through

which the heated damp air escapes, and there are also ventilators below, so that there is a constant current of air circulating through the building. It is of the greatest importance that the air charged with vapour should be carried off, for if this be not effectually done, the moisture would be recondensed upon the powder, when the temperature is lowered.

9. "*Finishing.*"

The drying process produces in all kinds of grain gunpowder a small portion of dust, which it is necessary to remove; but the finishing process has upon fine-grain powders a much greater effect than the mere removal of dust; it gives a final glaze or "colour," as it is called, which is of considerable importance.

Finishing is performed in a horizontal reel (*see* Pl. IX) consisting of a cylindrical wooden frame 8 feet 2 inches long by 2 feet 2 inches in diameter, covered with 18-mesh canvas; it makes 45 revolutions per minute, and the charge is about 300 lb. for each reel. Each reel is enclosed in a wooden case to catch the dust; there is a hopper at the top of the case for loading through an opening in the side of the reel, but the latter is unloaded by lowering and unscrewing one end.

R.F.G.[2] is reeled for $2\frac{1}{2}$ hours, and has, when finished, a very glossy appearance without using any graphite.

R.L.G.[2] and R.L.G.[4] powders are finished in a similar reel for $1\frac{1}{2}$ hours.

10. "*Blending.*"

For many years past advantage has been taken of every opportunity in the processes of the manufacture of gunpowder to mix or "blend" the grain together so as to obtain more uniform results at proof. For example, filling the set of glazing barrels or drums from a batch of grain can be so done as to get a "glazing" of about 16 barrels quite uniform. Formerly, two or more glazings used to be mixed when filling the trays for the stove and loading the reels for the finishing process, but now a far more exact mode of blending has been adopted. The machine for carrying out this process is of the simplest construction, consisting of a wooden hopper, divided into four equal compartments. At the bottom of each separate compartment, passages leading into a central shoot can be opened or closed simultaneously by sliding valves of wood or gun-metal. The *modus operandi* is equally simple: a barrel of powder is placed in each compartment of the hopper, and by opening the valves, four barrels of uniform mixture can be taken from the shoot below. Thus, starting with the uniform glazing as a unit, a large batch of uniform quality can readily be obtained. The above mode of blending is found to give very even results with all descriptions of powder, and especially with the smaller sizes of grain.

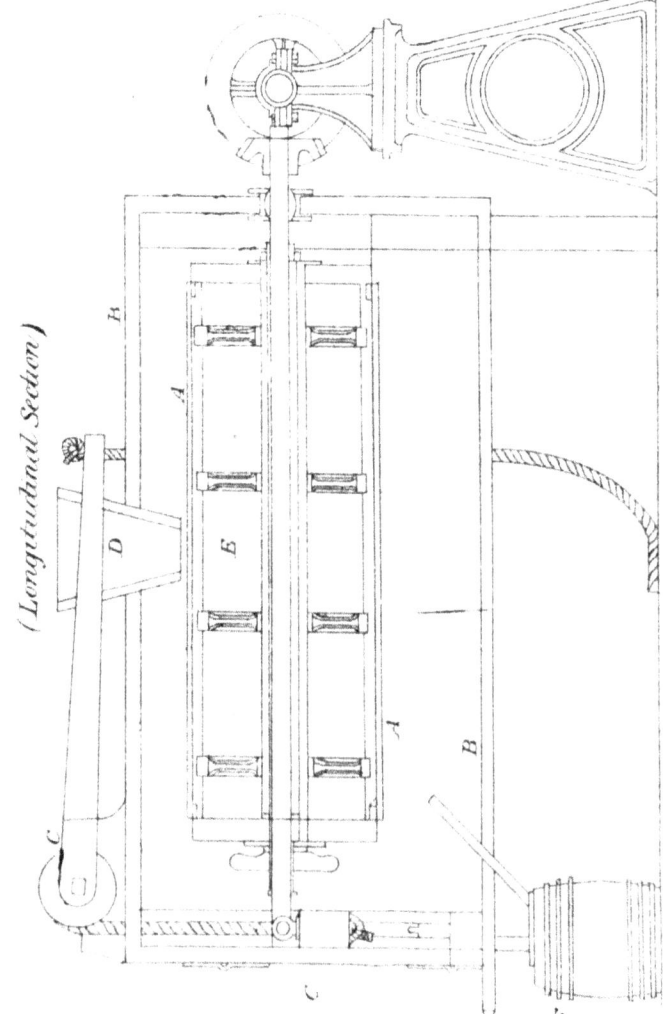

HORIZONTAL FINISHING REEL.
(Longitudinal Section)

PLATE LX.

A. Cylindrical reel.
B. Reel case.
C. Apparatus for lowering one end for unloading.
D. Hopper for loading.
E. Opening in reel for loading.
F. Barrel for unloading into.

All granulated powders are blended as follows:—

(1) Before stoving, four glazings are blended together in the four-way hopper, making about 64 (open) factory barrels of about 100 lb. each. The powder is then placed on the canvas "cases" or trays in the stove.

(2) After stoving, this batch or "stoving" is "finished" in horizontal reels. It is then blended into uniform batches of 50 barrels in a four-way hopper; these are again blended to make uniform batches of either 100 or 200 barrels.

Samples are drawn from each lot of 100 barrels and proved: from the results thus obtained two, three, or four batches are selected for the final blending; more frequently, however, four batches of 100 barrels each are blended together into a uniform brand of 400 barrels.

Class B or Cut Powders.

This class includes those natures of gunpowder in which the press-cake is "cut" with knife edges—either in a machine or by hand—first into strips and then into pieces of an approximately cubical shape; hence they are usually called cubical powders.

The first three processes of "mixing," "incorporating," and "breaking down" are conducted in precisely the same manner as for Class A powders. S.P. is made with four-hours' willow and alder charcoal, and is incorporated for three hours, and is worked with rather more moisture than the smaller cannon powders.

4. *Pressing.*

No press-box is used for S.P. powder.

The "meal" is pressed between metal plates, which are built up horizontally on the ram of the hydraulic press.

The exact quantity for each slab of press-cake is obtained by placing a wooden frame, $1\frac{1}{4}$ inches high, on each plate in succession; the meal is carefully filled into this frame, and scraped off level with the top by a wooden straight-edge. The frame is then removed, another plate put in position, and the frame replaced as before. There are 27 plates for each pressing, forming 26 slabs.

An arrangement is made in the frame which forms a groove in the cake, and thus allows the latter to be easily broken in two for convenience in cutting.

5. *Cutting.*

S.P. is "cut" from the press-cake in machines which essentially consist of two pairs of phosphor-bronze rollers, armed with *longitudinal* knife edges, and placed in a strong wooden frame, so that the axes of the second pair are at right angles to those of the first, the axes of both pairs being in vertical planes.

The knife-edges are set apart at an interval corresponding to the size of the powder to be cut.

The slabs of press-cake are fed by hand horizontally between the first pair of rollers, by which they are cut into strips; these strips are conveyed by a band to a copper plate, they are then pushed by hand on to a second band at right angles to the first, which conveys them to the second pair of rollers, which cuts the strips into cubes.

The powder then falls into barrels, and is conveyed to the glazing house.

At least 90% of almost perfect cubes are obtained by this machine; the remainder are removed by hand during the operation of cutting.

6. *Glazing.*

S.P. powder requires no separate dusting process, but is taken at once from the cutting machine or knives to the glazing barrels (*see* Pl. VIII). They hold about 500 lb.

This process, although it does not give to these heavy powders the glaze so apparent in the fine grain, yet rubs off the sharp corners and edges of the cubes. Moreover, the friction—combined with the very considerable amount of heat evolved—produces a hardening of the surface which is very valuable, as it tends to retard ignition, and also prevents the formation of dust. S.P. is glazed for four hours. After being glazed, the powder is sifted on a ⅜-inch mesh wire sieve to remove the small pieces.

7. *Stoving.*

The operation of drying S.P. is conducted in the same manner as for granulated powders, but a much longer time is required; it is stoved about 36 hours at 130° F. The "glazings" are kept separate in the stove.

8. *Finishing.*

A special "skeleton" reel (*see* Pl. X), made of wood, is used to finish S.P. powder; it is barrel-shaped, and large enough to hold 16 barrels at a time, the "ribs" being at such a distance apart as to confine the powder being finished, while the dust and broken pieces fall into the outer casing. It is run for about forty minutes, when pure graphite—in the proportion of 2 oz. to each 400 lb. of powder—is introduced in small muslin bags, and the powder is finished for twenty minutes more.

9. *Blending.*

By taking eight "glazing"* and mixing two barrels of each at a time in the skeleton reel, a fairly even batch of 102 barrels of 125 lb. each is obtained.

---

* A glazing consisting of 16 barrels of 100 lb. each.

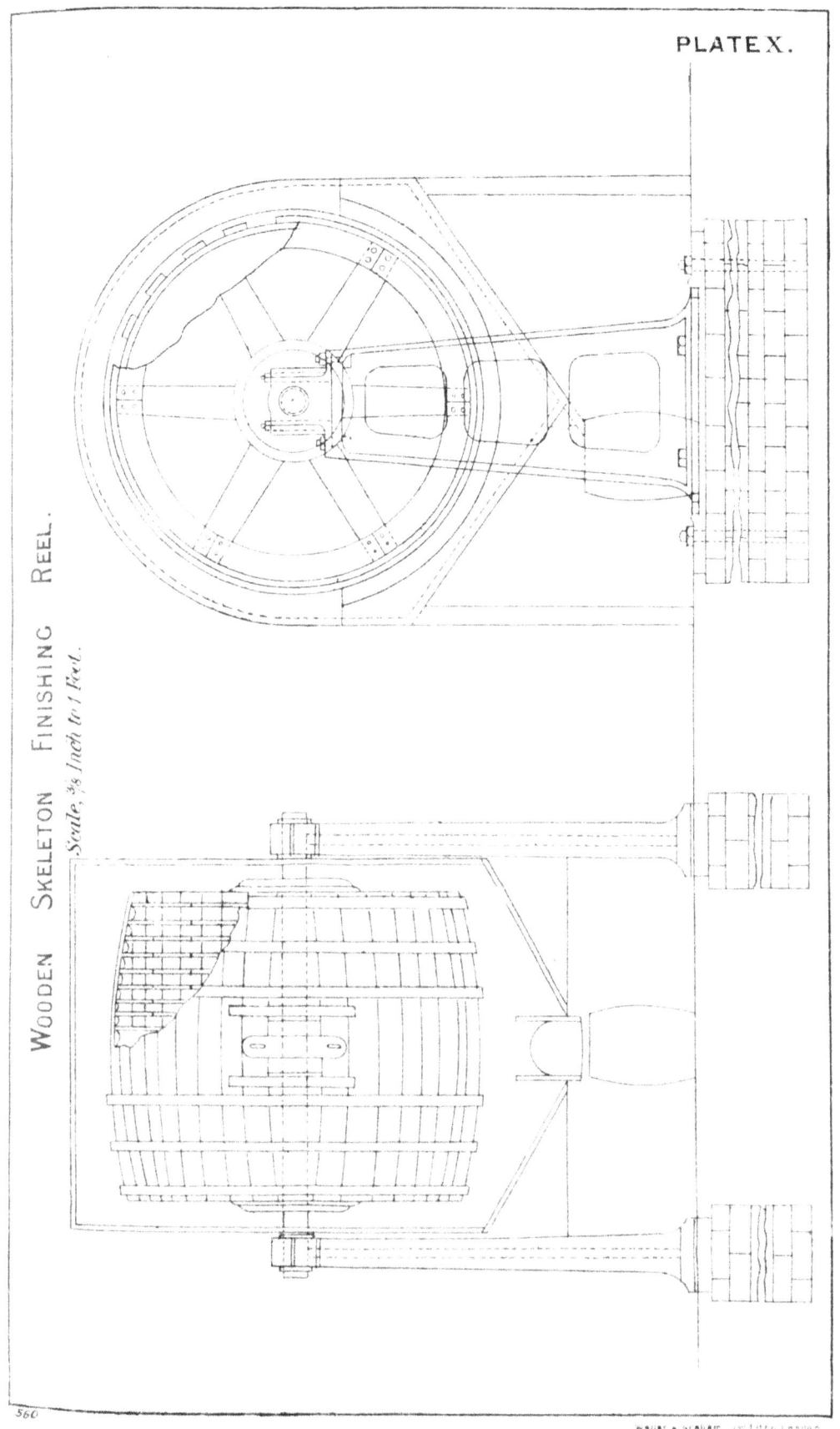

PLATE X.

WOODEN SKELETON FINISHING REEL.
Scale, ⅜ Inch to 1 Foot.

PRISMATIC

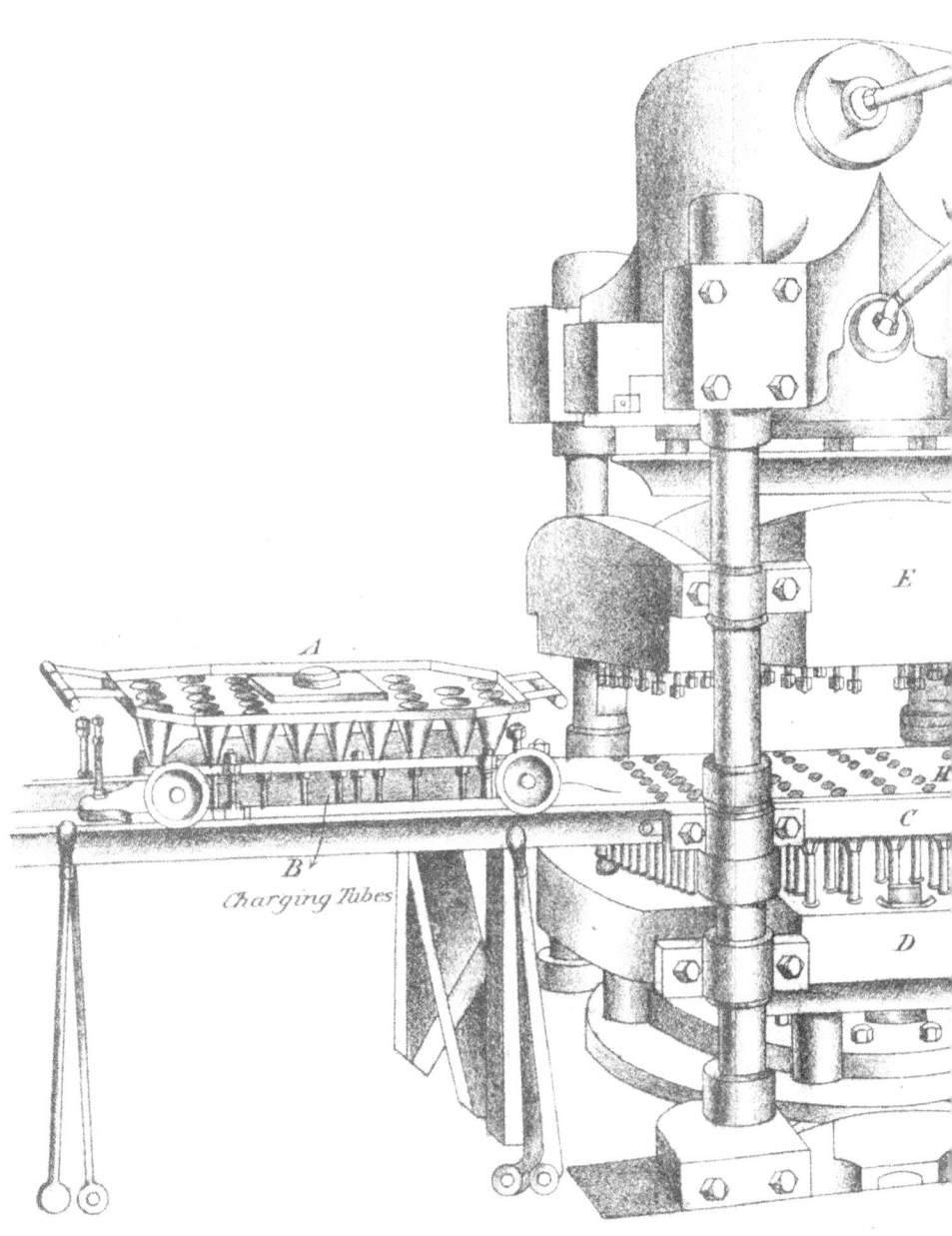

DER MACHINE.

PLATE XI.

Weller & Graham, Ltd. Litho London

(1) The 102 barrels are blended into uniform batches of 51 barrels each, in a four-way hopper, similar to that used for blending Class A powders.

(2) One barrel from each uniform batch of 51 is taken, and blended in the four-way hopper into a perfectly uniform lot of 102 barrels.

Class C or Moulded Powders.
(Prismatic Powder.)

THIS class comprises gunpowder, each grain or piece of which is moulded and pressed *separately* in a metal mould. The following Prism powders are now in the service—Prism[1] Black, Prism[1] Brown, S.B.C., and E.X.E. To make Prismatic powder in any kind of machine, there is needed, (1) a mould or " bouche," in which is placed the granulated powder, a certain number of bouches being usually contained in one metal plate; (2) "plungers," to fit the bouches accurately, in order to give the necessary compression; (3) phosphor-bronze "pins," to form the perforations, passing through both plungers and bouches; (4) a "charger" for loading the bouches simultaneously with the *exact* quantity of *granulated* powder; (5) an arrangement for pushing the finished prisms out of the moulds.

Making the Grain for Prismatic Powders.—The processes of manufacture before moulding are carried out in precisely the same manner as in making granulated powder of the smaller sizes.

The press-cake is granulated in the usual manner, to a size of 8 to 16 meshes to the inch; the foul grain is then run through a slope-reel, and is afterwards carefully blended to ensure uniformity.

Prism[1] Brown, S.B.C., and E.X.E. powders differ in the following particulars :—

(1) The employment of special charcoal.

(2) The ingredients being in different proportions as follows* :—

For Prism[1] Brown and S.B.C., 79 saltpetre, 18 charcoal, and 3 sulphur.

For E.X.E., $77\frac{6}{15}$ saltpetre, $17\frac{9}{15}$ charcoal, 5 sulphur.

8. *Moulding, or Pressing the Prisms.*

The operation of moulding, or pressing the grain into prisms, is performed either in hydraulic or "cam" machines.

Hydraulic Machine.—The hydraulic machine is shown in Pl. XI; it produces 64 finished prisms at one operation, the necessary power being supplied by an accumulator. There are two rams, the bottom one, to which is attached the lower plunger-

---

* From 1·7 to 2·2 per cent. of water is also present, being now recognised as an ingredient.

block D, and the top ram, which works the upper plunger-block E, the bouche-block C being placed between them. The operations of pressing are as follows:—The "charger" A, being run back, the 64 hoppers are carefully filled with grain powder; the charger-carriage is then run upon the top (H) of the bouche-block and locked in position. The 64 "charging tubes" B, are now exactly over the 64 phosphor-bronze bouches or moulds in the bouche-block, and by the movement of a lever, the powder in the hoppers is caused to fall into the charging tubes below; these latter are set so as to hold the exact quantity of powder required for any particular density of prism. Then, by moving another lever, the contents of the tubes are emptied into the bouches, and the charger is run back clear of the machine. The operator at the valves now allows the water to flow into the top ram, which closes the holes above, he then allows the water to flow into the bottom ram.

Pressure is kept on for from ten to twenty seconds, according to atmospheric conditions and the density required; the top plungers are then lifted, the prisms forced out of the moulds by raising the lower plungers, and cleared off the surface of the bouche-block on to a wooden table, when the charger is again pushed on to reload the bouches. The axial perforations through the prisms are formed while pressing by means of phosphor-bronze rods, or needles, which pass through the lower plungers, and also fit into corresponding holes in the upper set, so that the powder-prisms are pressed around the rods. In raising the lower set of plungers to eject the prisms, the latter are likewise forced off the rods. The time taken for a complete pressing is about two minutes.

Cam Machine.—In the cam machines (*see* Pl. XII) the compression is applied by means of an eccentric and crank pin, A and A_1, on a shaft, B, driven by water power. This machine works automatically and very rapidly, pressing six prisms at a time; there is a small hopper, C, for the granulated powder, with a self-feeding apparatus, the charger, D, sliding backwards and forwards, so as to be alternately underneath the hopper and the plungers. The charger, D, is actuated by a bell-crank lever, E, off the cam, F. The powder is compressed in the bouche-block, G, by phosphor-bronze plungers, H and H_1, attached to upper and lower cross-heads, I and I_1. The holes in the prisms are made by means of phosphor-bronze pins, J, attached to cross-head I_2. The eccentrics exert for a very short space of time an enormous pressure, which not only gives the required density, but finishes off the prisms with a very hard smooth surface, which ignites more slowly, and thus causes less *initial* pressure in the bore of the gun than in the case of the rougher surface of the prisms pressed in an hydraulic machine.

9. *Stoving.*

Prismatic powder is placed upon the stove cases, and carefully dried at two different temperatures. First, for 24 hours at 90° F., and, secondly, for 36 hours at 140° F.

PLATE XII.

CAM MACHINE.

A A. Eccentrics.
B. Shaft.
C. Hopper.
D. Charger.
E. Bell Crank Lever.
F. Cam.
G. Bush Block.
H H₁ Plunger.
I, I₁ Plunger, Crosshead.
I₂ Pin Block.
J. Phosphor Bronze Pins.

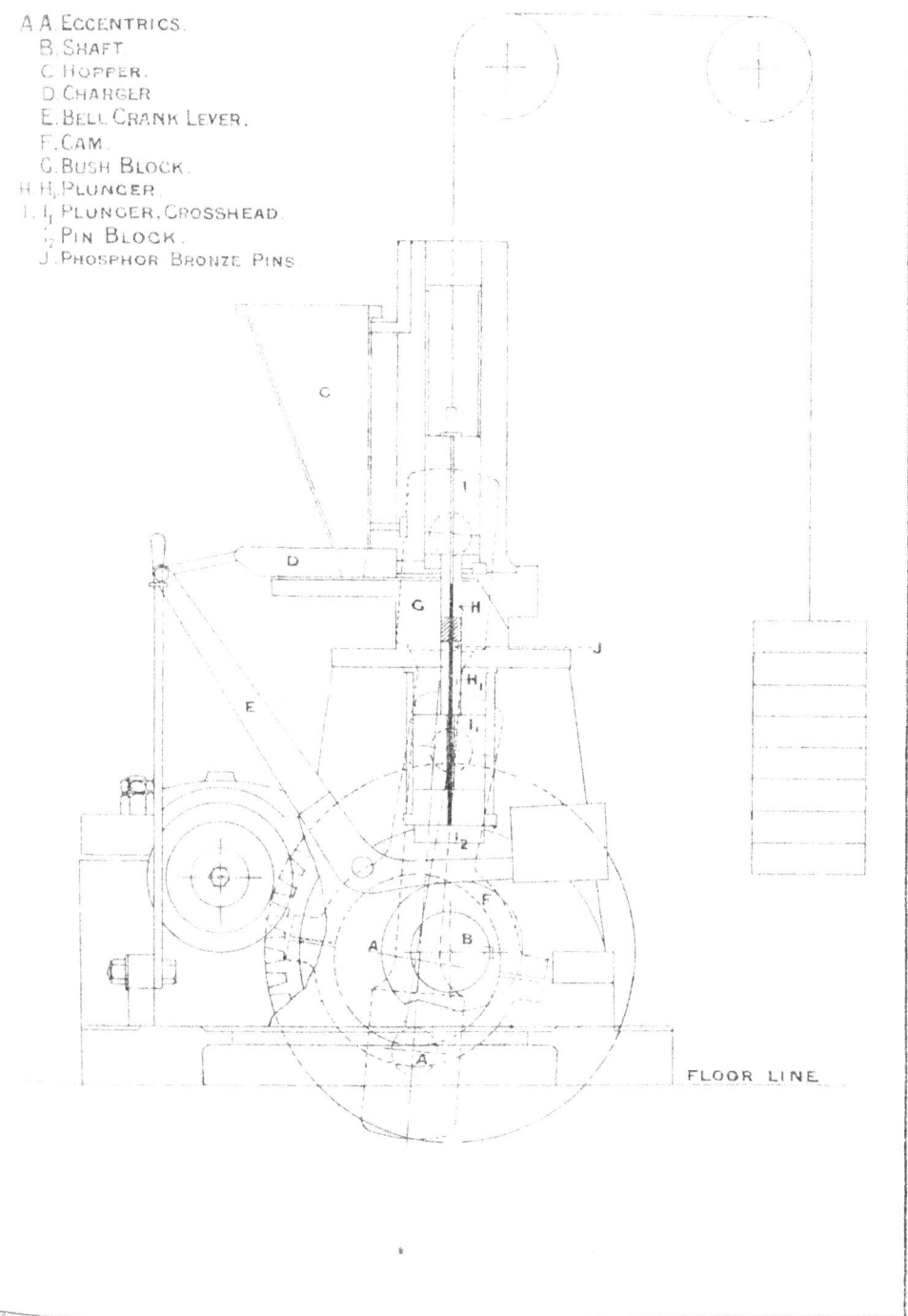

FLOOR LINE

10. *Blending and Packing.*

The finished prisms are carefully blended by hand into batches of 100 boxes of 100 lb. each.

S.B.C. and E.X.E. are made in uniform lots of 612 cases. To distinguish these powders from Prism[1] Black, and Prism[1] Brown, the top of each prism is grooved as shown in the sectional diagrams—

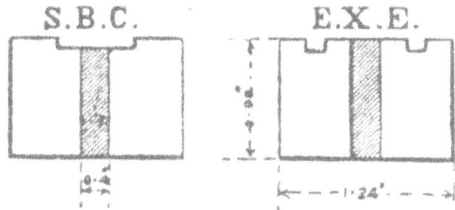

The colour of S.B.C. powder is similar to that of Prism[1] Brown; E.X.E. is a dark slate colour.

CHAPTER III.

EXAMINATION AND PROOF OF GUNPOWDER.

The tests to which powder is subjected are intended to ascertain—

1. *If the powder have a proper colour, a proper amount of glaze, sufficient hardness and crispness, and if it be free from dust.*
—These points can be judged by the hand and eye alone, and require a certain amount of experience in the examiner. The cleanness of the powder can be easily tested by pouring a quantity from a bowl held two or three feet above the barrel in a good light. If there be any loose dust it will be readily detected.

2. *If it be properly incorporated.*—This is tested by "flashing;" that is, burning a small quantity on a glass, porcelain, or copper plate. The powder is put into a small copper cylinder, like a large thimble, which is then inverted on the flashing plate. This provides for the particles of powder being arranged in pretty nearly the same way each time, which is very important. If the powder has been thoroughly incorporated, it will "flash" or puff off when touched with a hot iron, with but few "lights" or sparks, and leaving only some smoke marks on the plate. A badly incorporated powder will give rise to a quantity of sparks, and also leaves specks of undecomposed saltpetre and sulphur forming a dirty residue. Although a very badly-worked powder can be at once detected, yet, as a *comparative* test, "flashing" needs an experienced eye to form an accurate judgment, for powder made from slack-burnt charcoal will never flash so well as that in which the charcoal is prepared at a fairly high temperature. Powder once injured by damp will flash very badly, no matter how carefully it may have been incorporated. This arises from a partial solution of the saltpetre.

3. *Size, shape, and proportion of the grains.*—The *size* of grains, or pieces, in large *uniform* powders "cut" or "moulded" by machinery, is usually tested by actual measurement. Prismatic powder is also tested for size by means of a metal frame, into which a certain number of prisms must accurately fit. A *granulated* powder can be readily sifted on the two sieves which define its highest and lowest limit of size; it must all pass the one and be retained on the other. For example, R.F.G.^{2} powder should pass through a sieve of 11* meshes to the inch,

---

* The size of R.F.G.^{2} powder is from 12 to 20 meshes to the linear inch, but, *in sifting it by hand*, a sieve covered with 11-mesh copper wire cloth is employed; this is on account of the smaller force which can be then applied.

and be retained on one of 20 meshes. This sifting, however, conveys no idea of the *proportions of different sized grains* contained in the powder. For instance, a sample of R.F.G.[2] powder *may* consist *entirely* of grains just small enough to pass the 11-mesh sieve, or just large enough to be retained on the 20-mesh; and these two powders would give very different results. To obviate this, a sample is sifted on three sieves, an 11-mesh, a 16-mesh, and a 20-mesh. All must pass through the first; out of 16 parts, 12 should be *retained* on the 16-mesh sieve; of the remainder, not less than 3 parts should be retained on the 20-mesh sieve; not more than one-sixteenth part may *pass* the 20-mesh sieve. The *shape* of granulated powders is judged by the eye; the grains must be compact, not flaky nor flat.

4. *Density.*—100 grammes of the sample to be tested is weighed in a beaker and transferred to the globe of a Bianchi densimeter, an apparatus by which the air can be pumped out of a removable glass globe fitted with stop-cocks above and below. The air is then exhausted, and the mercury allowed to fill the globe and tube. The cocks are then closed, the nozzle taken off, and the globe removed from the densimeter and accurately weighed. The difference in the weight of the globe filled with mercury alone, and filled with mercury and powder (under precisely similar conditions), being obtained, the density of the sample of powder may be read off from a table giving the densities corresponding to differences of weight. Gunpowder of larger size than R.L.G.[2] is broken up in a mortar and the dust sifted out before weighing.

Then if—

S = Specific gravity of mercury at time of experiment,
W = Weight of globe filled with mercury alone,
W^1 = Weight of globe filled with powder and mercury.

$$\text{Density of gunpowder} = \frac{S \times 100}{(W - W^1) + 100}$$

Example of the calculation of the density in the absence of a table; suppose—

Weight of globe full of mercury	4,138 grammes.
,, ,, ,, and powder	3,434 ,,
Difference	704 ,,
Specific gravity of mercury at 80° F.	13·56
Weight of powder	100 ,,

Then—

$$\frac{13 \cdot 56 \times 100}{704 + 100} = 1 \cdot 689 \text{ density required.}$$

The density of Prismatic powder is more conveniently obtained by means of a simple immersion densimeter. This machine consists of a light tubular standard, or rod of brass, which is free to move vertically *with great ease* between two sets of three friction rollers, arranged one set above the other. This standard is provided at the bottom with three claws to hold the powder, a needle-point being fixed in the centre between the claws to indicate the exact depth to which the powder should be immersed in a bath of mercury placed below; at the top it has a pan for the weights. To take a density by this machine, several pieces, say ten, of the powder are weighed in air, the results noted and divided by 10 to obtain the mean weight; then each piece is placed successively between the claws of the densimeter and pressed under the mercury, by placing weights in the pan at top, until the needle-point is brought in contact with the surface. The sinking weight required for each piece is noted, and the sum of the weights divided by 10 to obtain the mean. The mean weight in air of the pieces of powder, and the mean sinking weight being thus obtained, the corresponding density is read off from a table.

In the immersion densimeter the sinking weight takes the place of the difference of weights, and we have the variable mean weight of the 10 prisms, or cubes, instead of the definite weight of powder used with the Bianchi densimeter—

If the weight of powder be .. .. 481·8 grammes.
„ sinking weight .. .. .. 3140·0 „
„ specific gravity of mercury at 80° F. 13·56 „

Then—

$$\frac{13·56 \times 481·8}{3140 + 481·8} = 1·803 \text{ (nearly) density required.}$$

5. *Moisture.*—A portion of the gunpowder is coarsely crushed in a mortar, and 100 grains is then accurately weighed on a pair of ground watch-glasses of known weight. The covering-glass being underneath the one containing the powder, the sample is dried in a water-oven for one hour for black powder, and for three hours for brown powder, at a temperature of 160° F. The powder is then covered with the underneath glass, removed from the oven, and placed under a bell-glass to cool for about 20 minutes. At the expiration of that time it is again carefully weighed, and the loss of weight represents the percentage of moisture which the sample contained.

6. *Hygrometric Test.*—The powder to be tested is placed in a double box, an inner one of sheet copper, and an outer one of stout wood, the space between being packed closely with some non-conducting material. The boxes are closed with a double lid, having a perforation to allow of a thermometer being introduced. The samples to be tested are placed on a movable tray of copper wire about half way up the inner box. On a level with the tray, all round the box, is a shallow trough which contains a saturated solution of saltpetre; the bottom of the box is also covered with the solution.

A sample of 200 grains of each of the powders to be tested is put in a little tray with a fine wire-gauze bottom, and placed in the box, the lid being closely screwed down; a thermometer is inserted through the aperture in the lid, and the temperature noted. The sample is allowed to remain in the box 24 hours for the smaller powders and 48 hours for the larger sizes, which are tested in single pieces. At the end of the period, the temperature of the interior of box is again noted, before taking off the lid, and the powder taken out and weighed. The increase of weight gives the moisture *absorbed* during the exposure, which, added to that already contained in the powder, indicates its hygrometric quality.

Gunpowder made with charcoal carbonised at a low temperature absorbs moisture far more readily than that made with perfectly burnt charcoal; dogwood charcoal, burnt slowly, and the very slack-burnt straw charcoal are far more absorbent than common charcoal, burnt at a fairly high temperature, and the powders made therefrom are similarly affected. This shows the importance of keeping the R.F.G.[2] and Prism[1] Brown gunpowder in a dry place, or in air-tight cases.

7. *Firing proof.*—(a) *Muzzle velocity.*—Each description of gunpowder is fired in the small-arm, or piece of ordnance (approximately) with which it is intended to be used, under certain fixed conditions as to charge, projectile, and gravimetric density. The muzzle-velocities are taken with the Boulengé Chronograph (a description of which is contained in the *Treatise on the Construction of Ordnance*). At the time of proof, one or more rounds of an accepted brand of the same powder will be fired, in order to serve as a "Standard of Comparison."

(b) *Pressure in bore.*—All cannon powders must likewise give pressures not exceeding certain limits, measured by the compression of copper cylinders adjusted in crusher gauges, which are placed either in the metal of the powder chamber or in the base of the cartridge.

(c) *Accuracy.*—R.F.G.[2] powder, if intended for small-arm cartridges, is further tested by firing at Woolwich, after being made up into cartridges; and a record kept of the "Figure of merit" of the "target" made by each Lot at 500 yards range.

8. *Proportions and purity of ingredients.*—These are determined by analysis in the following manner:—

1st. *Sulphur.*—From 10 to 12 (0·5 to 1 grm.) grains are oxidised completely by digestion at a gentle heat with strong nitric acid and potassium-chlorate. The excess of nitric acid is then driven off by evaporation to dryness, and the residue dissolved in water. To the solution, barium chloride is added, and the precipitated barium sulphate completely washed by repeated boiling with small quantities of water, it is then ignited and weighed.

2nd. *Saltpetre.*—About 80 (5 grms.) grains are treated with boiling water, and the dissolved nitre, after filtration from the sulphur and charcoal, is evaporated to dryness and weighed.

3rd. *Charcoal.*—The quantity of this ingredient is represented by the amount required to make up 100 parts after deducting the percentage of sulphur and nitre found.

In 100 parts of ordinary service black powder, *dry*, are :—

Saltpetre	..	..	75·00
Sulphur	..	..	10·00
Charcoal	..	..	15·00

In the specification for powders it is laid down that they should contain not less than 75 nor more than 76 per cent. of saltpetre; also, that not more than one part of chlorine, nor more than four parts of sodium, are contained in 3,000 parts of the saltpetre. The limits of the proportion of sulphur allowed are from 9·5 to 10·5 per cent.

9. *Classification of Powders.*—Gunpowder is classified and marked according to the following table:—

Class.	Designation.		Description.
	General.	Detail.	
I.	Service	S.B.C. Prism¹ brown ,, black Prism² E.X.E. P.² P. S.P. Q.F.¹ M.G. L.G. R.L.G. R.L.G.² R.L.G.⁴ F.G. R.F.G. R.F.G.² Pistol.... Rifled pistol....	1. All new gunpowder. 2. All unused gunpowder, the packages of which have been opened for examination, and which has been found serviceable. This is to stand first in order for practice purposes. 3. Gunpowder returned into store (including the contents of cannon cartridges) which on examination may be found uninjured. 4. Gunpowder which, after repair, is found fit for service.
II.	Blank*	Blank L.G., reduced	1. L.G., R.L.G., R.L.G.², in bulk or from broken-down cannon cartridges, too dusty or broken in grain for Class I, and which cannot be repaired for the same.
		Blank L.G., new	2. Gunpowder, specially manufactured as blank L.G.
		Blank F.G., reduced	1. F.G., R.F.G., R.F.G.², and pistol, too dusty or broken in grain for Class I, and which cannot be repaired for the same.
		Blank F.G., new	2. Gunpowder, specially manufactured as blank F.G.

* Blank L.G. and F.G. are suitable for shell L.G. and F.G. respectively.

Class.	Designation.		Description.
	General.	Detail.	
III.	Shell	Shell, P.	1. P. and S.P. powder in bulk, or from broken-down cartridges, too dusty or broken in grain for Class I, and which cannot be repaired for the same. 2. Gunpowder specially manufactured as shell P.
		Shell, Q.F.	Q.F.[1] powder in bulk, or from Q.F. cartridges which has deteriorated or is no longer required in Class I.
		Shell, L.G.	L.G., R.L.G., R.L.G.[2], and R.L.G.[4], in bulk or from broken-down cannon cartridges, too dusty or broken in grain for Class II.
		Shell, F.G.	F.G., R.F.G., R.F.G.[2], and pistol powder too dusty or broken in grain for Class II.
		Q.F. shell, F.G.	Gunpowder specially manufactured for bursting charges of 3-pr. and 6-pr. Q.F. shells.
IV.	Doubtful		All gunpowder awaiting examination.
V.	Condemned		All gunpowder found unfit for any of the above Classes, but available for blasting purposes, or for sale.
VI.	Condemned for extraction		Gunpowder obtained from shells and S.A.A. or other cartridges or charges which contain their own means of ignition, except Q.F. cartridges, and which is to be immediately wetted.

Doubtful Powder.—(Class IV) is returned into store at Purfleet, for further examination. It will then either be distributed among the first three classes, or condemned into Classes V or VI. Powder marked "*repairable for service*" (Class I.D.), or "*repairable for blank*" (Class II.D.), is sent to Waltham Abbey to be repaired, as required; repaired "service" powder is always specially marked after being blended into *lots*, and is examined and proved in the same manner as new powder. Condemned powder of Class VI is either destroyed or sent to Waltham Abbey to have the saltpetre extracted for further use.

Brown Powders.

Brown powders differ from the ordinary black powder, mainly in the nature of the charcoal and secondly in the quantity of sulphur. The latter amounts to 3 per cent. or less.

The *raison d'être* of this class of powder is that they may be used in very large charges without straining the gun as is the case with ordinary black powders.

The mechanical operation of pressing the powder until it is very dense or close grained, as mentioned under prismatic powders, is for the purpose of delaying somewhat the initial burning. Up to moderate pressures this "densifying" of the powder grains is effective, but as longer ranges of the projectile became desirable and the size of guns and weight of projectile increased, it soon became apparent that the mechanically obtained density of a powder was useless or rather had attained its practical maximum. As a matter of fact it is possible to press the ordinary prism powder to a specific gravity of about 1·8. Now fully ¾ of the weight of a powder is saltpetre, and the density of this substance is only a trifle over 2 when in the pure crystalline state. Very few crystalline salts have been found to be compressible to any material extent.* Therefore, considering the composition of powder, it is very unlikely indeed that a much greater density could be obtained by any safe amount of pressure.

When powder is burning in a gun gases are produced under pressure. These gases are more than red hot. Up to a certain critical pressure they will not penetrate far into the close mass of powder, but the latter will burn away layer by layer regularly. But when the pressure arises above some particular amount, owing to magnitude of charge and weight of projectile, then the hot gases will at a certain period in the combustion of the charge penetrate through and ignite all the still unburnt part of the charge practically instantaneously.

The result is a sudden rise in the pressure curve before the shot has got "way," and the gun suffers. That is why it is impossible to use a coarse mechanical mixture like black powder however much compressed for high pressures.

Brown powders overcame this difficulty for the reason that the brown charcoal is a complex chemical molecule, in fact very slightly altered cellulose, which must undergo some further simplification before it can burn in the manner required.

Cellulose in any form, wood, straw, cotton, paper, does not burn as such, but is broken down in stages, before the final change into water and carbon dioxide.

Celluloses heated to about 250° C. lose water and become brown and very friable (the brown charcoal is made by heating a straw to about 300° C. only).

---

* Sir J. Dewar on compressing crystals.

At higher temperatures the water is followed by methane, carbon oxides, acetic acid, acetone, tar-like matters, pretty much in this order, until a decided red heat is reached when black charcoal is formed, and carbon monoxide only given off.

The slowness of ignition and burning of powders made with these "cocoa" or brown charcoals must be due to the absorption of heat energy for some at least of these "breaking down" stages of the cellulosic molecule at and during the explosion.

The chemical molecule is acting therefore as an impervious ingredient to the gas pressure.

S.B.C. means slow burning cocoa powder. (C. means cocoa coloured, not that coca or cocoa has anything to do with it.) The pressure curve of brown powders is much more regular than of black, and the total volume of gases for equal weights considerably larger. Brown powders give much more smoke than black on account of their larger content of nitre. The combustion, however, is more complete, and the residue or fouling contains little or no potassium sulphide, but nearly always some potassium nitrite.

In ordinary black powders the amount of sulphur, $10°/_{o}$, is somewhat large, and it exerts very considerable influence on the rate, especially the initial rate of burning of the powder. The reason for this is the volatile nature of sulphur. Some vapour is given off by sulphur even before it is heated to the melting point ($115°$ C.), and it is possible for this vapour to ignite at or below the melting point according to conditions. It undoubtedly burns always with a flame which being hot gaseous matter can under pressure enter the grains or pieces of powder. Reducing the amount of sulphur, other things being the same, reduces the rate of burning, especially at first. Increase of sulphur accelerates the rate, and the old common blasting powders differed only from gunpowders by having a larger quantity of sulphur.

It is true that sulphur may be boiled in a clean glass vessel and poured out boiling and with sulphur vapour escaping into the air without igniting. But contact with a metallic oxide or with charcoal, which nearly always contains a considerable amount of occluded atmospheric oxygen will cause sulphur vapours to ignite at comparatively very low temperatures.

CHAPTER IV.

PRODUCTS OF FIRED POWDERS AND CHANGES TAKING PLACE ON EXPLOSION.

THE chemical processes taking place when gunpowder is burnt, have been investigated by several authorities.

Bunsen and Schischkoff, Linck, Karolyi, Noble and Abel, have burnt powders in closed vessels so as to retain all the products (which were then analysed and measured), and at the same time allow of the pressures and temperatures being ascertained.

Most of these investigators have been content with expressing the results obtained in percentage form; but as Debus, in several very valuable papers to the Royal Society and in Liebig's *Annalen*, has shown, it is possible to get from these results a very clear expression of the actions taking place, when any powder is fired, in the usual chemical equation form. This is particularly valuable, for from such equations the theoretical capability of a powder can be calculated.

The results of one of Abel's experiments with Waltham Abbey F.G. powder, gave for one gramme of the powder, the following quantities of products in decimals of a gramme and in relative fractions of an atom or molecule proportion:—

Potassium carbonate	·2615 G.	or	·00189 M.
,, sulphate	·1268 ,,	,,	·00072 ,,
,, hyposulphite	·1666 ,,	,,	·00087 ,,
,, sulphide (K_2S_2)	·0252 ,,	,,	·00017 ,,
Sulphur	·0012 ,,	,,	·00004 At.
Carbonic acid	·2678 ,,	,,	·00608 M.
Carbon monoxide	·0339 ,,	,,	·00121 ,,
Nitrogen	·1071 ,,	,,	·00765 At.
Hydrogen sulphide	·0080 ,,	,,	·00023 M.
Hydrogen	·0008 ,,	,,	·0008 ,,
Potassium sulphocyanate	·0004 ,,		
Nitre	·0005 ,,		
Ammonium carbonate	·0002 ,,		

Calculating back from these figures, the composition of the F.G. powder employed, may be represented by

$$16\ KNO_3 + 20·09\ C + 6·70\ S + ·76\ N_2{}^* + 1·0\ H^* + 5·69\ O.^*$$

A similar calculation for a pebble powder gives its composition as

$$16\ KNO_3 + 21·83\ C + 6·31\ S + ·67\ N + 1·02\ H + 1·05\ O.$$

---

* The charcoal, it will be remembered, contains this oxygen and hydrogen and nitrogen.

The mean composition of Waltham Abbey powder from the analyses of Noble and Abel, may be represented as:

$$16 \, KNO_3 + 21\cdot18 \, C + 6\cdot63 \, S.$$

This neglects, of course, the small amounts of water and nitrogen in the charcoal.

A powder having approximately this composition when burnt in a closed steel cylinder, so that all the products are for a little time in contact in a gaseous or fluid state, gives these final products:—

$$16 \, KNO_3 + 21\cdot35 \, C + 6\cdot63 \, S =$$
$$4\cdot98 \, K_2CO_3 + 0\cdot9 \, K_2SO_4 + 2\cdot10 \, K_2S_2 + 0\cdot84 \, S + 13\cdot13 \, CO_2 +$$
$$3\cdot23 \, CO + 17\cdot34 \, N + \cdot67 \, H_2S.$$

This equation may be simplified to

$$16 \, KNO_3 + 21 \, C + 5S =$$
$$5 \, K_2CO_3 + 13 \, CO_2 + K_2SO_4 + 3 \, CO + 2 \, K_2S_2 + 8 \, N_2$$

which shows the main products of the burning.

These are *end* results. What actions take place *during* the actual burning is difficult to say. The experiments of Károlyi show that pressure has an influence on the relative quantities of products.

The combustion also takes place in at least two stages; the first being one of oxydation at the expense of the oxygen in the nitre, and the second a reduction of the potassium carbonate and sulphate by the excess of sulphur and carbon.

In the earliest stage of burning of a powder perhaps of any kind, the products are free from sulphides or other reduction products. This may be the stage when a shell explodes. There is not time for a secondary action to begin before the products are dispersed. In a cannon of moderately long bore this second or reduction process has commenced, but here again the time is too short for its completion. A closed vessel is not exactly like the condition in a gun.

Secondary reactions:

α. $4 \, K_2CO_3 + 7 \, S = K_2SO_4 + 3 \, K_2S_2 + 4 \, CO_2$

β. $4 \, K_2SO_4 + 7 \, C = 2 \, K_2CO_3 + 2 \, K_2S_2 + 5 \, CO_2$

and

γ. $K_2CO_3 + K_2S_2 + O_7$ (free O still present) $= 2 \, K_2SO_4 + CO_2$.

The results of Noble and Abel may be expressed in one general equation, thus:

Let $x \, y$ and z represent positive values, and a the number of molecules of carbon monoxide formed when a powder is burnt, then—

$$x KNO_3 + yC + zS =$$
$$+ \, 1/28 \, (4x + 8y - 16z - 4a) \, K_2CO_3$$
$$+ \, 1/28 \, (20x - 16y + 4z + 8a) \, K_2SO_4$$
$$+ \, 1/28 \, (-10x + 8y + 12z - 4a) \, K_2S_2$$
$$+ \, 1/28 \, (-4x + 20y + 16z - 24a) \, CO_2$$
$$+ \, \tfrac{1}{2} x N_2$$
$$+ \, a CO.$$

Debus shows (*Annalen*, 213) that the above general equation can be employed for any sort of powder, and gives numerous examples of coincidence of theory and actual analyses of products.

With the powder (F.G.) before alluded to, the values calculated by this equation, setting $x = 16$, $y = 21{\cdot}18$, $z = 5$, and $a = 3{\cdot}23$, are—

$$16\ KNO_3 + 21{\cdot}18\ C + 5S = \begin{cases} 5{\cdot}01 & K_2CO_3 & 4{\cdot}98 \\ 0{\cdot}96 & K_2SO_4 & 0{\cdot}90 \\ 2{\cdot}01 & K_2S_2 & 2{\cdot}10 \\ 12{\cdot}93 & CO_2 & 13{\cdot}13 \\ 3{\cdot}23 & CO & 3{\cdot}23 \\ 8{\cdot}00 & N_2 & 8{\cdot}67 \end{cases}$$

(Theory. / Actually found by N. and A.)

Another conclusion from Noble and Abel's work, is that the pressure under which a powder is burnt exerts scarcely any influence on the *quality* of the products.

The composition however, does affect the quality of the products.

The general equation already given by Debus for the reactions, when powders are fired, can also be employed to give the capability or theoretical work obtainable from a powder. (*Annalen*, 265, 268.)

The mean composition of English powder is—

Saltpetre	74·77
Carbon	11·48
Hydrogen	0·44
Oxygen	1·84
Ash	0·28
Water	1·15
Sulphur	10·09
	100·0

These may be rounded off to KNO_3 74·8, C 11·5, and S 10·1. Dividing these by atomic and molecular weights, the combining proportions are given—

$$74{\cdot}8/101 = {\cdot}740;\quad 11{\cdot}5/12 = {\cdot}958;\quad 10{\cdot}1/32 = {\cdot}315$$

which, reduced to 16 molecules saltpetre, $\cdot 740 : \cdot 958 : \cdot 315 = 16 : 20{\cdot}71 : 6{\cdot}81$. Putting these values in the equation

*$16\ (KNO_3) + 20{\cdot}7C + 6{\cdot}8S = 3{\cdot}885\ (K_2CO_3) + 13{\cdot}81\ (CO_2) + 1{\cdot}428\ (K_2SO_4) + 3{\cdot}0\ (CO) + 2{\cdot}686\ (K_2S_2) + 8{\cdot}0\ (N_2)$.

The amount as gas is—

13·8	molecules	CO_2
3·0	,,	CO
8·0	,,	N_2
24·8		

---

* Taken in grammes, this amounts to 2082.
 $(16 \times 101) + (20{\cdot}7 \times 12) + (6{\cdot}8 \times 32) = 2082$.

Taking gramme weights for the basis of the calculation, then a molecule of any gas at 0° C. and 30 ins. B. = (760 mm.) occupies 22,380 c.cm. volume; so that 24·81 × 22,380 = 555,248 c.cm.

As the total weight of the powder used in the above equation is 2,082 grammes, one gramme of powder will give 266·7 c.cm. gases.

The amount of heat in calories = (1 gramme water 1° C.) is obtained by multiplying the coefficients in the general equation by their heat of formation.

```
                           Calories.
   3·885  (KNO₃)  × 279,530 = 1,085,974 calories
   1·428  (K₂SO₄) × 344,640 =   492,146    „
   2·686  (K₂S₂)  × 108,000 =   290,088    „
  13·810  (CO₂)   ×  97,000 = 1,339,570    „
   3·0    (CO)    ×  29,000 =    87,000    „
                                ─────────
                                3,294,778
Deducting heat of formation
     of 16 molecules KNO₃      1,911,680
                                ─────────
                                1,383,098 calories
```

given by 2,082 grammes powder, so that one gramme will give $\frac{1,383,098}{2,082}$ = 664·3 calories.

Berthelot proposed to multiply the volume of gas given by a powder, by the heat of formation (in calories), as a measure of *relative* strength or capability of doing work (energy).

In this case the gas from 1 gramme = 266·7 c.cm. × 664·3 = 177,169.

By the employment of this method it can be shown whether, and to what extent, the work differs when a powder is burnt so that no CO is formed, and when it is formed.

*The product of the gas volume and heat is, however, only about half a per cent. higher when all the carbon is oxidised to CO_2, but the difference depends on the contents of carbon in the powder.

Considering the manner in which the experiments of Noble and Abel were carried out, the practical results closely follow the theoretical.

Noble and Abel made some experiments with three sorts of powder—Waltham Abbey, Curtis and Harvey, and a Spanish powder.

The calculated results are—

	Gas-volume.	Heat.	Product = capability.
W. A.	265·1	674·1	178,703
Sp.	235·4	720·0	169,488
C. H.	254·6	691·6	176,081

---

* The product of gas volume and heat quantity differs to a greater extent practically than here stated.

Experiment gave—

W. A.	..	269·0	.. 720·0	..	193,680
Sp.	..	233·0	.. 762·3	..	177,616
C. H.	..	238·2	.. 755·5	..	179,960

Debus shows further, that when the saltpetre and sulphur are constant, an increase of carbon increases the relative energy of the powder, and when saltpetre and carbon are constant an increase of sulphur diminishes the energy of the powder.

Rule for calculating the gas-volume and heat from composition of a powder. (H. Debus.)

In the equation $16\,KNO_3 + yC + zS$, if the C be increased by one atom the weight of powder is increased by 12 parts and the gases by 15985·7 c.cm., the heat diminishes by 16925·2 calories; one atom sulphur increases weight of powder 32 parts, gas-volume 12788·5 c.cm., and lessens heat by 8,788 cals.

Example—
$$16\,KNO_3 + 17\,C + 8\,S = 2,076 \text{ parts byweight.}$$

It will give 501871·5 c.cm. gases, and 1,469,125 cals.

How much gas and heat will a mixture $16\,KNO_3 + 21\,C + 7\,S$ give?

There are $+ 4$ atoms C and $- 1\,S$.

$2,076 + 4 \times 12 - 32 = 2,092 =$ change in weight.
$501871\cdot5 + 4 \times 15985\cdot7 - 12788\cdot5 = 553,026$ change in heat.
$1,469,125 - 4 \times 16,925 + 8,788 = 1,410,213$.

	Gas.	Cals.	Product.
One gramme gives	264·3 :	674·1 :	178,164.

Sulphur undoubtedly increases *the rate* of burning of powder. According to Proust the rate of burning reaches a maximum when the weight of sulphur is one-sixth of that of the nitre. Increase in sulphur beyond this slows down the burning and also attacks the material of the gun very much.

For blasting powder the injurious action of sulphur may be neglected.

Sir F. Abel and Sir A. Noble, in their papers, "Researches on Fired Gunpowder," communicated to the Royal Society, sum up their mean results as follows:—

(A) *When Fired in a Confined Space.*

(1) The products of combustion are about 57 per cent. by weight of *ultimately* solid matter, and 43 per cent. of permanent gases.

*(2) The permanent gases at 0° C. and 760 mm. barometric

* Here are some other results for comparison :—

Authority.	Volumes of permanent gas generated.	Temperature. °Fahr.	Pressure of gases in atmosphere.	Pressure in tons per square inch.
Robins	244	—	1,000	6¾
Hutton	250	--	2,000	13½
Gay-Lussac	450	1,850°	2,137	14·3
Bunsen and Schiskoff	193	5,980°	4,374	29
Noble and Abel	280	4,000°	6,400	42

pressure, occupy about 280 times the volume of the original powder.

*(3) The pressure of the products of combustion when the powder entirely fills the space in which it is fired, is about 6,400 atmospheres, or 42 tons per square inch.

(4) The temperature of explosion is about 4,000° F. (2,200° C.).

(5) The chief gaseous products are carbon dioxide, nitrogen, and carbon monoxide.

(6) The solid residue is mainly composed of potassium carbonate, sulphide, and sulphate.

(B) *When Fired in the Bore of a Gun.*

(1) The products of combustion, at all events so far as regards the proportions of solid and gaseous matters, are the same as in the case of powder fired in a close vessel.

(2) The work on the projectile is effected by the pressure due to the gases formed.

(3) The reduction of temperature due to the expansion of the gases is, in a great measure, compensated for by the heat stored up in the liquid (afterwards solid) residue.

†(4) An expression is obtained showing the law connecting the pressure of the products of combustion with the volume they occupy.

†(5) Expressions are also deduced for the work that gunpowder is capable of performing in expanding in a vessel supposed impervious to heat, and for the temperature during expansion.

> [Hence is calculated a table showing the total work gunpowder is capable of performing in the bore of a gun, in terms of the volumes of expansion and of the density of the products of combustion. *See* Appendix II., p. 122.]

(6) The total theoretic work of gunpowder gases when indefinitely expanded (for example, in a gun of infinite length) is about 486 foot-tons per lb. of powder.

It will have been seen that the objects to be attained by a gunpowder for artillery and small arms are—

> (*a*) A maximum muzzle velocity with moderate and regular pressures properly distributed throughout the bore of the gun.

---

* Pressure of gases is measured in atmospheres. Increasing the quantity of a gas in a vessel by 100 % doubles the pressure on the sides, and so on. Heating through 273° C. or 480° F. doubles the pressure or volume, as the case may be.

† A note in former editions gave some theoretical calculations for the work done by a pound of powder or other gas, expanding adiabatically from its initial to its final volume, or to infinite volume, but this has been omitted in the present volume, as the calculation is given at length in all treatises on Thermodynamics, such as Maxwell's *Theory of Heat.*

(b) Uniformity of action, in order to ensure similarity of results.
(c) Freedom from fouling (especially in small-arm powders).
(d) Durability; being able to bear transport and to keep well in store.

The advantages of gunpowder are—

(a) Its rate of combustion is gradual; also, by altering the proportions of the ingredients and varying the mechanical processes of manufacture, its explosiveness can be considerably modified.
(b) The ingredients are easily produced.
(c) They are comparatively cheap.
(d) Gunpowder is, with proper precautions, safe in manufacture, in store, and in transport; it also keeps well.

CHAPTER V.

HISTORY OF GUNPOWDER.

NOTHING approaching a history of gunpowder can be here attempted. A very learned book was published in 1904 by Col. Hime (Longmans, Green, and Co.) on gunpowder and ammunition: their origin and progress. A monumental work on the same subject by Mr. Oscar Guttmann (Artists Press, Balham, S.W.) has just been published, 1906. Both works will repay consultation.

The early history of gunpowder is veiled in great obscurity, and this obscurity is heightened by the fact that many of the most ancient references seem, on close examination, to point, not to a *propelling* agent, but to some combustible or incendiary composition of the nature of the so-called Greek fire. For instance, probably the most ancient reference of all is in the Gentoo code of laws (Halhed's translation), supposed by some authorities to be coëval with Moses; it runs thus: "The magistrate shall not make war with any deceitful machine, or with poisoned weapons, or with cannon and guns, or any kind of firearms." The translator remarks that this passage may serve to renew the idea, founded on a statement of Quintus Curtius, that Alexander the Great was opposed in India by some such weapons; but the terms translated "cannon and guns" may, as certainly was the case with the word "artillery," have reference to ancient mechanical engines of war, while the word rendered "firearms" is literally a weapon of fire, and may mean a dart or arrow tipped with some combustible composition.

One fact is tolerably clear—that gunpowder was *not* invented, as has been often stated, by the German monk, Bertholdus Schwartz, about A.D. 1320, for Roger Bacon, who was born A.D. 1214, refers, about 1267, in unmistakable terms, to an explosive mixture of the nature of gunpowder as known before his time, employed for purposes of diversion, producing a noise like thunder, and flashes like lightning; he even suggests its application to military purposes. In his treatise, *De Secretis Operibus Artis et Naturæ et de Nullitate Magiæ*, he says "that from saltpetre *and other ingredients* we are able to make a fire that shall burn at any distance we please." In chap. xi of the same work, these other ingredients are veiled in the thin disguise of an anagram : " Sed tamen salis petræ *lura nope cum ubre* et sulphuris, et sic facies tonitrum et coruscationem, si scias artificium"; the unmeaning words in italics have been interpreted as *carbonum pulvere*. Robins, in his work on Gunnery (1742), suggests that Bacon may have derived his knowledge from the MS. of Marcus Græcus preserved in the National Library in Paris, entitled, *Incipit Liber Ignium a Marco Græco prescriptus, cujus virtus et efficacia est ad comburendum hostes, tam in mari quam in terra.* Marcus Græcus lived about the end of the 8th century, and gives the following among other modes of launching fire upon an enemy :—" One pound of live sulphur, two of charcoal of willow, and six of saltpetre, reduced to a fine powder in a marble mortar, and mixed together; a certain quantity is to be put into a long, narrow, and well-compacted cover, and then discharged into the air." This is evidently the description of a rocket, and an epistle by Ferrarius, a Spanish monk, and a contemporary of Bacon, which is preserved in the Bodleian Library at Oxford, gives recipes for Greek fire, rockets, and " thunder." There is also a treatise on gunpowder in the library of the Escorial, written about A.D. 1250, which seems to describe both rockets and shells. Rockets were undoubtedly employed during the reign of the Greek Emperor Leo, about A.D. 880, and indeed seem to have been long known in India, some of them having been made of great size.

Greek fire seems to have been the generic name given to several different combustible compositions, although Arabian writers speak of them as Chinese fires. Greek fire was apparently introduced into Constantinople about A.D. 670, being used in the defence of that city in the seventh and eighth centuries. It was discharged upon the enemy by means of various engines of war, and, in smaller quantities, attached to arrows or darts; it was also vomited, in a liquid form, through long copper tubes attached to the bows of vessels of war. The secret of its manufacture afterwards passed into the hands of the Saracens, and it was used by them against the Crusaders. Joinville, who was an eye-witness, describes its effects in quaint and awe-struck language; however, the actual destructive effect seems to have been very slight compared to the terror it occasioned. One description of this wildfire was composed of resin, sulphur, naphtha, and probably saltpetre.

Apart from vague references in various classical writers, the researches of all modern authorities seem to point to the far east as the birthplace of an explosive composition of the nature of gunpowder, and that it was used there from time immemorial, although its application as a propelling agent is probably of far later date. In all probability the germ of the science of explosives lay in the accidental discovery of the peculiar properties of the nitre so plentifully found mixed with the soil upon the vast plains of India and China. By means of the charred embers of wood fires, used for cooking, the two most important ingredients of gunpowder might easily be brought into contact, and, under the action of heat, more or less deflagration would ensue; in fact, the accidental dropping of some of the crude saltpetre into the coals would show its remarkable power of supporting and accelerating combustion. The combination of saltpetre and charcoal into a more or less powerful mixture can therefore be easily conceived, the sulphur being an after addition, and not necessary to cause explosion. Our present gunpowder is only the improvement of such a mixture.

Saltpetre was early known as Chinese snow, and it has been claimed that gunpowder was used in China for military purposes long anterior to the Christian era. There is no doubt that they had fiery compositions in use very early in our era which seem to have been known by such names as " devouring fire," " earth thunder," &c.; but Colonel Anderson, C.B., in his book on gunpowder (London, 1862), adduces evidence tending to show that, although some such mixture had been used in rockets, fireworks, and perhaps even in the bursting of large shells, for about 2,000 years, yet that its application to the propulsion of shot was a comparatively late introduction. It seems certain that the Chinese were first instructed in the scientific casting of cannon by Jesuit missionaries in the 17th century, and the analysis of their powder in the present day shows proportions of the three ingredients almost identical with those employed in Europe, which were only arrived at after some centuries of experience.

The same may be said as regards the use of gunpowder in India. The *Institutes of Timur*, written about the middle of the 14th century, contains no mention of cannon or gunpowder, although full particulars are given of the equipment of his troops; it is, however, related that, when Timur engaged the army of Mahmoud under the walls of Delhi, rockets were thrown and wildfire scattered in every direction. It may also be noted that the names given to pieces of artillery in the days of Baber and the Mogul conquerors of Hindoostan, almost invariably point to a European or at least a Turkish origin: the fact that Akbar and Aurungzebe had Englishmen and other Europeans in their service to teach the art of gunnery, is well authenticated.

Whatever obscurity may hang over the early history of gunpowder, there is little doubt that its first employment as a propelling agent in Europe was by the Moors in Spain. They are said to have employed some description of artillery a century or more earlier, but Condé (*Hist. Dom. Arabs in Spain*) states positively that Ismail Ben Feraz, King of Grenada, who, in 1325, besieged Baza, had among his warlike machines "some that cast globes of fire, with resounding thunders and lightnings, resembling those of the resistless tempest; all these missiles caused fearful injuries to the walls and towers of the city." The first reliable contemporary document relative to the use of gunpowder in Europe, and which is still in existence, bears date 11th February, 1326; it gives authority to the Priors, the Gonfalonier, and Council of Twelve of Florence, to appoint persons to superintend the manufacture of cannons of brass and iron balls for the defence of the territory of the Republic.

As regards the introduction of gunpowder into England, it was stated by John Barbour, Archdeacon of Aberdeen, who wrote in 1375, that cannon, which he called "crakys of war," were employed during the invasion of Scotland by Edward III in 1327; they are, however, not mentioned in the accounts of the expenses of that war preserved in the Record Office. The first distinct reference to gunpowder occurs in 12 Edward III, 1338, when it is mentioned as being among the stores in the Tower. Under date of that same year a document, now in the National Library in Paris, refers to a weapon in the arsenal at Rouen, called "pot de fer," together with some saltpetre and sulphur to make powder for the same: at this period it seems that the ingredients were usually kept separately and mixed when required. From the year 1345, 19 Edward III, we have preserved in the Record Office, reliable accounts of the purchase of ingredients needed for making gunpowder, and of the shipping of cannon for France, whether it be true or not that cannon were used at Crécy in that year; Napoleon III (*Etudes sur le passé et l'avenir de l'Artillerie*) maintains that such was the case. It may be noted that Petrarch, writing about the year 1344, in his dialogues *De remediis utriusque fortunæ*, speaks of "brazen globes cast forth by the force of flame with a horrible sound of thunder," as being apparently as common as any other kind of warlike engine.

In 1377, being the first year of Richard II, Thomas Norbury was ordered to buy, amongst other munitions, saltpetre, sulphur, and charcoal, to be sent to the Castle of Brest. In 1414, Henry V decreed that no gunpowder should be taken out of the kingdom without special licence; in the same year this monarch ordered twenty pipes of powder made of willow charcoal, and various other articles, for the use of his guns.

It was not, however, until the reign of Elizabeth that the manufacture of gunpowder can be said to have been established in England. The greater portion of the supply required had been previously procured from abroad, and the trade had been an open one; the threatening attitude of Spain, however, compelled the Government to provide improved means of defence, and patents were issued by the Crown for the manufacture of gunpowder, constituting it a monopoly. Early in this reign also, saltpetre began to be artificially produced in England, but in small quantity, the bulk of that required being imported from the continent and from Barbary. In 1623, ostensibly in order to prevent the sale of weak or defective powder, a Proclamation was issued by James I, prohibiting its manufacture, as well as that of saltpetre, except under the King's commission, and directing that all gunpowder should be proved and marked by the sworn proof-master. A little later, in 1626, the East India Company had commenced the importation of saltpetre, and also erected powder works in Surrey. The Company's renewed Charter in 1693 contained a clause providing that 500 tons of saltpetre should be furnished to the Ordnance annually, and from this time forward we hear of no difficulty, at least in England, of obtaining the chief ingredient of gunpowder, although on the Continent great attention has had to be paid to its artificial production; this was especially the case in France during the reign of Napoleon I, when the supremacy of Great Britain at sea prevented for many years the importation of saltpetre by her enemies.

About the year 1590, George Evelyn, grandfather of the celebrated John Evelyn of Wootton, received the royal licence to set up powder mills at Long Ditton and Godstone. The Evelyns are said to have brought the art from Holland. The works at Faversham, afterwards for so many years the Government powder factory, also date from Elizabeth's reign, but were then of secondary importance to those at Godstone. There seems reason however to suppose that powder mills existed at Waltham Abbey so far back as 1561, for in that year we find John Thomworth, of Waltham, in treaty on behalf of Queen Elizabeth for the purchase of saltpetre, sulphur, and staves for barrels. In any case, Fuller, appointed Vicar of Waltham in 1641, refers (*English Worthies*, i, 338) to the powder mills at that place as having existed for years. In 1787 these works were sold to the Crown by John Walton, Esq., when they were enlarged and reorganised under the superintendence of the famous Sir William Congreve, and became the Royal Gunpowder Factory. The old royal factory at Faversham was given up after the peace of 1815, the more inland site being preferred; Faversham was first let, and afterwards sold, to the well-known firm of Messrs. John Hall and Sons, and a third Government factory at Ballincollig, in Ireland, was disposed of a few years later.

For some centuries gunpowder remained in the form of dust, or "meal." Granulating or "corning" the powder was a great step in advance, but it is doubtful whether this operation was intended to increase its strength, or merely to render it more convenient for charging small-arms, for which purpose alone it was used for many years, whilst meal powder was still employed with heavy guns; the latter was called "serpentine" powder in the time of Edward VI, in allusion to the name of one of the principal natures of ordnance then in use. However, during the reign of Elizabeth the experience of the great additional strength imparted by the corning process, owing to ignition being accelerated by the free passage of the flame between the grains, occasioned the universal introduction of corned powder, except for priming—both in cannon and small-arms—for which purpose meal powder remained in use as late as the reign of Charles I.

The earliest gunpowder used in cannon in Europe consisted of equal parts of saltpetre, charcoal, and sulphur, ground up and roughly mingled together, and must have proved a mixture very inferior in strength to some of those given by Marcus Græcus. Probably the reason of such a weak composition being used long after better proportions had been ascertained, was the weakness of the cannon from which it was fired. The earliest guns now in existence were made of longitudinal bars hooped round with wrought-iron coils—a construction remarkable as approaching that of the R.M.L. guns, so far as the coils are concerned. The welding, however, was most imperfect, and tubes of thin iron, or even of wood or leather, having rope coiled round them, were sometimes used. Indeed, the most effective employment of gunpowder as a propelling agent involves a whole series of inventions and improvements in mechanical science and art, although when cast-iron and bronze guns were introduced there seems to have been almost a pause of some three centuries. During this period, however, the quality of gunpowder was being slowly improved. In 1380, equal parts of the three ingredients were still in use, but about 1410 the proportions were 3 saltpetre, 2 charcoal, and 2 sulphur. The relative amount of saltpetre was gradually increased, and Tartaglia (*Quesiti e Inventioni diversi*, Venice, 1546) mentions twenty-three various compositions as having been used at different times; he gives the following as the gunpowders then in use:—

	Saltpetre.	Charcoal.	Sulphur.
Cannon powder	4	1	1
Musket „	48	8	7
or	18	3	2

It is remarkable that Robins, writing in 1742, states that the above proportions were very nearly those of his day, although Baptista Porta, who was one of the first to make accurate investigations on this subject, had—in the sixteenth century—fixed on the modern French proportions as the best. For a long period it was customary to put considerably more saltpetre in the fine grain or musket, than in cannon powder. Also, the proportion of saltpetre seems to have been reduced as the piece of ordnance became heavier; this was doubtless with the object of obtaining a slower burning powder for large charges. However, by the end of the last century, what was called "common war powder" was almost universally composed of 6 saltpetre, 1 charcoal, and 1 sulphur, and these are the proportions still in use by France and many of the continental nations. Exhaustive experiments were carried out by Beaumé, Chaptal, Proust, and other chemists, at the instance of the French Government, which resulted in the recommendation of proportions of saltpetre varying from 76 to 80, of charcoal from 13 to 17, and sulphur from 5 to 9. These figures may seem to give rather a wide margin, but this will surprise no one who is acquainted with the great differences in results caused by comparatively slight variations in the processes of manufacture—or in the conditions of experiment—with powder of the same description.

During the five centuries which have elapsed since gunpowder was introduced into Europe, it has been composed of the same three ingredients, although the proportions have varied considerably at different times, and in different countries. The following table gives the composition of the chief black gunpowders in use at the present time in this country, and on the Continent:—

Country.	Saltpetre.	Charcoal.	Sulphur.
Austria	75·5	14·5	10
Belgium	75	12·5	12·5
England	75	15	10
France	75	12·5	12·5
Germany	74	16	10
Holland	70	16	14
Italy	75	15	10
Portugal	76	13·5	10·5
Russia	75	15	10
Spain	75	12·5	12·5
Sweden	75	15	10
Switzerland	76	14	10
Turkey	75	15	10
United States	76	14	10

In our service, the proportions had not varied for a very long period. The experiments initiated by the Special Committee on Gunpowder, and afterwards carried on by the Committee on Explosives, were considered to demonstrate that the variations in the mechanical and physical properties of gunpowder, produced by processes of manufacture, exert even more influence upon its action than a comparatively considerable difference in composition.

This conclusion was however disturbed by the introduction of slow-burning prismatic powders, containing different proportions of the three ingredients, as follows:—

Prism[1] Brown and S.B.C., 79 saltpetre, 18 charcoal, and 3 sulphur.

E.X.E., $77\frac{6}{16}$ saltpetre, $17\frac{10}{16}$ charcoal, 5 sulphur.

From 1·7 to 2·2 per cent. of water is also present in these powders, being recognised as an ingredient. The charcoals for these powders are prepared in a special manner.

CHAPTER VI.

Explosive Compounds.

All the varieties of gunpowders proper are simply mixtures of a combustible, with a substance capable of supplying oxygen and perhaps incidentally nitrogen and other substances. Some of these may add to the volume of gases or be merely heat producers.

When a nitrate as potassium nitrate (KNO_3) is brought into contact with strong sulphuric acid, an interchange as expressed by the chemical equation:—

$$M.NO_3 + H_2SO_4 = MHSO_4 + HNO_3,$$

takes place. HNO_3 represents nitric acid or a nitrate of hydrogen.

Nitric acid is a very decidedly endothermic compound, and can exist only below a certain not very high temperature without suffering some decomposition. Absolutely pure nitric acid is very difficult to obtain and keep. Light decomposes it to some extent. It is a colourless liquid which gives off vapour and also absorbs water from moist air. The ordinary strongest acid is about 94 per cent. only. Such acid is obtained by gently distilling a mixture of sodium nitrate and strong sulphuric acid. This acid boils at 125° to 130°, and is usually coloured yellow or reddish from partial decomposition. When heated, as a vapour, to quite a moderate temperature above its boiling point it decomposes in the sense of $2HNO3 = H_2O + 2NO_2 + O$.

Metallic nitrates contain a metal in place of the hydrogen of the acid.

Other substances besides metals combine with nitric acid, for instance, ammonia. The compound formed is represented by the formula NH_4NO_3, and is known as ammonium nitrate. It is a crystalline solid, somewhat resembling ordinary nitre. On gently heating this nitrate melts and then commences to give off gases and presents the appearance of boiling. It is really decomposing into water, and one of the oxides of nitrogen and the action is exactly represented by $NH_4NO_3 = {^2}H_2O + N_2O$. This action is "*internal*" combustion. There is a total rearrangement of the elements in the compound, and some heat is developed. If the substance be rapidly heated to considerably above its melting point, the decomposition becomes more violent, and actually accompanied by flame. Under certain conditions ammonium nitrate may also be detonated (see later), and for this reason it is employed somewhat largely in a number of blasting compositions.

NEARLY ALL the explosive compounds in practical use owe their explosive properties to this kind of internal combustion, above represented, which is brought about at some particular temperature or in some cases by friction or percussion.

It is, of course, absolutely necessary that the oxygen compound be of the endothermic class. Ammonium sulphate, for instance, although it produces water by a similar internal combustion of some of its hydrogen cannot be induced to show any signs of burning nor can it be exploded.

This behaviour of ammonium nitrate is shared by many substances containing the arrangement—NH_2. These compounds are known as amine bases. They combine with acids in a similar manner to ammonia. For instance *urea* $CO\genfrac{}{}{0pt}{}{NH_2}{NH_2}$, or aniline $C_6H_5NH_2$, the nitrates of which behave in a precisely similar manner to ammonium nitrate when heated to certain temperatures.

A very considerable number of compounds of carbon, with the two elements hydrogen and oxygen, are found as natural products of plant life, and many others can be obtained by synthetical processes.

It is usual to classify these substances into families or groups according to their general properties or constitution.

The alcohols or hydrates of the paraffinic hydrocarbons constitute one of the simplest of these groups.

Methyl alcohol, or wood spirit, CH_3OH, is the hydrate of the hydrocarbon methane or marsh gas CH_4.

Under suitable conditions nitric acid reacts with this substance as shown by $CH_3OH + HNO_3 = H_2O + CH_3NO_3$, an action quite on the same lines as $KHO + HNO_3 = H_2O + KNO_3$.

CH_3NO_3 or methylnitrate can undergo internal combustion (perhaps as represented by the expression—

$$4(CH_3NO_3) = 6H_2O + 4CO + 2NO + N_2)$$

but not necessarily so simple as here expressed, the conditions of pressure exerting a great influence on the relative amounts of the various products and therefore on the mechanism of the reaction. Most of the nitrates of this class are liquids at the ordinary temperature.

Another large class of substances are known as carbohydrates, it comprises many members as the celluloses, starches, sugars, &c.

The internal structure of these substances undoubtedly resembles to a certain extent that of the alcohols. They give, under appropriate conditions, nitrates of a more complex structure than those from the alcohols proper and in some cases containing more than one molecule or group of the nitric complex NO_3. For instance, mannitol ($C_6H_{14}O_6$) (a kind of sugar) can give a hexanitrate $C_6H_8(NO_3)_6$.

All these are capable of internal combustion and are also more or less responsive to friction or percussion.

Nearly all the nitrates of this class are solids at the ordinary temperature, some are crystalline and also soluble in water.

A totally different kind of product is obtained from the action of nitric acid on the hydrocarbons and also other substances of the class known as benzenoïd. The typical action in this case is shown by the expression $C_6H_6 + HNO_3 = H_2O + C_6H_5NO_2$. This means that the hydrocarbon benzene has reacted with the acid to form water and another substance which is neither a nitrate nor a nitrite, although the formula $C_6H_5NO_2$ would indicate the latter. Many substances of this nature are known. They are capable of exhibiting internal combustion, but not with the ease of the nitrates, and always leave much unconsumed carbon in the process. They constitute a class known as nitro-compounds.

GUNCOTTON.

HISTORY, CHEMICAL AND PHYSICAL PROPERTIES OF GUNCOTTON.

In 1832 Braconnot discovered that starch, woody fibre, and similar substances, when treated with nitric acid, were converted into highly combustible bodies; to which he gave the generic name of "*xyloïdine*." Six years later (in 1838), Pélouze repeated the experiments, and extended his researches to include paper, linen, and cotton, which he found when treated with cold, concentrated nitric acid, and the free acid afterwards removed by careful washing, were changed into substances possessed of explosive properties without any apparent change of structure.

No practical result, however, came from these preliminary researches, till Schönbein, in 1846, announced the discovery of "cotton-powder" or "guncotton," which he proposed as a substitute for gunpowder, as possessing the advantage over the latter of burning without any noticeable residue, and consequently without smoke. It was prepared by immersing carded cotton wool in the strongest nitric acid and then carefully washing it. Immediately afterwards the same substance was discovered independently by Böttger and Otto. Later on Knop introduced the improvement of adding concentrated sulphuric acid to the nitric acid.

Guncotton at once became an object of great scientific and practical interest, and nearly every European country took up the matter with the view of utilising the new explosive for war purposes, factories being established for its production on a large scale. Messrs. Hall and Son, of Faversham, commenced its manufacture in this country, and they also attempted to diminish its unwieldy bulk by compressing it into paper cases. However, a terrible explosion which took place at their works, together with other accidents both in this country and abroad, inspired so much alarm and distrust, which was increased by the impossibility of satisfactorily accounting for them in the then state of knowledge of the substance, that the manufacture of guncotton in this country and in France at all events, was given up for several years.

A more perfect acquaintance with the properties of guncotton has clearly demonstrated that these calamities were ascribable either (1) to the incomplete purification of the guncotton from free acid; or (2) to the presence of small quantities of nitrogenous matters—formed from resinous or fatty substances retained in the raw cotton fibre, even when treated with alkali. These substances are much more ready to undergo decomposition by exposure to heat or light, than the cellulose products themselves. It is also now known that if dry guncotton be packed in considerable quantities, the heat generated by such chemical changes may rise to the ignition point, or even cause detonation.

In Austria, General von Lenk of the Artillery, a firm believer in the future of guncotton, still continued to carry out experiments with it, and succeeded in considerably improving its manufacture and purification. The attempts to use it as a substitute for gunpowder for military purposes had been unsuccessful, owing to the impossibility of controlling and making its rate of combustion uniform. After extensive trials however, von Lenk succeeded in so altering its mechanical condition as to modify its rate of combustion in air, and therefore, as was believed in Austria, to have rendered its application for military purposes possible. In fact its manufacture in that country was approved, and in 1862 Austria armed 30 field batteries with guncotton cartridges. Von Lenk's system consisted in making guncotton from yarn and thread of various sizes and degrees of compactness spun from long staple cotton, and then twisting and plaiting the guncotton yarn in various ways and winding it more or less tightly upon reels or cores, or weaving it into cartridges of various shapes and sizes. The reason why this treatment affected the rate of combustion, at all events at about atmospheric pressures is simple and apparent.

Von Lenk's improvements were effectual in moderating the rapidity of explosion in air, or under slight confinement, but were after all, found of no practical utility when guncotton was confined in the bore of a gun, especially in considerable charges; the hot gases penetrating and inflaming the most closely plaited, or mechanically compressed, forms of guncotton so that little or no retardation was effected. In fact many serious explosions occurred. The Austrian experiments, however, led to the study of guncotton being resumed in England in 1863, about the time it was being abandoned in Austria, and the results of very extensive experiments, carried out under the direction of Sir Frederick Abel, ultimately resulted in the adoption of a method of manufacture, which ensures a more complete purification from acids, and other impurities than was previously possible. The method consists in reducing the material to a very fine state of division and subsequent compression, into thoroughly compact, homogeneous masses. The advantages of this process, which in the following chapter will be described in detail, are so considerable that it may be as well to notice them here, *seriatim* :—

(1.) The cost of production is much decreased by the use of the waste cuttings from the cotton mills, in lieu of the expensive long stapled cotton yarn before employed.

(2.) By the use of machinery to separate the fibre and cut the cotton waste into short lengths, it is more entirely exposed to the action of the acids than could possibly be the case with the skeins of yarn, which had to be kept whole.

(3.) The operation of reducing the converted guncotton to a fine state of division, corresponding to the pulping process in papermaking, allows of its better purification from free acid, and from other foreign substances.

(4.) The guncotton pulp can be compressed, by means of hydraulic power, into dense and compact masses of any desired shape.

(5.) Lastly, although not least in importance, by this process the greatest possible amount of safety is secured; not only can the guncotton be manufactured throughout in a wet state, but it can be transported and stored, and even exploded in the same condition.

All the advantages that would accrue from compressing guncotton could not have been foreseen when the process was first introduced in 1865, although it was evident from the experiments of von Lenk and subsequent ones made with compressed guncotton pulp, that the more compact and uniform its mechanical state, the more probability there was of the action being moderated and controlled. Apart from the question of using guncotton as a propelling agent, its value for purposes of destruction was universally admitted; but to develop the full explosive effect it was necessary that the charge should be strongly confined, and this much reduced its range of application. However, all necessity for confinement ceased when it was discovered in 1869, by the late Mr. E. O. Brown, of the Chemical Department, Royal Arsenal, that compressed guncotton could be fully detonated by fulminate of mercury in a totally unconfined state. At first supposed to apply only to dry guncotton, the discovery was greatly increased in value when it was ascertained later on that wet compressed guncotton, although quite uninflammable, could be detonated by using a small "primer" or initiative charge of the dry material; indeed, even the latter may be dispensed with if a larger quantity of the fulminate be employed. Sir Frederick Abel demonstrated, by means of Noble's chronoscope, that wet guncotton is detonated even more rapidly and therefore more promptly than dry guncotton.

From the earliest days of its discovery, the employment of guncotton for propulsive purposes had been attempted. Until about twenty years ago, however, the only real success in the way of employing guncotton for propulsive purposes, and that a partial one, was the Schultze powder, which had a basis of nitrated wood fibre, and was suitable only for sporting purposes. It was not until about the year 1885–86, when the introduction of small calibre magazine rifles was beginning to occupy the attention of the principal European countries, and the use with them of a smokeless powder became an absolute necessity, that a method of treating nitrated cellulose was arrived at, which reduced it to a condition in which it could be depended upon to give regular and reliable results for military purposes. To convert it into a substance absolutely devoid of all porosity was the result to be striven for, and it was eventually obtained by subjecting the nitrated cellulose to the action of suitable volatile agents which will gelatinise it, and then on evaporation leave a compact, homogeneous non-porous colloidal material, capable only of burning from the exterior inwards. The gelatinised material, before the evaporation of the solvent forms a more or less plastic mass which can be rolled out or pressed into sheets, cords, or other desired form, and when dry may be cut up into discs, tablets, cylinders, &c. On these lines many smokeless powders have been proposed and produced and a goodly number are in general use. They differ in details of manufacture, and frequently contain, in addition to the nitrated cellulose, other explosive or non-explosive ingredients. Those not actually service explosives in this country will not be further considered here.

Cellulose is one of the most widely distributed and important plant constituents. Its external appearance varies considerably, depending on the plant. For instance, flax, cotton,* hemp, and pith of various woods are mostly cellulose. In woods it is more or less intimately mixed with "lignin," sometimes as much as 50 per cent. of the latter, and with numerous other compounds as well as mineral salts absorbed by the plant from the soil and carried up into the tissues and deposited.

The simplest formula for cellulose as derived from its composition per cent. of carbon, hydrogen, and oxygen, is $C_6H_{10}O_5$. It is, considering its composition, an exceedingly insoluble and highly resistant compound against ordinary chemical re-agents.

It dissolves, or, at least, forms a gelatinous mass, in cupramine (a solution of oxide of copper in ammonium hydroxide) and in a strong solution of zinc chloride in hydrochloric acid. Both these "solutions" or gels are decomposed by much water or by solutions of salts, and the cellulose is again obtained practically without loss or chemical change, but in altered physical state. It reappears in a gelatinoid form. This behaviour is made use of to obtain filaments for electric lamps, &c.

The substances and structures generally occurring intermingled with cellulose in plants, wood, &c., can be removed, generally very completely, by treating the materials with alcohol to remove resinous and oily bodies, and then with acids and alkalis alternately. Cellulose can be obtained in a moderate state of purity from sawdust by warming it to 40° C. with a mixture of 1 volume oil of vitriol and 3 volumes of 25 per cent. nitric acid and then washing with water.

Good filter paper which is nearly pure cellulose may be

---

* The specific gravity of cotton = 1·27 of flax 1·45.
$C_6H_{10}O_5$ produces 678·0 calories on combustion.
White filter paper is a very pure form of cellulose.

heated to 220° for some time before browning. On heating with water to 200° C. it becomes brown, and several decomposition products result.

Cellulose dissolves in cold concentrated sulphuric acid. The solution becomes dark brown, and finally black, from a separation of a charcoal-like substance, after a short time. If dissolved in the strong acid and the solution diluted largely with water and heated, dextrin, glucose and other substances are formed. In a mixture of sulphuric acid, with one-third of its weight of water, cellulose dissolves, forming a sulphate and other substances.

The act of solution of cellulose in sulphuric acid is due to the formation of sulphates the composition of which is not with any certainty known. These sulphates, on contact with water, especially when heated, undergo a series of changes, sulphuric acid being more or less completely reformed along with substances other than the original cellulose.

Very strong sodium or potassium hydroxide solutions decomposes cellulose, brown charcoal-like products resulting.

Cotton wool or filter paper heated to 180° C., with excess of acetic acid anhydride, forms a tri-acetate $C_6H_7O_2(CH_3CO_2)_3$, which is insoluble in water, alcohol, and ether. Lower, that is mono and di-acetates, can also be obtained.

The evidence from this tri-acetate is that in cellulose there are three hydroxyl molecules, $(OH)_3$, as in the case of some metallic hydroxides, for instance $Bi(OH)_3$.

A penta acetyl compound (?) was obtained by Cross and Bevan (Chem. Soc. $\frac{57}{2}$) by heating cellulose with acetic acid anhydride and a very little zinc chloride. This is also insoluble in water and can be gelatinised on warming with nitro benzene, &c.

Some idea of the internal structure of many substances can be obtained by the action of acetic acid CH_3COOH or its anhydride, especially as to the existence and number of (OH) or hydroxyl groups. Acetic acid combines with substances containing this arrangement, as a rule, without any further or secondary actions, and is used therefore as a measure of the presence or number of OH groups in compounds where other evidence may not be obtainable.

From the existence of the penta acetate it might be concluded that five OH groups were contained in cellulose so that a constitutional expression $C_6H_5(OH)_5$ might seem justified. This is very doubtful. The zinc chloride it is necessary to employ as a help to the acetic anhydride is a very powerful re-agent and can break into and dislocate other arrangements of atoms in carbon compounds, besides the hydroxylic group.

If cellulose contained five definite hydroxyl groups it might be possible to obtain some compounds similar to the penta acetate with other acids. This, however up to date, does not seem to be the case.

Nitrates.—Cellulose, when boiled with nitric acid of 50–60 %, can be oxydised into oxycellulose, oxalic acid and other substances.

In contact with cold nitric acid of 75% to 91% (the strongest commercial acid) nitrates and water are formed practically without any other action. In this action temperature, time of contact and strength and volume of acid are all important factors. The product is generally a mixture of at least two nitrates, possibly more.*

No satisfactory method of separation of these nitrates formed by nitric acid alone is known.

The chemical action may be considered to be taking the lines $C_6H_{10}O_5 + HNO_3 = H_2O + C_6H_9O_4NO_3$ and $C_6H_{10}O_5 + 2HNO_3 = 2H_2O + C_6H_8O_3(NO_3)_2$. It cannot be carried out with the quantities here shown, viz., 162 (cellulose) to 63, acid, or 162 to 126. Much more acid is necessary as water commences to be formed at the earliest stage of the reaction and goes on progressively diluting the remaining acid until a stage of dilution is reached which, at ordinary temperatures, has no action whatever on cellulose.

Imagine, for instance, 162 parts of cotton-wool immersed in 63 of nitric acid.† At the point when 81 parts of cellulose are made into mono-nitrate ($C_6H_9O_4NO_3$), 31·5 parts of (real) nitric acid will be combined and 9 parts of water formed and mixed with the remaining 31·5 of nitric acid, reducing its active strength to about 70% only.

Also, all chemical actions are reversible under proper conditions; here the water formed tends to reverse the action of the acid.

When cotton wool or filter paper is immersed in a considerable excess of strong 94 per cent. nitric acid at the ordinary temperature for one or two hours, and the product washed thoroughly with water, a substance is obtained which approximates *very roughly* to the composition $C_6H_8O_3(NO_3)_2$.*2

There is a strong tendency for the products to gelatinise if the acid be strong and in large excess and the time of contact extended. At a moderately high temperature (50° C.) complete gelatinization can be obtained. The products are, however, not pure *cellulose* nitrates.

These products of the action of nitric acid are soluble in a mixture of ether and alcohol from which they separate on the evaporation of the solvent in a gelatinous form known as collodion.

It is doubtful whether any excess of nitric acid would produce appreciable amounts of a higher nitrate than that roughly represented by the formula $C_6H_8O_3(NO_2)_2$.

For the stage of nitration known as guncotton, it is absolutely necessary to employ sulphuric acid as a dehydrating agent.

In making guncotton, therefore, a mixture is employed. A theoretically perfect mixture would be $HNO_3 + H_2SO_4$, that is 63 of nitric to 98 of sulphuric. Its action should then be shown by

$$C_6H_{10}O_5 + HNO_3 = C_6H_9O_4NO_3 + H_2O \text{ and } H_2O + H_2SO_4 = H_4SO_5.$$

---

* The strongest commercial acid generally contains some nitrous acid which acts simply as an oxidising agent, the oxidation products contaminating the nitrates produced.

† Commercial strongest acid is seldom more than 94%.

*2 The simplest formula, $C_6H_{10}O_5$, for cellulose will be retained as the basis for representing these nitrates.

Now neither of the acids as usually obtainable are pure, or 100 per cent. The nitric may be only 90 per cent. Commercial sulphuric is generally 98 per cent. When weak nitric acid is mixed with sulphuric, the latter probably takes away the water, forming a hydrate, and leaving the nitric in a pure or 100 per cent. state in solution in the excess of sulphuric acid.

Thus when a mixture of the two acids is employed the cellulose is practically brought in contact with 100 per cent. nitric acid and there is still sufficient excess of sulphuric acid to combine with the water as it is formed in the reaction.

The acid mixture actually employed contains considerably more than the (above mentioned) theoretical proportion of sulphuric acid.

Celluloses of whatever sources when placed in this mixture of acids show no external change, although they increase in weight.

Considerable differences of opinion exist in regard to the composition and representation by chemical formulæ of the nitrated cellulose produced by variations in composition of the nitrating acid mixture and temperature.

Some chemists regard the cellulose molecule as $C_{12}H_{20}O_{10}$, and express some nitrates as

$$C_{12}H_{14}O_4(NO_3)_6, \text{ and } C_2H_{15}O_5(NO_3)_5, \&c.$$

Vieille, Berthelot and others proceed on the assumption that $C_{24}H_{40}O_{20}$ represents cellulose and formulate some products as $C_{24}H_{28}O_8(NO_3)_{12}$, and $C_{24}H_{29}O_9(NO_3)_{11}$, &c., &c.

As a matter of fact nitrated cellulose products can be obtained which have a nitrogen content corresponding to almost any one of them. These products when examined by solvents, &c., appear to be mixtures of nitrates of various degrees of nitration.

A broad distinctive term in common use in the manufacture of guncotton is "soluble" or "insoluble," which refers, as a rule, to their solubility or not in a mixture of alcohol and ether.

It has long been thought that there exists in cellulose nitrates, when tested by solvents, a relation between their solubility or insolubility in ether-alcohol on the one hand and their nitrogen content on the other. It was indeed thought that the most highly nitrated form, the tri-nitrate, $C_6H_7O_2(NO_3)_3$ (on the $C_6H_{10}O_5$ basis) was insoluble whereas products represented by $C_6H_8O_3(NO_3)_2$ (or $C_6H_9O_4NO_3$) were soluble. More recent experiments, in which widely varying acid mixtures have been used, have shown that there is still a limit in the percentage of nitrogen below which the nitrates increase in solubility, and also that there is a limit above which an increase of nitrogen is accompanied by decreased solubility.

As a matter of fact, the percentage of nitrogen in cellulose-nitrate wholly soluble in ether-alcohol may be much higher than that in the products corresponding to the old dinitro-cellulose ($C_6H_8O_3(NO_3)_2$, to the tetra-nitro-cellulose of Eder

($C_{12}H_{16}O_8(NO_3)_4$) or to the ennea-nitro-cellulose ($C_{24}H_{31}O_{11}(NO_3)_9$) of Vieille and Berthelot.

As the degree of nitration depends principally on the strength of the nitric acid, should the nitric acid used be not sufficiently concentrated, or the proportion of sulphuric acid be too small, the water contained in the former, together with that produced by the reaction itself, will cause the formation of a lower or soluble nitrate. As the higher the degree of nitration the greater the explosive force of the product, every care is taken to reduce, in the manufacture of guncotton the amount of soluble product as much as possible by using a mixture of nitric and sulphuric acid containing a large excess of the latter, having the acids largely in excess of the amount of cotton to be treated, using the cotton as dry as possible, keeping down the temperature of the acid bath, and by other minor precautions. With every care however, it is not possible on a manufacturing scale to obtain guncotton, or insoluble nitrate, which does not contain a percentage of collodion or soluble guncottons, just as it is impossible to produce soluble guncottons without a proportion of the insoluble.

When carefully made and purified guncotton is odourless and tasteless, and neutral to the acid and alkali test papers. Water alcohol, ether, glacial acetic acid, and some other liquids, exert no appreciable solvent action. Nitro-glycerine does not dissolve guncotton, whereas soluble cotton or collodion cotton is more or less soluble or gelatinizable therein. Dilute hydrochloric, sulphuric, and nitric acids (20 per cent. about) have no action, but dilute alkalis and alkali carbonates have a slight decomposing action especially when warm, and afterwards contain traces of nitrite and nitrate. Ammonia is much more active. Guncotton warmed to about 70°C in ammonia gas becomes browned, and then as a rule explodes. Damp ammonia gas at the ordinary temperature slowly decomposes guncotton, producing some brown products which dissolve in water, to some extent, yielding a solution containing both nitrate and nitrite in considerable amount.

Strong alkali solutions, or solid potassium or sodium hydroxides decompose guncotton very rapidly. The solutions become brown, and as the reaction goes on the temperature may rise to the boiling point. A mixture of nitrate and nitrite of the alkali results and the cellulose molecule is completely destroyed. The solid hydroxides are particularly dangerous. Air-dry guncotton placed in contact with the solid hydroxides, in the ordinary moist atmosphere, inflames almost immediately.

Cold concentrated sulphuric acid slowly dissolves guncotton. Nitric acid is liberated and if the sulphuric acid be in tolerable excess dissolves therein and a sulphate of cellulose is also probably formed. [This is the first stage of action in the nitrometer.].

When warmed very slightly with strong sulphuric acid nitric acid fumes are first evolved followed by oxides of nitrogen; an oxidation of the cellulose with rise of temperature commences and the action may become violent with moderately large quantities. Dilute sulphuric acid becomes easily concentrated on heating or long exposure to a dry and warm atmosphere. A very little sulphuric acid left, by imperfect washing, in guncotton may cause it to inflame during some drying process. This is the commonest danger in connection with guncotton.

Quite a number of the so-called reducing agents* will decompose guncotton quietly, in some cases liberating the whole of the nitrogen as gas, so that it may be collected and measured, thus giving a measure of the amount of nitration of the cotton. A very strong solution of a ferrous salt (ferrous sulphate) and sulphuric acid of about 50 per cent. is a practical re-agent for this purpose. Contact with a metal like zinc, in a moist state, results in decomposition at the point of contact. The action is somewhat slow.† Alkali and other soluble hydrosulphides as KHS or NH_4HS quietly remove and reduce the NO_3 groups from guncotton. The cellulose is in these cases restored.‡

Several carbon compounds gelatinise or dissolve guncotton without any chemical action. Some of these are volatile substances, which on their evaporation leave the guncotton in a totally altered form. All the fibres and cells of the original cotton have disappeared, and the material left is, when dry, hard and non-porous, like glue without its stickiness. It is now in the colloid state.

Acetone is, perhaps, one of the most convenient substances for effecting this change. Many substances of the class " Ester " or etherial salt, as methyl, ethyl and amyl acetates, ethyl benzoate, &c., and also some benzene compounds as nitrobenzene, behave in the same way. Acetone has some advantages over many of these, especially as regards volatility and ease of production.

Aniline and some other compounds at a slightly elevated temperature also dissolve guncotton, but their action is a chemical one, a mutual destruction quietly taking place, resulting in the formation of water, oxides of nitrogen, carbon-dioxide, and some liquid and solid non-explosive compounds.

Cotton gains about 70 per cent. in weight when converted into guncotton, Quite dry guncotton becomes very easily electrified by friction. It does not absorb moisture from the air, but in the "ordinary" dry state contains a little less than 2 per cent. moisture. The normal amount of moisture increases as the degree of nitration decreases.

The specific gravity of guncotton = 1·63. When pulped and hydraulically compressed the density = 1, about.

---

* Substances which absorb oxygen or give off nascent hydrogen.

† Ammonia is liable to be formed in these circumstances, and then the action is not so local.

‡ The so-called artificial silk, and one of the methods of making incandescent lamp filaments depends on the same action,

When thoroughly wetted guncotton cannot be inflamed, but when damp—that is, containing a few per cents (3 per cent.) of water—it may be fired, but it is not very sensitive to heat. With 12-13 per cent. it ceases to be inflammable. When dry—that is air dry—it will take fire at about 170° C., or even lower. A good deal depends on the rate of heating. It is possible, by careful washing with alcohol-ether, to get guncotton not igniting before 185° C. is reached. Many commercial guncottons will, however, ignite at 150° C.

In the open air the flame is yellowish and practically smokeless, and little or no residue is left. Compressed, but unconfined, guncotton burns comparatively slowly if in small quantities, say one or two pounds, but in much larger amount the combustion goes on at a very rapidly accelerating rate, and may end in violent explosion. Guncotton when warm and dry, especially if heated to about 100° C., will often explode when first ignited.

There is little doubt but that the best and most carefully made guncotton undergoes a slow decomposition when kept for a long time at ordinary temperatures. When maintained at about the temperature of boiling water it also undergoes slow decomposition, and may end after some time (which depends on the quality of the guncotton, &c.) in inflaming. Many products result from this slow decomposition, as fatty acids, esters, ketones, &c. Direct sunlight starts a slow decomposition, and the substance becomes darker in colour.

Several "heat" tests have been proposed to test the stability of guncottons—that is, if they would be reasonably safe to keep in store for an indefinite period. Whether the methods are absolutely reliable is not quite settled.

Guncotton when dry and warm is very easily detonated by friction on a moderately hard surface or by percussion. Even when slightly damp the blow of a hammer on guncotton resting on an anvil will detoriate the portion struck. Sometimes the remainder will fire, but not always.

Unconfined compressed guncotton, slabs or blocks, can be fully detonated by a charge of mercury fulminate. When the

---

In all the cases of slow decomposition, water, carbon dioxide and oxides of nitrogen are produced. This is well shown when guncotton is heated in a vacuum vessel and the gases pumped away by a Sprengel pump as fast as they are formed.

Under these circumstances, the gases collected are quite colourless until they come in contact with air, when they become red. Therefore the oxide of nitrogen given off is nitric oxide or NO, which, on contact with air, becomes NO_2 or N_2O_4, this in contact with water giving a mixture of nitric and nitrous acids. (A little nitrogen dioxide—NO_2—is also formed, but is mainly absorbed by the mercury of the pump.)

There seems to be a distinct connection between the quality of the guncotton and the time it may be heated to some moderately high temperature before explosion or very *rapid* decomposition takes place.

Guncotton imperfectly washed, or not very completely nitrated, certainly decomposes more rapidly and in less time than well-nitrated and carefully-washed samples.

guncotton is dry a small fulminate charge only is necessary. Dry guncotton detonated in contact with the wet compressed will also bring about complete detonation. Wet compressed guncotton explodes more perfectly than the dry, the resilience of the contained water no doubt aiding in the transmission of the explosive wave.

Service guncotton is always stored, containing about 17 per cent. water or 20 parts of water to 100 of guncotton; the degree of moisture in guncotton being defined as the number of parts by weight of water added to 100 parts of dry guncotton. With this amount of admixed water guncotton placed in a fire will merely smoulder away as the outer portions become dried. At any rate, experiments made officially on a large scale showed that when a building containing a ton of wet guncotton was fired the contents gradually smouldered away as above stated. It is not known, however, whether in the event of very large quantities strongly confined being subjected to great heat for a length of time, explosive action might not ensue. It very probably would. In the wet state the safety of guncotton from a transport and storage point of view is very much increased, as is also the ease and safety with which it can be manipulated and employed, seeing that, as already pointed out, it can be detonated when wet just as readily us when dry.

In a suitable medium, such as water, a charge of guncotton may be detonated by the detonation of another charge a considerable distance away. This has been shown in experiments with mines and torpedoes.

As stated (*ante*), it is doubtful whether *dry* guncotton can be kept indefinitely in any quantity without undergoing slow decomposition. It has however now been most thoroughly established by the experience of many years, that *wet* guncotton, when properly made and purified, can be kept in any climate, and for any length of time, without undergoing spontaneous chemical change. Service wet guncotton is issued in air-tight metal-lined cases, so that the necessity for re-wetting it will seldom arise, but should it become requisite, means of, and full instructions for, re-wetting are provided. With the idea of further ensuring its stability, service guncotton is rendered alkaline to the extent of from $\frac{1}{2}$ to 2 per cent. with sodium carbonate before it is moulded and pressed.

Sodium carbonate is only a weak alkali, and its function is to combine with and neutralise any acid that might be produced by a slight decomposition of the guncotton.

As stated (*ante*), the function of the sulphuric acid in the acid mixture employed for nitrating should be that of combining with the water contained in the nitric acid and also with the water produced in the reaction of the latter with the cellulose. Unfortunately it does not confine itself to these duties, but produces some small quantity of a sulphate of cellulose. Most of this sulphate undoubtedly undergoes hydrolysis during the washing and boiling processes to which the guncotton is subjected. But a little seems to escape destruction, either because it is in the innermost portions of the cells, for it must be remembered the cells are not destroyed, or is in some degree protected by the very insoluble nitrate enclosing it. The cellulose sulphates known are extremely unstable substances and decompose at moderate temperatures liberating the acid. As before stated, dry guncotton, in the ordinary sense, contains a small amount of moisture, sufficient to act as a hydrolysing agent on the sulphate, so that in keeping for some time at ordinary temperatures hydrolysis may be taking place. The sulphuric acid as fast as liberated will commence, especially at a slightly elevated temperature, to decompose some guncotton, liberating nitric acid and starting a little oxidation of the cellulose, and especially of the cellulose wh... was combined as sulphate.

Most commercial guncottons when boiled with solution of ammonia for one hour will yield up some sulphuric acid which can be detected by the formation of barium sulphate, when the filtered solution is made acid and a soluble barium salt added. Many bases as aniline, toluidine, urea, &c., decompose guncotton, and can be used in place of ammonia for the "sulphuric acid testing."

Guncotton can also be decomposed by alcoholic potassium hydroxide solution and the residue after evaporation to dryness taken up with dilute nitric acid and this tested for sulphuric.

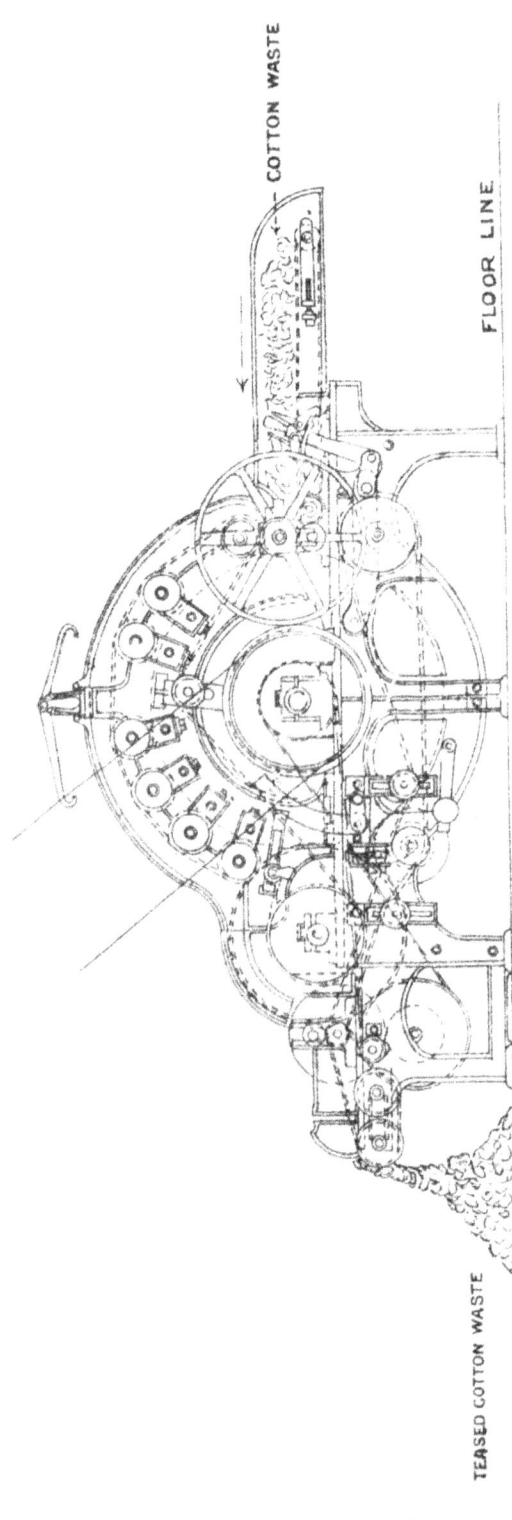

PLATE XIII.

COTTON WASTE TEASING MACHINE.

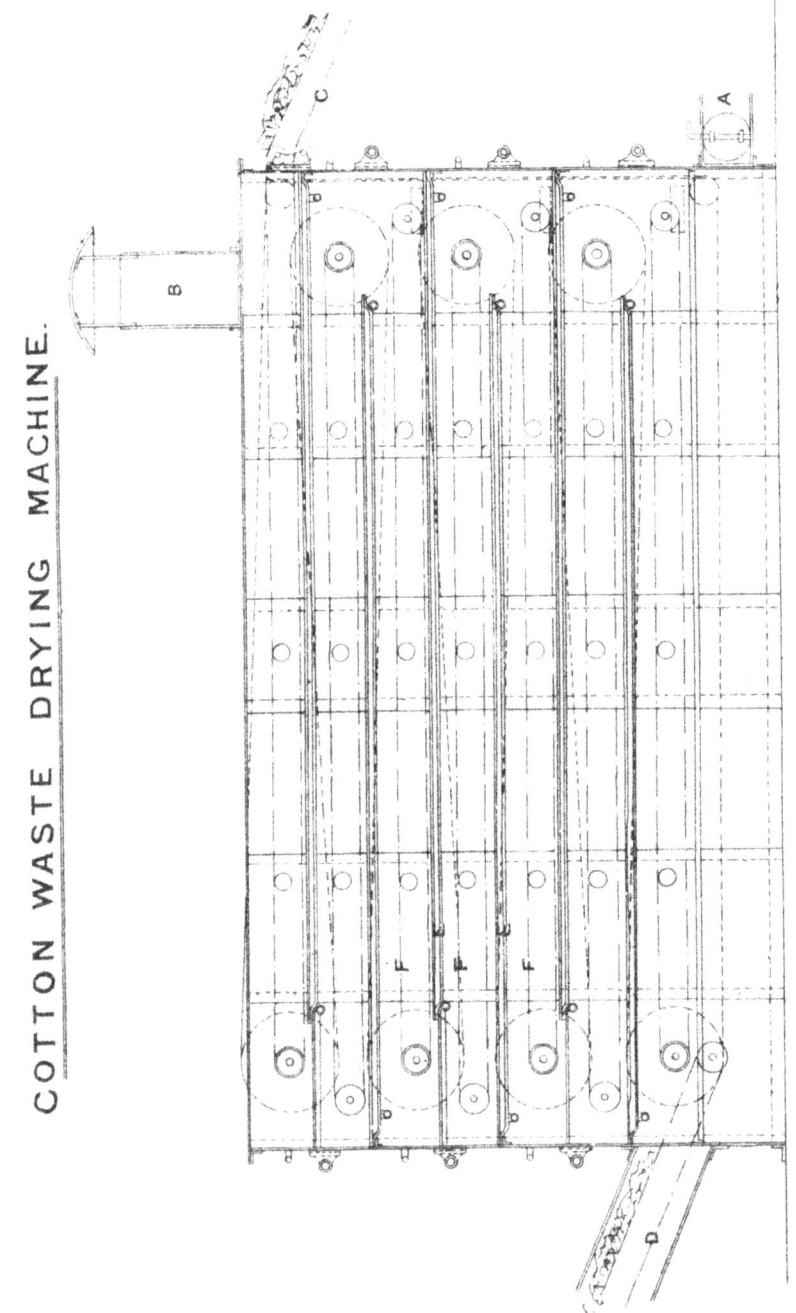

PLATE XIV.

COTTON WASTE DRYING MACHINE.

A. Hot Air Inlet.
B. Hot Air Outlet.
C. Cotton Elevating Band, Inlet.
D. Cotton Elevating Band, Outlet.
E. Steam Trays.
F. Endless Bands.

CHAPTER VII.

MANUFACTURE OF GUNCOTTON, ORDINARY OR OLD PROCESS.

For the manufacture of guncotton the best cotton waste is alone employed. Its preparation, consisting essentially of a treatment with alkalis for the removal of grease and oils, and of bleaching, is a speciality, and is carried out by the contractor before the waste is supplied to the factory. As supplied, it should contain not more than 1·1 per cent. of oily matter, nor more than 8 per cent. of moisture.

(1) *Picking Over.*—The first process consists in picking the cotton over by hand and removing all foreign substances, such as pieces of wood, cane, wire, string, &c.

(2) *Teasing.*—The cotton waste is then passed through a "teasing machine" (*see* Pl. XIII) which, by means of a combination of rollers armed with iron teeth, separates the fibre of the cotton, and opens out at the same time all knots and lumps. It is again picked over as it issues from the machine.

(3) *Cutting.*—In order to get a short-stapled cotton, and so facilitate the operations of drying, and dipping the cotton waste in the acids, it is cut, if necessary, by a description of guillotine, into 2-inch lengths. After this cutting it is again passed through the teasing machine, and picked over.

(4) *Drying.*—The cotton is placed upon an endless band, which conducts it to the stove, or drying closet (*see* Pl. XIV), a chamber heated by a hot-air blast and steam trays to about 180° F. Falling upon a second endless band placed below the first, it travels back again through the length of the stove, and so on, backwards and forwards, until delivered at the bottom of the further end on to another endless band, travelling out at right angles to the machine, which carries it into a large wooden bin. The speed at which the cotton travels is 6 feet per minute, and, as the lengths of the bands traversed amount in all to 126 feet, the operation of drying takes about 21 minutes, and reduces the amount of moisture to below 1 per cent.

(5) *Weighing.*—The cotton waste having been thoroughly dried, is weighed into charges, each of which is at once placed in a tin box provided with a tight-fitting lid to exclude the air. A truck, fitted to receive a number of these boxes, conveys the cotton along a tramway into a cool room, where it remains cooling in the covered boxes until the next day, when it is ready for dipping.

(6) *Mixing the Acids.*—The strength of the acids is a matter of much importance; the nitric acid must not be below 1·5

sp. gr. at 60° F., and must not contain more than 1·5°/₀ of nitrous acid; and the sulphuric acid must not be below 1·842 sp. gr. at 60° F., and must contain not less than 96°/₀ by weight of sulphuric monohydrate (H_2SO_4).

The sulphuric acid is obtained from the trade and is received in glass carboys, each containing 105 lbs. of acid. The nitric acid is made at Waltham Abbey Gunpowder Factory. A mixture of new sulphuric and nitric acids, together with a proportion of waste acid extracted from the guncotton after the nitrating processes are complete, is employed. The mixing is effected as follows:—The sulphuric acid is emptied from the carboys into an egg-shaped steel vessel known as a *monte-jus*, and is forced from it by means of compressed air through lead pipes into a cylindrical steel tank placed on high pillars. The nitric acid as it is produced is run into an earthenware egg, from which it is forced, also by compressed air, into the same tank. The waste acid is finally added through the sulphuric acid egg. The proportion of nitric to sulphuric acid is as 1 to 3. The contents of the tank are thoroughly mixed by means of jets of compressed air, and the mixed acids then run by gravity into the acid store tanks, in which they are allowed to thoroughly cool down, the temperature having risen considerably from the heat generated by the absorption of water by the sulphuric from the nitric acid. The store tanks have outlets at the bottom with earthenware cocks, all communicating with a common main pipe which conveys the acids to the dipping pans. The main pipe runs along in front of the pans and is provided with small branch pipes with cocks for each individual pan.

(7) *Dipping.*—Each "dipping-pan" is supported in an iron tank, through which cold water is kept flowing, in order to carry off any heat generated by the chemical action of the conversion of the cotton into guncotton; the temperature is kept below 70° F. The dipping-pans are provided with gratings for pressing out the superfluous acid from the charge. The charge of cotton having been removed from its tin box, is placed by the dipper into the mixed acids as rapidly as possible.

After remaining in the acid bath for about eight minutes, the cotton is removed to the grating, and a portion of the acids squeezed out by means of a lever having a plate attached to one end. After each charge has been removed from the dipping-pan a quantity of the mixed acids is run into it in order to replace the amount removed with the charge.

The charge, now weighing with the acids about 17½ lbs., is placed in an earthenware pot provided with a cover, and transferred to the cooling pits, through which a stream of cold water constantly flows, and where it is allowed to remain for eight hours. The cotton waste has thus time to digest in the excess of acid, so that it may be entirely converted into guncotton. This process is sometimes modified, the cotton being dipped a second time at the end of four hours. In addition to the danger of enough heat being generated to cause

PLATE XV.

BEATING ENGINE.

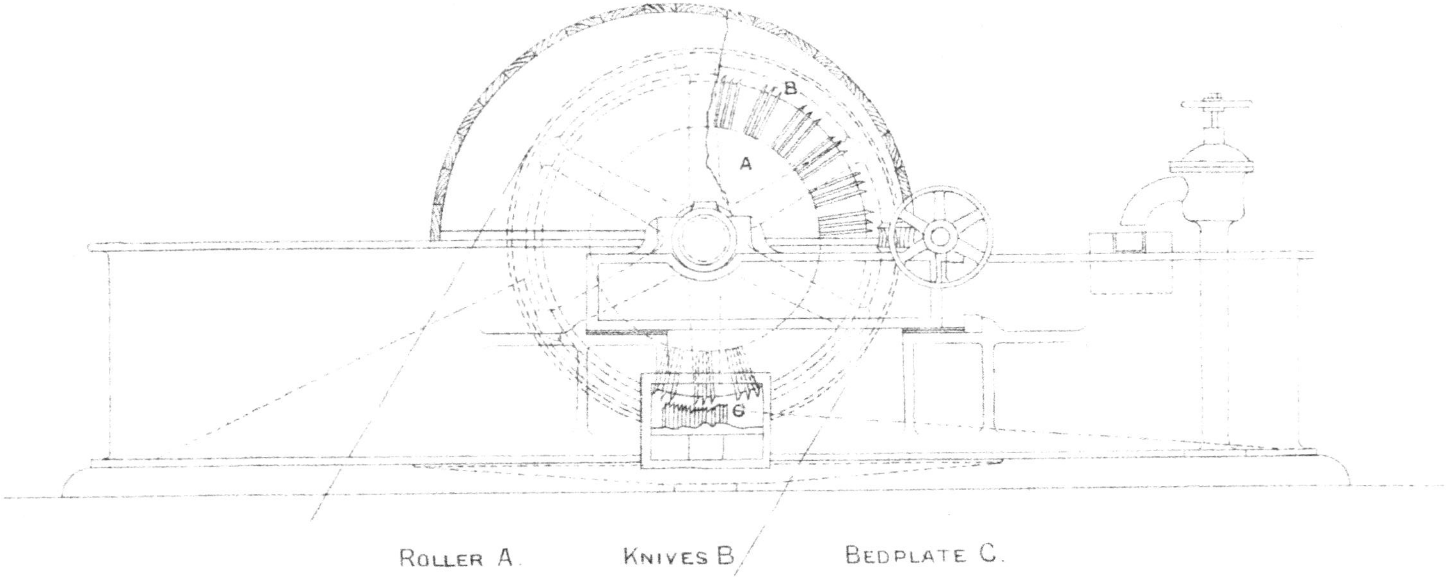

ROLLER A.   KNIVES B.   BEDPLATE C.

the cotton to be completely decomposed with the evolution of dense nitrous fumes, it is of great importance to keep the temperature as low as possible, as thereby there will be a less percentage of *soluble* nitrates formed. The pots are covered so as to prevent any moisture being absorbed by the sulphuric acid from the atmosphere, and also any water splashing into them, which, through the heat generated by the action of the sulphuric acid on the water, would cause decomposition, and consequent fuming-off.

(8) *Extracting the Acids.*—When the cotton has been completely converted, a large amount of superfluous acid still remains in each charge. The contents of six pots are therefore transferred to an "acid extractor," consisting of a centrifugal wringing machine, provided with a perforated iron cage which revolves at the rate of 1,200 revolutions per minute. After being whirled in this machine for five minutes, about $11\frac{1}{2}$ lbs. of waste acids are removed from each charge dipped.

(9) *Immersing.*—The guncotton is removed from the centrifugal machine by a workman, who uses for the purpose a couple of short-handled, flat, iron forks, and is placed by him in an iron pan provided with a long handle. When full, this pan is carried quickly across to the "immersing machine," and its contents thrown into the water, a workman standing by the tank of the machine pushing the guncotton at once under the water with a stout wooden paddle. The immersing must be done as quickly as possible, for if the guncotton were allowed to come gradually in contact with water it would be liable to fume off. The immersing machine is fitted with a perforated copper plate to allow the water to escape, so that fresh water is constantly passing through the machine. The guncotton is kept well stirred up by means of the paddle. When 2 cwt. of guncotton have been immersed, the inflow of water is stopped and the tank drained down; when all the water has run off, the tank is filled up again with fresh water. This is repeated six times, after the sixth washing the guncotton is tasted, and if there is no taste of acid another washing is given, $\frac{1}{2}$ lb. of soda ash being added to the water; this last washing is not given however until there is no acid taste.

(10) *Wringing.*—The guncotton is removed to another centrifugal wringing machine, provided with a wire cage, in which it receives a further washing with a jet of water, the cage meanwhile revolving. The inflow of water is then stopped, and the moisture wrung out for four minutes, at 1,200 revolutions per minute.

(11) *Beating or Pulping.*—The guncotton is next reduced to a very fine state of division in a "beating engine" (*see* Pl. XV), somewhat similar to that employed for pulping rags in the manufacture of paper. It consists of a roller, A, armed with knives, B, and a bed-plate, C, similarly furnished; the guncotton being made to pass between them. The roller is gradually lowered nearer to the bed-plate as the operation proceeds. There are two sizes of beaters in use, one holding

4¼ cwt., the other 2¼ cwt. of guncotton, and the operation of beating takes from four to five hours. At the start bicarbonate of soda is added, 2½ lb. for the small, and 5 lb. to the large beater, to neutralise any acid set free during the process.

Pulping is one of the most important processes in the treatment of guncotton.

(12) *Boiling.*—On completion of the beating process the guncotton is run by gravity through iron pipes into large wooden vats, where it undergoes several boilings by means of steam. The water is syphoned off after every boiling, and the vat filled up each time with fresh boiling water. The early boilings are shorter than the end ones, the entire boiling process lasting about one day. After the final boiling the guncotton pulp is run through an outlet valve at the bottom of the tank, into a common main, from which it is lifted by means of a Cortin's elevator into an overhead iron pipe.

(13) *Poaching.*—The pulp is carried by this pipe through "grit traps," in which sand, stones, pieces of iron and metal, &c., are caught, into large oval iron tanks called "poachers" (see Pl. XVI), which hold 1,500 gallons each, and are provided with paddle wheels to keep the finely-divided guncotton agitated in a large volume of water; in this way it is thoroughly washed, and all minute impurities removed. The contents of two vats, *i.e.*, about 18 cwt. of guncotton, is run into each poacher. After being washed two or three times in the poacher, samples of the pulp are removed for testing.

(14) *Adding Alkali and Drawing into Stuff-chest.*—When the pulp has passed the requisite tests successfully, and just before being required for moulding, 500 gallons of water are run out of the poacher, and the same quantity of limewater is added, also 9 lb. of whiting and 9 lb. of caustic soda; this mixture is of a strength calculated to leave in the finished guncotton from 1 to 2 per cent. of alkaline matter.

No lime water, whiting, or caustic soda are added to guncotton intended for the manufacture of cordite.

The pulp is then drawn up into the "stuff-chest" by means of a vacuum. This stuff-chest is a large cylindrical iron tank, sufficiently elevated on iron standards to allow room for the small gauge-tanks and moulding apparatus below; it will hold the contents of one poacher (18 cwt.), and is provided with revolving arms to keep the guncotton pulp stirred up so that it may be uniformly suspended in the water.

(15) *Moulding.*—By means of the small measuring tanks above referred to, which are provided with glass gauges, any required amount of guncotton pulp can be drawn off from the stuff-chest, and run into moulds of the shapes and sizes required. A large proportion of the water is drawn off through the hollow plungers of the moulding machine, by means of tubes connected with the vacuum engine, the tops of the plungers being covered with fine wire gauze in order to prevent the pulp from passing through. Hydraulic pressure of about 34 lb. on the

POACHER.

PLATE XVI.

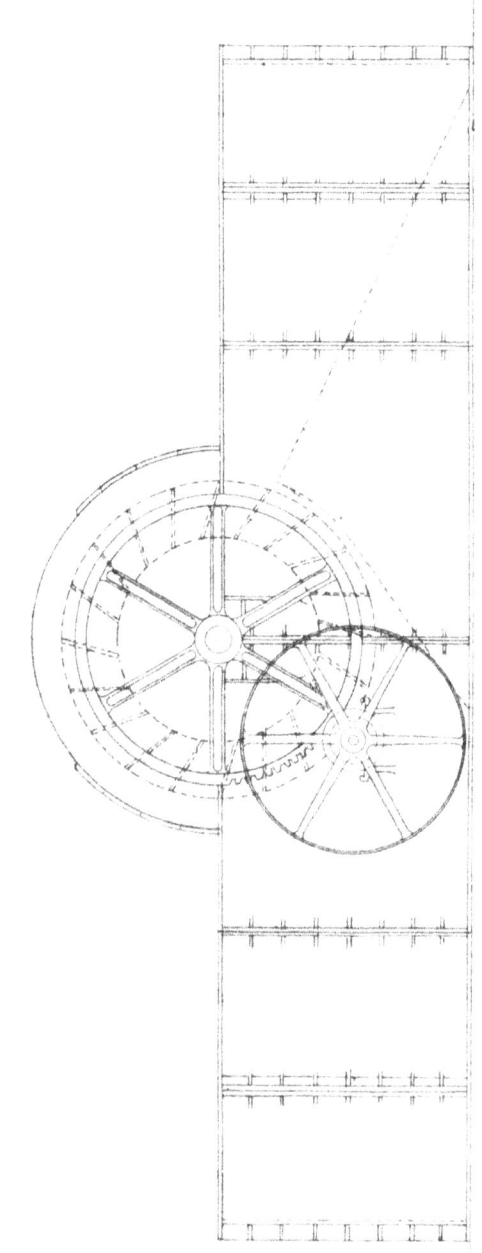

PLATE XVII

GUNCOTTON HYDRAULIC PRESS.

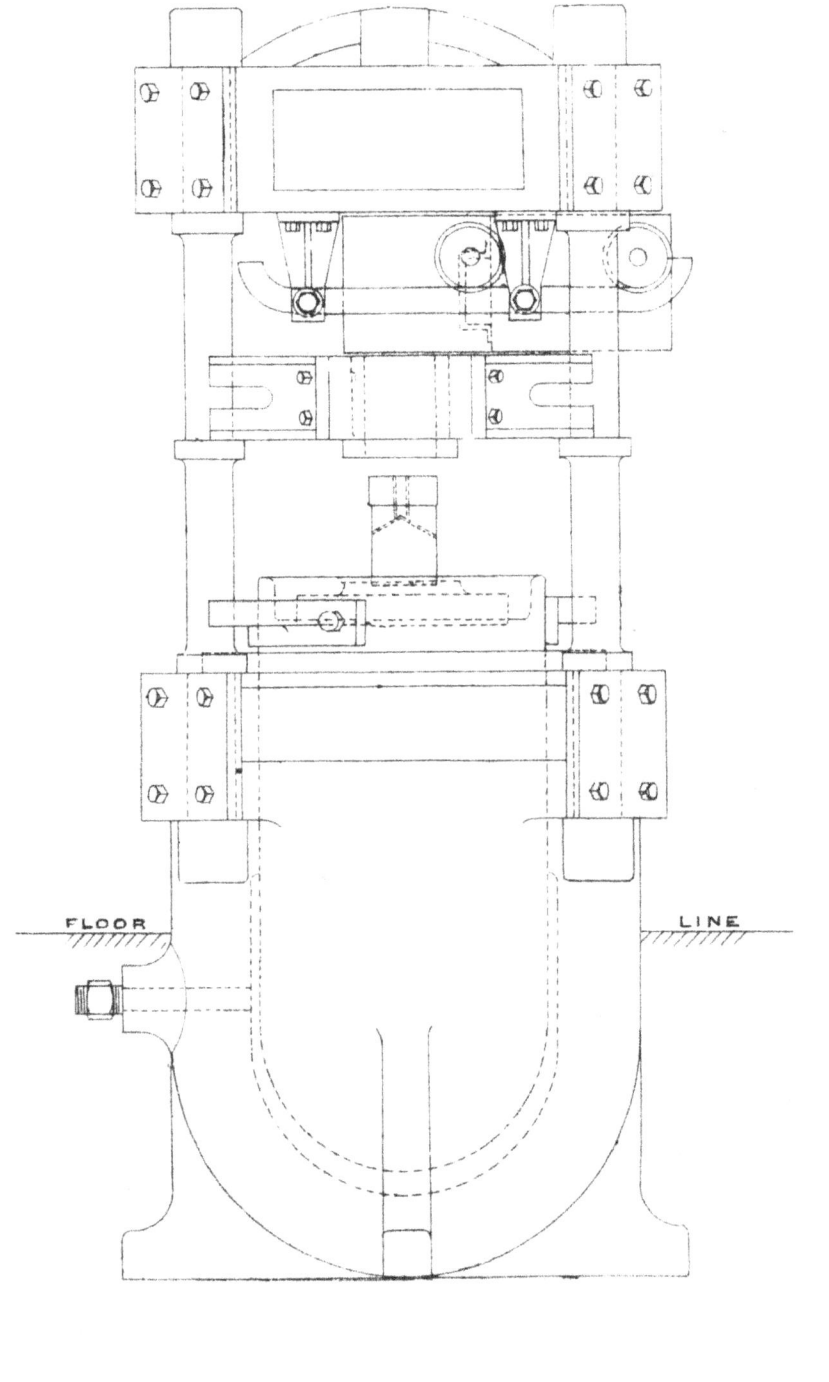

square inch is then applied, which has the effect of squeezing the pulp into a state in which it has sufficient consistency to be handled with care, at the same time expelling a portion of the remaining water.

This 34 lb. pressure is only applied in the moulding machine itself, to slabs, and to "A" primers; "B" primers are pushed from the moulding machine into a separate mould or carrier in which they are conveyed to a small hydraulic press, where they are compressed also by a pressure of about 34 lb. on the square inch. "C," "D," "E," "F," "G," "H," and "J" primers are moulded, one at a time, in a hand machine. Guncotton intended for the manufacture of cordite is moulded into "B" primers.

(16) *Pressing.*—The moulded guncotton is placed in boxes, and removed to the press house (*see* Pl. XVII). The "moulds" of guncotton are here subjected to powerful hydraulic pressure, amounting to about 6 tons upon the square inch, which has the effect of compressing them to about one-third their former height; the slabs, or primers thus formed, are kept a certain time under pressure in order to give them the requisite density. They should, when finished, be firm and compact, not perceptibly yielding to pressure between the finger and thumb, and *just* sinking when placed in water when dry.

The slabs or primers are of different dimensions, and weigh from $2\frac{1}{2}$ lb. down to 1 oz., according to the purpose for which the guncotton is required. These slabs or primers frequently have holes bored in them, while in the wet state, to receive primers of dry guncotton or else the fulminate of mercury detonators. The wet compressed guncotton is also cut by means of a band saw, or turned in a lathe into the shapes requisite to fill the charge cases of torpedoes and mines; these cutting and turning operations are not however, carried out at Waltham Abbey.

Plate XIX shows the forms, dimensions, and weights of guncotton pressed at Waltham Abbey.

(17) *Packing Wet Guncotton.*—The finished slabs and discs are dipped into a solution of caustic soda and carbolic acid; they are then packed in special wood metal-lined cases. When the guncotton is to be sent abroad, the metal lining, which is made of tinned copper, is carefully soldered down. Both the outer wooden case and the metal inside case, are fitted with air-tight screw plugs, so that when necessary, water can be added without unfastening the cases.*

Re-working Guncotton.—Guncotton sent back to Waltham Abbey for re-working, either on account of being in a broken condition, from alteration of pattern, or from other causes, is boiled by steam in order to soften it, and also to remove the alkali, and is then run through a beater into a poacher, where it is poached. From the poacher it is drawn into the

---

* For regulations for the inspection, wetting, &c., of guncotton, *see* "Regulations for Army Ordnance Services."

"stuff-chest," moulded, and pressed in the same manner as new guncotton.

Samples of pulp from the poachers, or of the finished guncotton, are tested with the following objects :—

(*a*) *Alkalinity Test.*—To determine the proportion of alkaline matter contained in the finished guncotton, which should not be less than 0·5, nor more than 2 per cent.

(*b**) *Solubility Test.*—To ascertain the percentage of soluble nitrate contained in any sample. Shaking a carefully weighed quantity for a length of time in a mixture of ether and alcohol, dissolves out all the soluble nitrated cotton, the percentage of which is ascertained by weighing the residue after evaporating off the ether-alcohol; it must not exceed 12 per cent.

(*c*) *Nitrogen Test.*—To ascertain the percentage of nitrogen in the guncotton, which must not be less than 12·5 for service guncotton, and not less than 12·8 nor more than 13·1 for guncotton intended for the manufacture of cordite. To determine this an apparatus called a "Nitrometer" is used.

(*d*) *Heat Test.*—In order to determine its freedom from uncombined acid. This is an exceedingly delicate test, depending upon the length of time very finely divided guncotton, dried at a low temperature, can be exposed in a test-tube to a steady heat of 170° F. by means of a water bath, in close proximity to a moistened strip of paper impregnated with iodide of potassium and starch, without producing discolouration of the latter. When this test is properly performed under exact conditions, good guncotton should show no more discolouration than that of the standard tint paper for *at least ten minutes.*

(*e*) *Test for Unconverted Cotton.*—The complete conversion into guncotton may be tested by taking a very small quantity and shaking it for some time with acetic ether or acetone, in which it should slowly dissolve, forming a gummy fluid; unconverted cotton is not affected by these solvents.

The above tests have to be carried out with the greatest care and under certain strictly defined conditions, of which the above affords a mere outline or indication. A full description of the methods of performing the tests is laid down in the Specification for Guncotton.

Making Guncotton by the Displacement Process,
(Nathan and Thompson).

The method just described has been recently considerably improved upon. The displacement process, as it may be termed,

---

* When *finished* guncotton is submitted to tests (*b*) and (*d*), it must first be washed free from all alkaline matter.

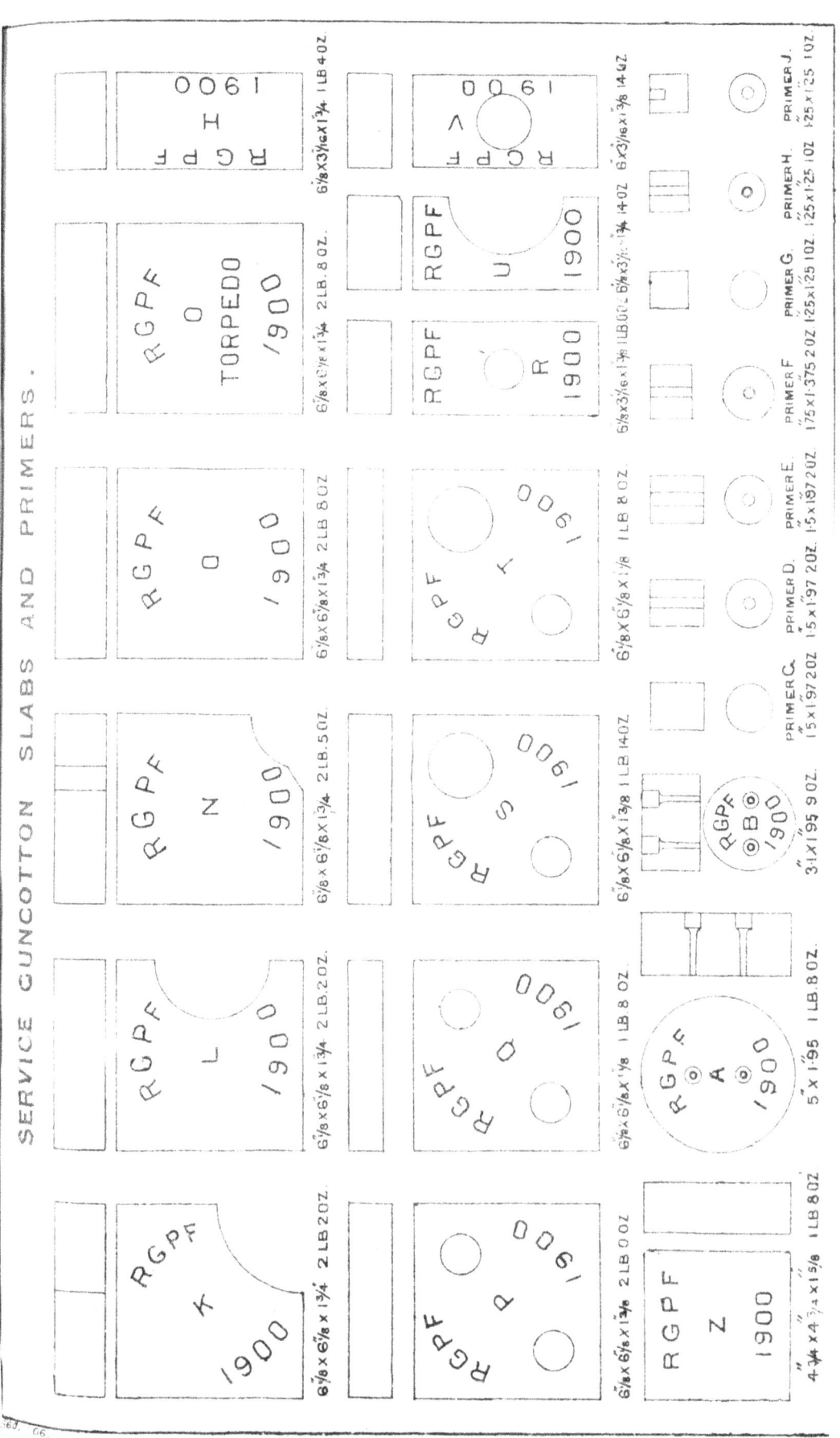

being simpler, safer, and decidedly more economical for the same output of guncotton. The diagram of the apparatus itself almost explains the whole process.

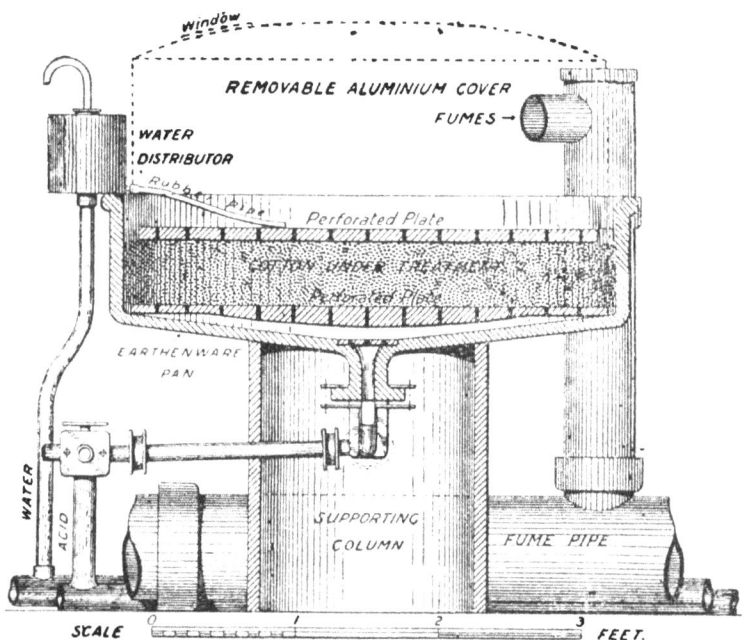

Section showing the New Apparatus of Nathan and Thompson.

The cotton material is placed in a considerable bulk of the nitrating acids, and remains in the same vessel not only until the nitration is completed, but also until washed sufficiently free from adhering acids to undergo the boiling process (ante).

The apparatus in which the nitration and first washing is conducted consists of a circular earthenware pan 3 feet 6 inches inside diameter, with a perpendicular side of 10 inches, below which the bottom slopes slightly funnel-like to a central pipe the opening of which is three-quarters of an inch diameter. The pan is supported about 2 feet above the floor by an earthenware cylinder or pipe. In working, the central pipe opening is covered with a small perforated plate, and above that is placed a large perforated plate which forms a complete level false bottom.

Acid from the nitrating supply at a temperature of from 10° to 15° C., is admitted to the pan until within a few inches of the top. The charges of cotton waste, prepared as usual, are then added and immersed and covered with perforated plates, which are divided into segments for ease of manipulation. The plates help to push and keep the cotton under the acids.

Four of these pans are connected, so as to form a set, by lead and aluminium pipes, and during the time that cotton is being introduced that pan is covered by an aluminium fume-hood which is connected to a draught flue.

When all the charge has been added, water, at a temperature of from 5° to 10° C. is run over the surface of the perforated plates in a very thin layer, which soon completely seals the acids, stopping fuming, and the fume-hoods can be removed to the next set of pans.

The nitration then proceeds for $2\frac{1}{2}$ hours. The tap leading to the gauge-box is then opened and the waste acids allowed to run off at the rate of about 17 lbs. per minute. Water flows on to the top of the charge at about the same rate as the outflow of acid. The first portion of waste acid is returned to the acid store tanks to be refreshed with strong sulphuric and nitric acids. The second weaker portion passes to the acid factory for denitration and concentration, and the last portions containing very little acid flow to waste. Weak acids down to 1·10 specific gravity can be economically concentrated. Twenty pounds of cotton can be nitrated in each pan, for which 600 lbs. of acid is required in the space above the large perforated plate or false bottom. There is about 100 lbs. of acid below this which is unused and passes back with the waste acid to the store tanks to be refreshed or revivified. Each charge passes through all the processes, and is placed in the boiling vat in between seven and eight hours from starting.

This modified process has been found to give a higher yield and more uniform nitration than the process previously described (the Abel method).

Its great recommendation is its economy in time, plant and working.

The waste acids are recovered, the nitric being distilled off, and residual sulphuric concentrated in a Kissler concentrator.

This process can be also carried on by having two nitrating vessels only placed side by side, and joined at their lowest points by a pipe provided with a stop-cock, each vessel having also a tap for emptying. The vessels are used alternately, thus: One of the vessels is charged with the nitrating acid, and the cellulose immersed in the usual manner, whereupon a thin layer of weak sulphuric acid is allowed to flow over the surface of the acids to prevent fuming. After standing for two or three hours, or until the desired nitration is complete, water is slowly and carefully run on to the acids, so as to avoid mixing. The stop-cock between the two vessels is opened, and the acids allowed to flow at the same easy rate into the empty vessel as the water flows into the charged one. The whole of the acid in the first vessel is driven by water into the next one, where it is revivified by addition of fresh acids, and again used for a nitration, after which it is returned to the first vessel, and so on alternately.

The after treatment of the nitrated cotton is practically the same as with the original Abel process.

NITRO-GLYCERINE.

Glycerol trinitrate, $C_3H_5(NO_3)_3$, was discovered by Sobrero in 1847 (Ann. $\frac{64}{398}$). It is obtained by the action of a mixture of nitric and sulphuric acids on glycerine, and the process may be carried out in several ways. The highest yield of product is said "to be obtained by mixing 10 parts of glycerine with 30 of nitric acid, specific gravity 1·49 and 6 parts sulphuric acid, specific gravity 1·84, all being cooled down to below 15° C. The reaction is completed in a few minutes, the product rising to the top of the acid mixture from which it is separated and washed with water until acid free."

When pure, nitro-glycerine is a colourless oily liquid, but generally it shows a slight yellow tint. It crystallizes at a low temperature, but statements as to this differ considerably, $-20°$ C. is given for the pure substance and 4° for the ordinary product. The confusion arises no doubt from the fact that it exhibits the phenomenon of superfusion as also does glycerine. In its solid state its specific gravity is given as 1·735. Its specific gravity at 4° C. = 1·6144, at 15° C. 1·600, at 25° 1·591. 800 cubic centimetres of water dissolve 1 gramme. It is much more soluble in absolute alcohol and also in methyl alcohol, but not soluble in glycerine. It mixes in all proportions with ether, glacial acetic acid, phenol, chloroform, acetone, ethyl acetate, and a number of other liquid organic compounds.

The boiling point of this substance has not been determined with certainty—when heated to about 130° C. it begins to decompose, giving off oxides of nitrogen along with its own vapour. The boiling point may be somewhere about 170–180° C.?*

It gives off a little vapour at ordinary temperatures and in a vacuum it distils very readily below 100° C. It is also volatile in a current of air at this temperature. Handling or breathing the vapour causes violent headache, sometimes accompanied by sickness. It is poisonous either as liquid or vapour, but in small doses is most valuable in cases of angina pectoris and other cardiac affections.

It is very sensitive to percussion. A drop soaked into paper and struck on an anvil detonates very violently, but, as a rule, only the portion struck is affected. It is more sensitive when warm than at the ordinary temperature, and is "said" to be very insensitive when in a frozen—solid—state, a detonation scattering the crystals instead of exploding them. When moderately slowly heated on a piece of metal, it will begin to decompose with production of red vapours and finally detonate. If the metal surface be very hot it will simply inflame quietly. This applies to small quantities only. When soaked into filter paper or other porous combustible substances it burns quickly but quietly with a greenish yellow flame. When dissolved in some of the solvents mentioned, it is difficult, if not impossible to explode. Solutions of nitro-glycerine in ether, acetone and some other inflammable liquids will burn away

---

*140° at 760 mm. (Hodgkinson).

quietly when the amount of nitro-glycerine contained is not large.

The very various descriptions of dynamite consist essentially of nitro-glycerine soaked into some more or less porous substance, which may be either of a mineral and inert nature, or of a combustible and even explosive nature.

In the liquid form nitro-glycerine may be detonated by percussion between hard surfaces, but the action is seldom complete, some of the liquid being merely scattered about, thus becoming a source of danger. When soaked into a porous solid it may be very completely detonated by a fulminate primer or by other detonators.

The original dynamite, invented by Nobel in 1867, consists of a porous "infusorial earth" known as Kieselguhr, impregnated with so much nitro-glycerine that it just does not exude. In this form it can be transported and used as a blasting agent with comparative safety. Contact with water spoils dynamite, displacing the nitro-glycerine from the Kieselguhr.

Glycerine is a substance of the class *alcohol*, and is closely related in its nature and constitution to the simplest alcohols known, viz., methyl-alcohol, CH_3OH, and ethyl-alcohol, C_2H_5OH, and more so to propyl-alcohol, C_3H_7OH. Its constitution is expressed by the formula,

$$H_2COH$$
$$HCOH$$
$$H_2COH$$

from which it will be seen to contain three of the characteristic groupings or arrangements OH, which are considered as conditioning the "hydroxide" nature of a substance. The alcohols are hydroxides or hydrates of hydrocarbons. Glycerine is considered to be derived from the third member of the paraffin series of hydrocarbons, propane C_3H_8, to which it can also be by appropriate means reduced back.

Technically, glycerine is obtained from either vegetable oils or animal fats, which are mainly compounds of glycerine with certain so-called fatty acids, by the process of saponification or hydrolysis. This may be performed by heating with a strong solution of sodium hydroxide (soda) or by treatment with superheated steam.

Consequent on the presence of three OH groups, three classes of salts are obtainable from glycerine by the action of some acids. Nitro-glycerine is the trinitrate, the terminal product of the action of nitric acid. The mono and di-nitrates may be obtained, but as they are comparatively soluble in water, and have no particular qualifying properties, they have scarcely received practical notice until recently. Nitro-glycerine is dissolved and decomposed by cold strong sulphuric acid into nitric acid and glycerine sulphate. When warmed with the acid a complex decomposition which may end in the detonation of even moderate quantities sets in. Strong solutions of, or solid hydroxides of sodium or potassium also decompose it in a dangerous manner. Ammonia appears to be without action, and *weak* solutions of alkali carbonates as sodium carbonate exert no decomposing action. Soluble sulphhydrates as KHS or CaS reduce nitro-glycerine back to glycerine, the sulphur of the sulphide being partly oxidised partly precipitated in the process. Aniline and similar substances also decompose it moderately quietly a number of non-explosive compounds being formed. Other amines seem to act in the same way. Exposure to bright sunlight starts a decomposition. It becomes yellow from formation of oxides of nitrogen and oxidation products and may eventually explode. Nitro-glycerine can be ignited both by a naked flame and electric sparks, but not easily or with certainty. Both are certainly dangerous methods of ignition.

CHAPTER VIII.

MANUFACTURE OF NITRO-GLYCERINE.

THERE is more than one process in existence for the manufacture of nitro-glycerine, with certain slight modifications in details, that most generally employed may be divided into—

(A) Nitrating the glycerine.
(B) Separating the nitro-glycerine from the waste acids.
(C) Preliminary washing of the nitro-glycerine.
(D) Washing or final purification of the nitro-glycerine.
(E) Filtering the purified nitro-glycerine.
(F) Removal of nitro-glycerine from the washing waters.
(G) Removal of nitro-glycerine from the waste acids.
(H) Separation of the waste acids.

In the manufacture of nitro-glycerine it is desirable that it should flow from process to process by gravity, as it is too sensitive for pumping or carrying by hand. The tanks containing the glycerine and the mixed acids ready for use, are therefore at the highest point of the factory; the lowest building on one side is the "wash water settling house," on the other side the "after separating house." The various tanks are connected by "bends" of suitable materials, with one another, or with the gutters, usually of lead, which in their turn convey the nitro-glycerine, washing waters, or waste acid, from one house to another. All the acid, water, and compressed air pipes where exposed, are of lead or are lead covered; the apparatus and tanks are similarly of lead, or of wood, lead lined. The cocks are all of earthenware, and, to ensure their working smoothly, they are carefully lubricated with vaseline daily before work is commenced.

(A) *Nitrating the Glycerine.*

Mixing the Acids.—The acids employed are similar in all respects to those used in the manufacture of guncotton, the relative proportions are however different, being 62 lb. of nitric acid to 105 lb. of sulphuric acid, or one part of the former to about 1·7 parts of the latter. The acids are thoroughly mixed by means of compressed air, in large cylindrical steel tanks holding enough acid for six charges, a normal day's work. After mixing, the acids are allowed to stand to cool down, and for solid impurities to settle out. When required for use they are drawn off into steel bogie trucks, each truck holding half a charge. The quantity of acids for one 500 lb.

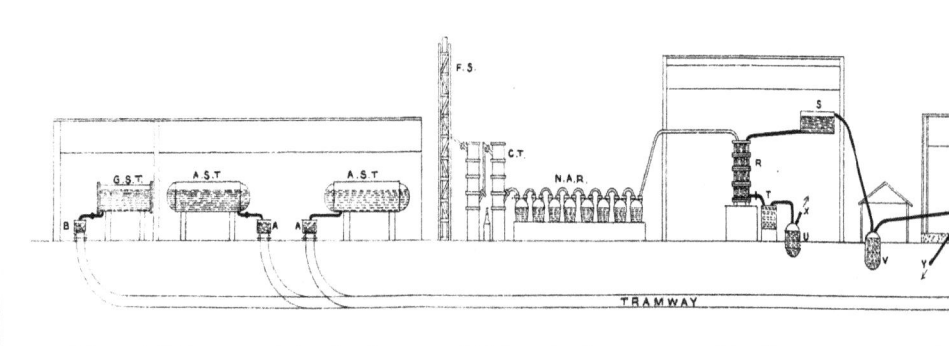

To face page 80

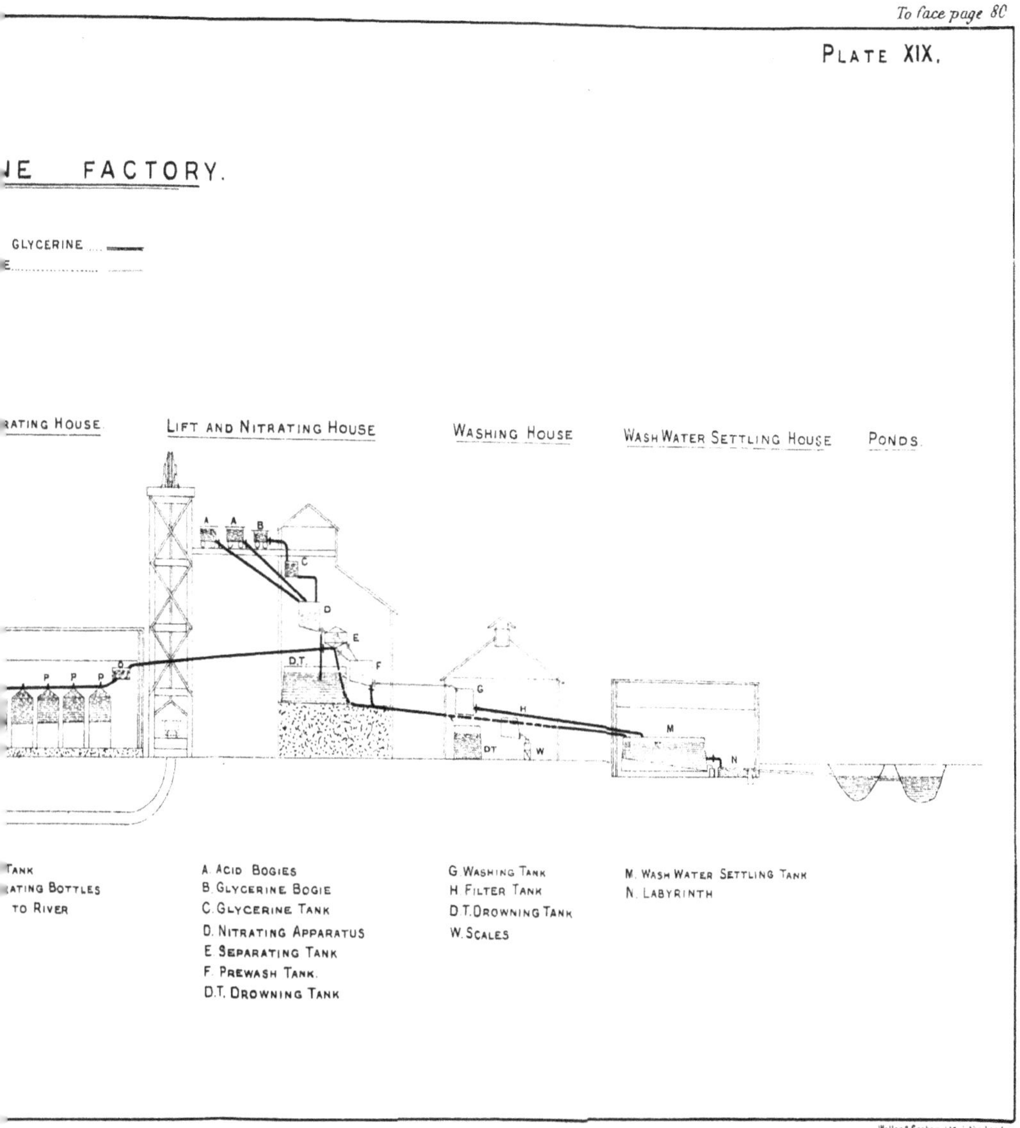
PLATE XIX.
...NE FACTORY.
GLYCERINE
...E
...RATING HOUSE.
LIFT AND NITRATING HOUSE
WASHING HOUSE
WASH WATER SETTLING HOUSE
PONDS.
A
A
B
C
D
E
F
D.T.
P
P
P
G
H
DT
W
M
N
...TANK
...ATING BOTTLES
TO RIVER
A. ACID BOGIES
B. GLYCERINE BOGIE
C. GLYCERINE TANK
D. NITRATING APPARATUS
E. SEPARATING TANK
F. PREWASH TANK.
D.T. DROWNING TANK
G. WASHING TANK
H. FILTER TANK
D.T. DROWNING TANK
W. SCALES
M. WASH WATER SETTLING TANK
N. LABYRINTH

Weller & Graham Ltd. Litho. London.

charge of glycerine is 1,485 lb. of nitric and 2,515 lb. of sulphuric.

Weighing the Glycerine.—The glycerine is obtained by contract; its specific gravity must not be less than 1·26, and it must contain no free acid or other impurities. It is stored in two cylindrical iron tanks, each capable of containing 4½ tons; these tanks are built into brick chambers, heated by means of internal steam pipes, and they are also provided with air pipes to agitate the glycerine while it is being warmed, and so ensure uniform heating. When required for use a charge is drawn from the tank through fine wire gauze, to remove impurities, into a small bogie truck, in which it is conveyed to the nitrating house lift. This lift, which is situated outside the nitrating house traverse, is a vertical one, with windlass and water counterweight. The glycerine bogie having been raised, is run along on a horizontal platform, until its emptying cock is directly over a lead pipe which conveys the glycerine into a tank above the nitrating apparatus. This tank is steam jacketed, it being necessary to keep the glycerine at a temperature of about 30° C., as below this it is too thick to run readily. The tank is provided with a gauge glass and scale to enable the operator to watch the outflow of glycerine, which takes place through a valve at the bottom of the tank, in connection with an indiarubber pipe leading to the glycerine injector.

Nitrating.—The nitrating apparatus is a large lead tank, cylindrical in shape. Inside are four lead coils through which cold water circulates; when necessary this water is artifically cooled by means of a carbonic acid refrigerating apparatus. Three pipes for the supply of air, at a pressure of 20 lb. on the square inch, are led down to the bottom of the apparatus. The top of the tank is closed by a domed cover of lead cemented on and provided with four glass inspection windows. The various air and water pipes, and the pipe conveying the acids, enter the apparatus through holes in the cover, in which is also a hole for the thermometer, and one in the centre for the glycerine injector. A fume pipe fitted with a glass tube, to allow the colour of the fumes to be seen, is also fixed in the cover.

The bogies containing the mixed acids are brought up similarly to the glycerine, and the water taps of the coils having been opened, the mixed acids are run into the apparatus and cooled down if necessary, by means of the cold water circulating through the coils and by air stirring, until the temperature has fallen to 16° C. (60·8° F.). The valve of the glycerine injector is then opened, and the glycerine enters the acids at the bottom of the apparatus in a small stream, sprayed by means of an air pipe led down inside the injector. The whole contents of the apparatus are kept in a state of agitation by means of the jets of compressed air, thus ensuring thorough mixing and preventing local heating, while the cold water circulating through the coils keeps down the temperature of the whole charge.

The workman in charge of the nitrating operation watches the thermometer, which reaches well into the liquid, and if the temperature should rise too quickly, he checks the inflow of glycerine by closing the valve on the injector, and on no account does he allow the temperature to exceed 22° C. (71·6° F.). If the temperature should rise beyond 22° C., the valve of the injector is completely closed, and additional air let in through the air pipes, and no further inflow of glycerine is allowed until the temperature has fallen below 22° C. The glass fume tube is watched, and if red fumes should appear, the injector is immediately closed and additional air let in until the red fumes cease; if they continue and cannot be stopped, the whole charge is run into the "drowning tank"—a very large wood tank nearly full of cold water, situated directly under the nitrating apparatus, with which it is connected by a lead pipe and earthenware cock. The drowning tank is also provided with an air pipe for agitating the contents of the tank during the drowning of a charge.

The time taken in nitrating the 500 lb. of glycerine depends mainly on the temperature of the cooling water in the coils, 30 to 45 minutes would be about an average time.

(B) *Separating.*

When the whole of the 500 lb. of glycerine has been injected into the apparatus, and the temperature of the mixture of nitro-glycerine and acids brought to that temperature which will equal as nearly as possible 15° C. (59° F.) when the whole charge reaches the "separating tank," the whole of the contents of the nitrating apparatus is discharged into the separating tank through a lead bend, by opening the cock at the bottom of the nitrating apparatus.

The separating tank is a strong lead tank supported by a wooden frame above and an iron lead-covered frame below. The bottom slopes downwards from all four sides to a hole fitted with a vertical glass cylinder, to which is secured a horizontal lead pipe branching in two directions, with an earthenware cock on both branches. Under the separating tank is another lead-lined wooden tank, for the purpose of catching the contents of the separator should the glass cylinder break from any cause; this safety tank is in connection with the drowning tank mentioned above. The separating tank has a glass cover, the sides of which slope upwards to a fume pipe for carrying off the fumes. Air pipes are led into the separator through the cover, one is laid round the bottom of the tank, another passes down into the glass cylinder at the bottom. In the cover are also two holes for thermometers. In one side of the separator is a glass inspection window, in another side is an earthenware cock situated about 4 inches below the surface of the nitro-glycerine, when it has separated out from the acids.

The charge of nitro-glycerine and acids is run into the separator, and the nitro-glycerine allowed to settle out; its specific gravity being 1·6, while that of the acids is about 1·735, it floats upon the top of the acids. The temperature in the separating tank, taken by two thermometers, one of which dips into the acids and the other into the nitro-glycerine, is not allowed to exceed 17° C. (62·6° F.) ; if the nitro-glycerine shows signs of heat, or should it give off red fumes, the air is turned on at once, and if the temperature cannot be kept down to 17° C., and red fumes are given off, then the charge is sent to the drowning tank, from the waste acid cock. When the separation is complete, which is usually in from 40 to 45 minutes, there are about $5\frac{1}{2}$ inches of nitro-glycerine on the top of the mixed acids. The cock in the side of the separator which is connected with the " preliminary washing tank " by means of a lead pipe, is then opened and the bulk of the nitro-glycerine is run off through it into the preliminary, or " pre-wash " tank as it is called, this tank is already about half full of cold water; air is kept on the pre-wash tank during the running in of the nitro-glycerine. The waste acids are next run away through the bottom pipe of the separator, to the " after separating house." The vertical glass cylinder connecting the separator with the horizontal pipe is watched during the running off of the acids, and as soon as the nitro-glycerine is seen coming down into the glass cylinder, the cock leading to the after separating house is closed, and the one leading to the pre-wash tank is opened, and the remainder of the nitro-glycerine run through a lead pipe into it.

(o) *Preliminary Washing.*

The " pre-wash tank " is a circular lead-lined tank with an air pipe running round the bottom ; there is also a pipe over the edge for supplying cold water. The bottom of the tank slopes downwards to a cock from which the nitro-glycerine is run, a small air pipe is led into this cock, and in the side of the tank is another cock, well above the level of the nitro-glycerine when settled, for drawing off the washing waters to the wash water settling house. A thermometer is supported in the tank, the bulb reaching well into the nitro-glycerine so that the temperature in the tank can be watched during the operation, it is not allowed to exceed 18° C. (64·4° F.). As already stated, the tank is half full of cold water, and the air turned on at a pressure of about 50 lb. on the square inch, before the first quantity of the nitro-glycerine is run into it from the separator. The nitro-glycerine is washed for a few minutes, the air then turned off, the nitro-glycerine allowed to settle to the bottom, and the washing water run off through the upper cock to the wash water gutter. The air is turned on again, fresh cold water run in, then the remainder of the nitro-glycerine from the separator, and the whole is washed again for two or three minutes. The air is again turned off, the nitro-glycerine allowed to settle, and the wash water run off as before. This is repeated twice more, making four washings in all; at the fourth washing, however, six buckets of warm dilute sodium carbonate solution are added, and the temperature in the tank brought to 15° C. When the washing water has been drawn off after the fourth washing, the nitro-glycerine is ready to go to the washing house.

(D) *Washing.*

The carbonate of soda solution for washing in the "washing house" a day's production of nitro-glycerine, is prepared overnight in a large tank outside the nitrating house. It is allowed to settle, and the clear solution is drawn off into a smaller tank inside the nitrating house, the tank communicating with the washing house gutters. The temperature of the solution is 50° C. (122° F.), and the strength 10° Twaddell, when used.

The washing house is connected with the nitrating house by means of a lead gutter, through which the nitro-glycerine and soda waters flow. In the washing house is a lead-lined tank (Pl. XXI) over the edge of which the gutter from the nitrating house projects. The washing tank is supported over a large drowning tank, kept nearly full of water. Cold water from the main, or warm water from a tank alongside, can be run through indiarubber branches into the washing tank. Air pipes supplying air at a pressure of about 50 lb. on the square inch, are laid round the bottom of the tank. The bottom of the tank slopes down to the nitro-glycerine draw-off cock in front. A short length of lead pipe projects through the side of the tank near the bottom, and on to this a length of indiarubber pipe is attached leading into the wash water settling house gutter. The lead pipe also projects into the tank, and attached to it by means of an indiarubber pipe, is the "skimmer," through which the wash water is skimmed off the surface of the nitro-glycerine as the latter sinks to the bottom of the vat. This skimmer (Pl. XXI) is a circular brass dish, having a jacket of stout indiarubber, with a hole in the centre to which a hollow lead elbow is fitted; over the other end of this elbow the indiarubber pipe is secured. The skimmer is suspended in the tank by means of a rope passing over a pulley and led outside the building where a counterweight is attached to it. Previous to running the nitro-glycerine from the pre-wash tank to the washing tank, a quantity of soda water is sent down through the nitro-glycerine gutter into the tank, and the air in the latter turned on. The nitro-glycerine is next run down into the washing tank, and then more soda water. The temperature in the washing tank is now brought to 30° C. (86° F.) by the addition of hot or cold water as required, the total quantity of soda water and plain water amounting altogether to about 42 gallons. On the completion

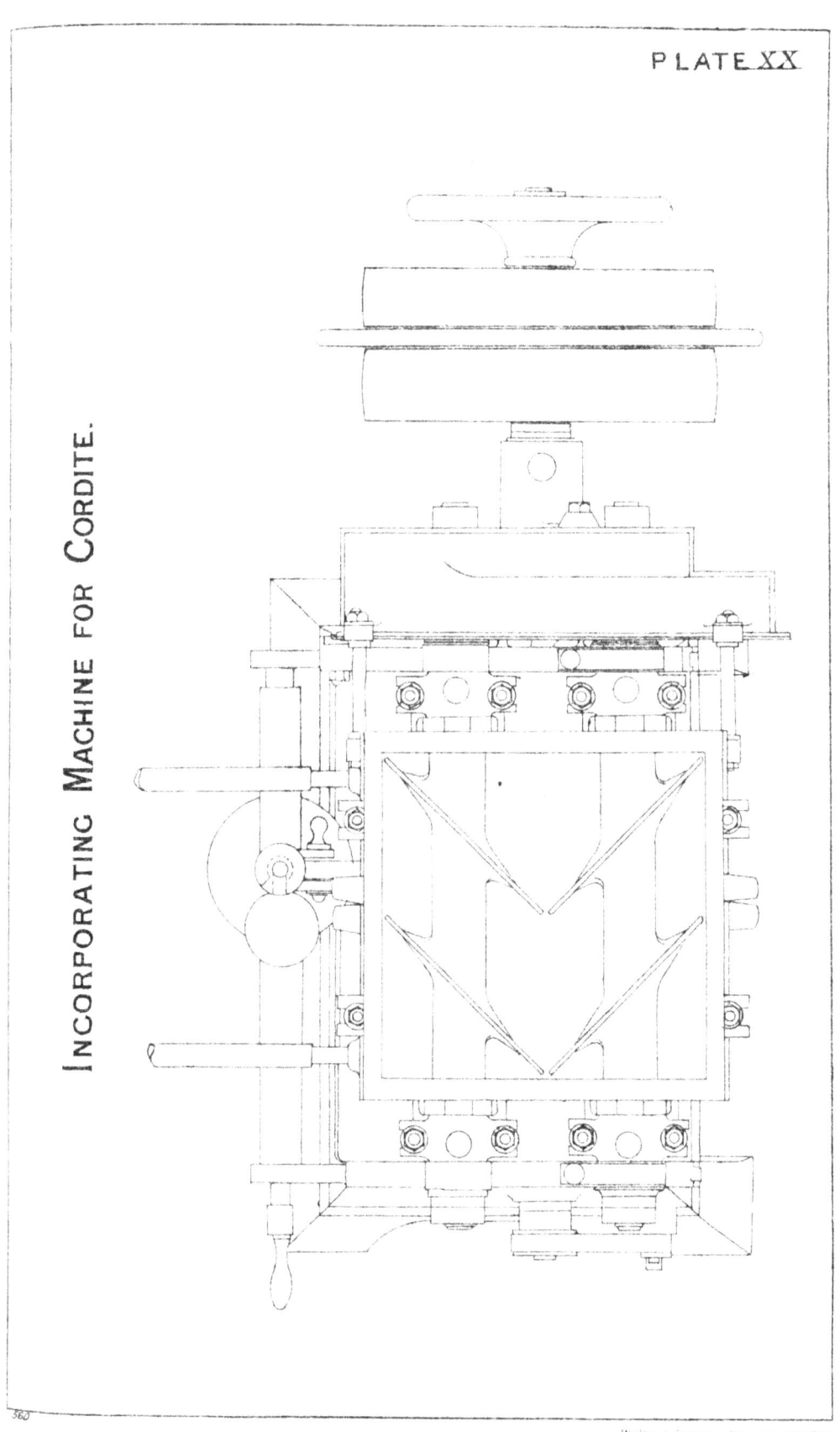

PLATE XX

INCORPORATING MACHINE FOR CORDITE.

To face page 65

PLATE XXI.

N/G. WASHING TANK.

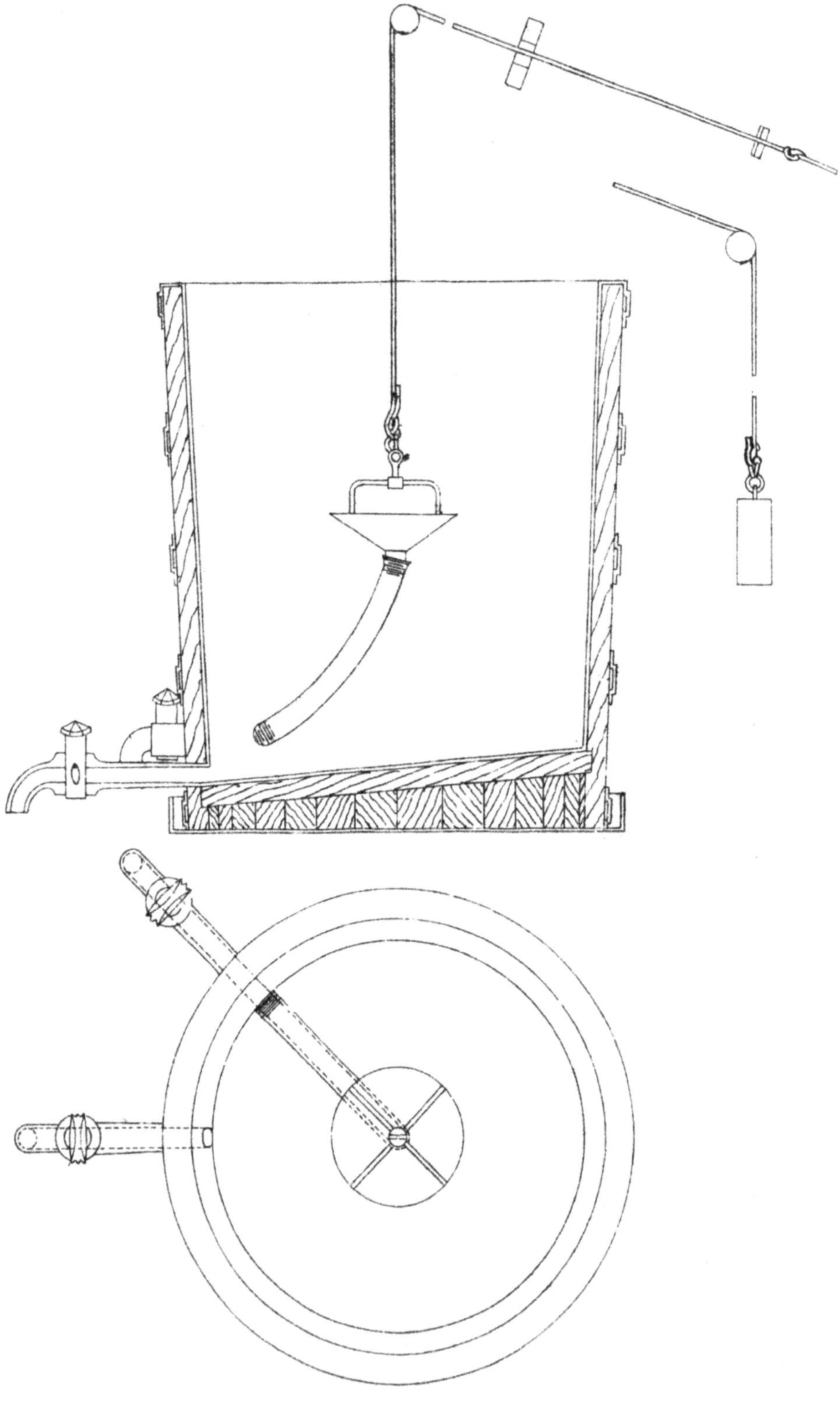

560 12 08

Weller & Graham, Ltd Litho London

of this first washing, the air is turned off, the nitro-glycerine allowed to settle down, and the washing water removed from the surface by means of the skimmer, which is gradually lowered, so as to allow the water to flow over the edge and away through the indiarubber pipe. The nitro-glycerine receives in the washing tank four washings, the duration of which vary, the last washing is with plain water only. The temperature in the washing tank is brought to 30° C. at the commencement of each washing. The final washing leaves not more than 0·01 per cent. of alkali in the finished nitro-glycerine.

(E) *Filtering.*

In front of, and below the washing tank, is a smaller lead-lined oval tank called the "filter tank." Attached to the cover of this tank, and projecting into it, is a sheet brass cylinder covered with gutta-percha open at the top and closed at the bottom with a sheet of copper wire gauze attached to a circular brass ring. A flannel bag filled with salt rests on the gauze, and is pressed out so as to fit closely to the sides of the cylinder. When the washing process is completed, the cock in the front of the washing tank is opened, and the nitro-glycerine run through a gutta-percha bend on to the bag of salt, through which it percolates into the body of the filter tank. The salt absorbs any water still clinging to the nitro-glycerine, and the flannel retains scum, flocculent matter, or other solid impurities which may be mixed with the nitro-glycerine.

The bottom of the filter tank slopes down to a cock in front, through which the nitro-glycerine is drawn off into gutta-percha buckets. These buckets stand on a pair of scales, and the amount of nitro-glycerine for a cordite incorporator charge is run directly into them.

(F) *Removal of Nitro-glycerine from the Washing Waters.*

There is a considerable quantity of nitro-glycerine mixed with the washing waters; this must be removed, partly because it can be used, but chiefly on account of the danger it would be, if allowed to run away with the water. All the water therefore used in the various washings of the nitro-glycerine itself, and in the washing out of the apparatus and tanks, is run down the wash water gutter, to a very large tank in the "wash water settling house." The bottom of the tank is always kept well covered with water, and air is turned on during working hours. Before the water is drawn off the air is shut off and the contents of the tank allowed to settle so that any nitro-glycerine may collect at the bottom of the tank. The bottom of the tank slopes from the back of the tank to the front; the nitro-glycerine therefore, as it settles down, collects in the front of the tank, and can be drawn off from a cock fixed at the lowest point. An air pipe runs round the bottom of the tank, and another one is led into the draw-off cock. Above this cock is another and much larger one for drawing off the water. This cock is connected with a "labyrinth," or nitro-glycerine trap, a long, narrow, oblong, lead tank; the bottom is constructed so that the two sides slope to a centre line, and this again slopes from back to front. The interior of the labyrinth is divided up into compartments by means of vertical lead plates, having rows of holes at the top and bottom of alternate plates; all the plates, however, have one hole at the lowest point, through which any nitro-glycerine which may separate out from the water as it serpentines through the labyrinth, can run to the cock fixed in the front end at the lowest point. The last compartment overflows into a shallow trough, from which a pipe leads the water to a drain running into a pond. Once a week some dynamite cartridges are exploded in this pond, to destroy any nitro-glycerine which might by any chance have collected in it.

The nitro-glycerine drawn from the wash water settling tank, or from the labyrinth, is carried over in indiarubber buckets to the "mud-washing house," in which are two lead-lined tanks. It consists of a few buckets of clear nitro-glycerine and a small quantity of thick dirty nitro-glycerine. The clear is washed, without any filtering, with dilute soda solution in one of the tanks which is furnished with an air pipe. The thick material is neutralised with soda solution and filtered through flannel into the other tank. After the clear nitro-glycerine has been drawn from the first tank any thick which remains in this tank is drawn off and passed through the flannel filter into the other tank. The clear nitro-glycerine collected in the tank after filtration, is washed in the tank with the air pipe. The cocks for drawing off the water from these two tanks are connected to a small labyrinth similar to the one described above, through which all the water is run to the pond. The clear and filtered nitro-glycerine drawn from the second tank in the washing shed, is taken up in indiarubber buckets to the washing house for final washing, for which purpose it is added to the charge in a washing tank before the first washing.

At the end of the week, after the water and nitro-glycerine have been run off from the wash water settling tank, a quantity of sediment is left at the bottom of this tank, consisting principally of sulphate of lead, nitro-glycerine, and water. This is drawn off in buckets and allowed to settle for a short time, the water is then poured off through the labyrinth, and the mud, &c., sent to the mud-washing house for treatment. This "mud," as it is called, is taken over to the mud-washing house, placed on flannel filters over the tanks referred to above, and as much nitro-glycerine as possible is washed out with water. The mud is then wrung in flannel to squeeze out as much of the remaining nitro-glycerine as possible, after which it is mixed with paraffin, spread out in a thin layer and set fire to; in this way the last traces of nitro-glycerine are destroyed.

(G) *Removal of the Nitro-glycerine from the Waste Acids.*

The waste acids from the separator in the nitrating house, are run to a lead-lined tank in the "after-separating house." On either side of this house are large cylindrical lead bottles with glass necks. Each bottle holds two charges of waste acid. The bottles are connected with the tank by a lead pipe, through which the acids are run into them. The nitro-glycerine still remaining in the acids rises to the surface, and collects in the glass neck, from which it is removed from time to time, and drowned in a small lead tank in the corner of the house; this tank is kept nearly full of water, and in it the nitro-glycerine gets a preliminary washing by means of air stirring. The nitro-glycerine drawn from this tank is sent down to the washing shed for neutralising, filtering, and further washing, in the same way as that drawn from the wash water settling tank, before it is sent to the washing house for final washing.

(H) *Separation of the Waste Acids.*

After remaining for at least 24 hours in the after-separating bottles, the waste acids are run into lead-lined tanks in a small, separate building, and from these tanks the acids are drawn as required into a steel egg, from which they are forced by air pressure into the supply tank of the "denitrating house." In the denitrating house the waste acids are run into tall towers of earthenware, or volvic stone, encased in iron. The towers are packed with broken glass, stoneware, &c., so as to spread the acids, which meet on their way down the towers, ascending streams of steam and air. The heat generated decomposes any trace of nitro-glycerine, or other nitro-bodies which may still remain, and also drives off the nitric acid, which is condensed in stoneware bottles, and finally in Lunge-Rohrman condensing towers. The sulphuric acid issues from the bottom of the tower, and is led through a lead cooling worm, standing in a tank of running water.

Testing Nitro-glycerine.

Samples of each charge of nitro-glycerine are drawn from the filter tank, and submitted to the heat test. The temperature at which the heat test is carried out is 180° F., and the time from the commencement to the completion of the test must not be less than 18 minutes. A proportion of the charges are also tested for volatile matter, which must not exceed 0·5 per cent., estimated by loss of weight on being placed in a desiccator over dry calcium chloride for 16 hours; and for alkalinity, which, calculated as sodium carbonate in the nitro-glycerine, is not to exceed 0·01 per cent.

Nitro-glycerine Manufacture at Waltham Abbey. Newer Process.

Considerable improvements have been made during the past few years in the nitro-glycerine manufacture at Waltham Abbey by the introduction of the Nathan, Thomson and Rintoul process.

In this the nitrating vessel is of the usual construction excepting that it has an inlet pipe for acid at the bottom and a glass separation cylinder with a lateral overflow pipe at the top. The other essential parts are a pre-washing tank, a washing tank and a final filtering tank.

Method of operation.—The charge of nitrating acid is run from a high level gauge tank into the nitrating vessel, where it is cooled and agitated while the glycerine is run in. When the nitration is complete and the temperature has fallen slightly, the agitation is stopped. The separation of the nitro-glycerine is allowed to proceed in the same vessel, and waste acid from a previous charge is caused to flow gently in from a high level waste tank through the inlet pipe at the bottom of the nitrator. The inflowing waste acid forms a layer at the bottom of the apparatus and gradually raises the whole charge till the level of the clear nitro-glycerine appears in the separation cylinder and flows over into the pre-washing tank where it is drowned in water. The rate of inflow of the waste acid is regulated so as to be equal to the rate of separation of the nitro-glycerine. This is easily done by keeping the upper surface of the acid layer at a constant level in the separation cylinder and just below the outlet. When the bulk of the nitro-glycerine has separated a sharp line of demarkation appears in the separation cylinder.

The subsequent manufacture is carried out in the usual manner. The above system of manufacture is fully described and specified in patent No. 15,983, 1901.

Now as to the treatment of the residual acids left in the nitrator after the bulk of the nitro-glycerine has been displaced.

The contents of the nitrator are allowed to stand until a short time before the apparatus is required for the next charge. This allows the recovery of as much of the nitro-glycerine as possible. A small quantity of the clear nitro-glycerine free waste acids, lying at the bottom of the apparatus, is run off. The level of the acids is thus sufficiently lowered to allow of their being air-stirred without splashing over. The acids are then strongly agitated and a small quantity of water, equal to 2 per cent. by weight of the acids formed is slowly added. The agitation of the mixture is continued until the temperature has begun to fall when the air current is stopped and sufficient waste acid is run in from the high level tank to raise the surface to a level with the separation cylinder. After remaining at rest for a short time to ensure that no nitro-glycerine remains undecomposed (unseparated) the acids are run off for storage or denitration.

A sufficient quantity is raised to the high level waste acid tank for use as displacing acid for a subsequent charge.

The apparatus is then in readiness for the next nitration. This method of treating acids is described in patent No. 3,020, 1903.

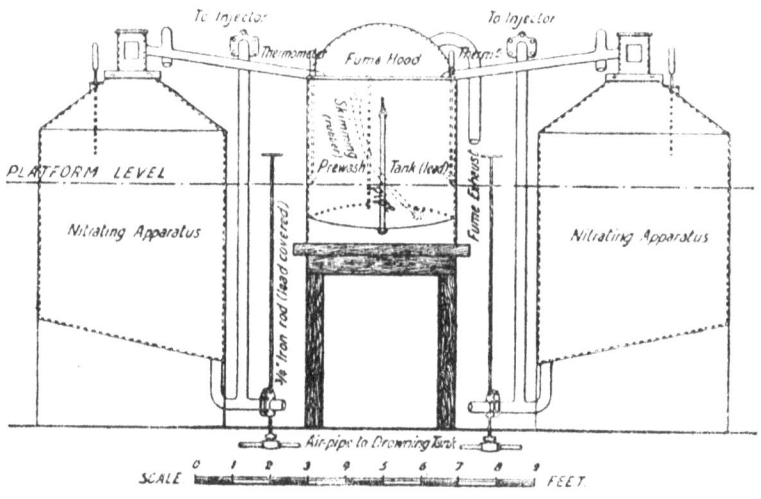

Fig. 1a.

Fig. 1a shows the general arrangement of a nitrating plant built in duplicate, and fig. 2a shows the various falls required and the economy effected in the necessary heights of the buildings.

The primary object of the new treatment is to obviate the necessity of passing nitro-glycerine through any form of cock, and so decrease the danger of manufacture.

Removing the nitro-glycerine from contact with the acids as soon as it separates, also increases the safety, as do the cooling coils in the separation and "after-separation" stage, the latter rendering it possible to check at once any undue rise of temperature. Less transference of both acids and nitro-glycerine is necessary.

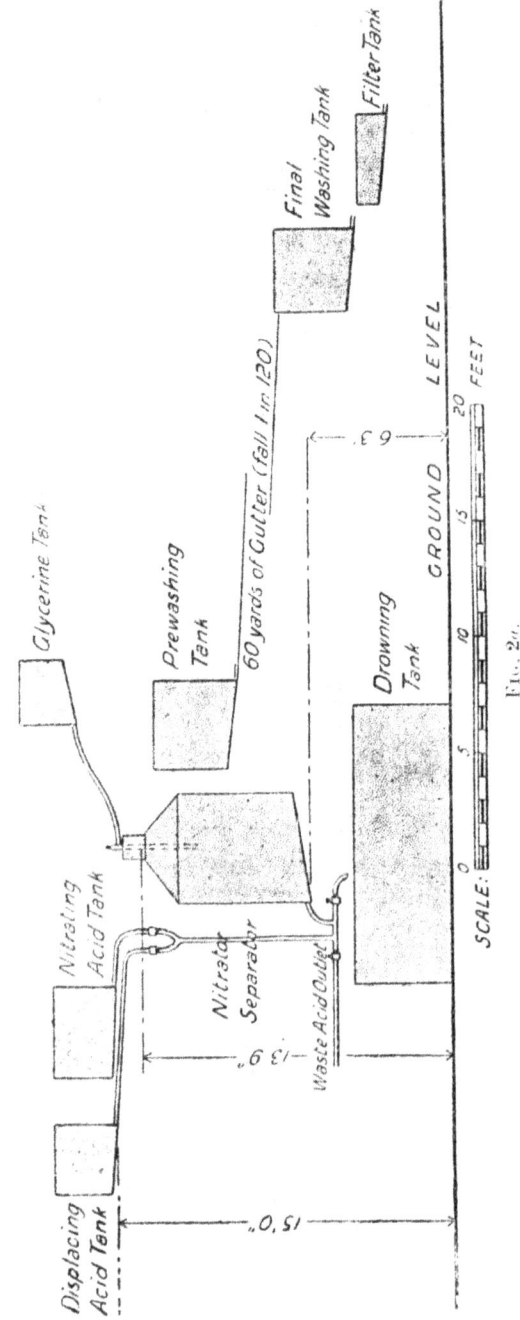

Fig. 26.

The essential explosive in all forms of dynamite is nitro-glycerine. The first dynamite was invented by A. Nobel immediately after he had found that nitro-glycerine could be detonated by a mercury fulminate charge. Nitro-glycerine in the liquid form is for reasons stated (*ante* p. 77 and *seq.*) quite impossible as a practical explosive, but when absorbed into a porous inert material it may be carried and stored with comparative safety, and much more perfectly detonated than in the liquid state. This was Nobel's discovery. The porous inert material most generally employed is "Kieselguhr," an infusorial deposit of a smooth and non-gritty nature. This after cleaning and drying can absorb about three times its weight of nitro-glycerine without appreciable exudation. This forms the original dynamite. Many modifications have been proposed. In some nitrates and other oxygen supplying substance are added, and in others the "Kieselguhr" is more or less replaced by salts such as sodium carbonate, barium sulphate, ammonium salts, charcoal, oxide of iron, &c.

The ingredients sanctioned are—

Sodium carbonate,
Barium sulphate,
Mica,
Talc,
Ochre.

} In all 8 parts (or less) by weight, in substitution for an equal amount by weight of kieselguhr.

An amount of ammonium carbonate not exceeding $1\frac{1}{2}$ parts by weight in every 100 parts by weight of the finished dynamite, is also allowed to be, and is generally added.

The kieselguhr is prepared by calcining, to drive off water and organic matter, and more or less of the accompanying sand is sifted away. It generally contains a little iron, which accounts for the more or less red tinge observable in ordinary dynamite. Nitro-glycerine is poured on to the prepared kieselguhr and the two thoroughly kneaded together into a plastic mass, which is then, in a special machine, pressed up into cylindrical cartridges of various diameters, to suit various sizes of bore holes for blasting, each cylinder being wrapped in parchment paper. Five pounds of cartridges make a packet, and 10 packets go to a box, which thus contains 50 lb. of dynamite. When ignited unconfined in small quantities, it burns away fiercely with a reddish flame; if the amount is sufficiently large, however, it ends by exploding. The usual method of exploding it is by means of a fulminate of mercury detonator. Contact with water quickly disintegrates it, separating out the liquid nitro-glycerine, and hence great care is required when using it in wet places; in this particular it compares unfavourably with blasting gelatine and gelatine dynamite. The exuded nitro-glycerine may find its way into cracks in the rock, and lie there for an indefinite time until called into fatal activity by a blow from a pick or a drill. Another great danger in the use of dynamite arises from its freezing at a comparatively high temperature (about 40° F.), and it remains frozen even at 50° F.; in its frozen state it is useless as a blasting agent, and has to be thawed or "tempered." This operation requires great care, and the instructions issued with every packet should be closely and carefully attended to. The safest plan is to place it in a tin inside another tin containing hot water, on the principle of a glue-pot, but the outer tin *must not* be placed on a fire or stove, and the inner tin must be watertight. Special "warming pans" on this principle are sold, jacketed with felt and canvas; this not only prevents the pan being placed on the fire, but keeps in the heat.

It cannot be too strongly impressed, that if dynamite or other nitro-glycerine preparations are gradually warmed up to a temperature approaching their igniting point they become extremely sensitive to the least shock or blow, and once that point is reached, they do not simply burn, but explode with great violence.

Blasting gelatine is a combination of nitro-glycerine and soluble cellulose nitrate. It is made by dissolving, with the aid of kneading and heat, finely divided soluble cellulose nitrates in nitro-glycerine. The product is a gelatinous mass about the colour of new honey, and varying in consistency from a tough leathery material, to a soft substance like jelly. Blasting gelatine No. 1, which is that practically in use, contains from 93 to 95 per cent. of nitro-glycerine, and is made up into cartridges like dynamite. Speaking broadly, the thinner the gelatine the more sensitive it is to detonation; but, on the other hand, a thin gelatine is more liable to liquefaction, and possibly also to exudation, and thus to cause a danger in storage and transport. Specially strong detonators are required to detonate it, or ordinary detonators with a primer of dynamite or gunpowder. Blasting gelatine, unlike dynamite and nitro-glycerine, is much more, instead of much less liable when frozen, to be exploded by a blow such as that given by a rifle bullet. It is, on the whole, less liable to freeze than dynamite. Blasting gelatine has the great advantage over dynamite of being practically unaffected by water. It is stored, therefore, under water, in suitable tanks, in the perforated boxes containing 45 lb., as received from the makers. It is more powerful than dynamite, not only as containing a higher percentage of nitro-glycerine, but also since this is associated with the explosive nitrated cellulose instead of with the perfectly inert kieselguhr. It is also, from its physical condition, cleaner and rather safer to use.

Gelatine Dynamite, and *Gelignite*, are two modifications of blasting gelatine which are now largely manufactured; they are cheaper, but not such powerful explosives.

Gelatine dynamite, of which there are two varieties, differing only slightly in composition, contains about 80 per cent. of explosives, while gelignite only contains about 60 per cent. The varieties principally in use, contain nitro-glycerine, nitrated cellulose, nitrate of potash, and wood meal. They much resemble blasting gelatine in appearance.

The liability of nitro-glycerine to freeze is a source of danger in the employment of dynamites of almost any kind, not because the nitro-glycerine is more sensitive in the frozen or solid state than when liquid. In fact, it has been shown by a number of observers that it is less sensitive in that condition, but the danger lies in the melting or "thawing" process.

Very early indeed in the history of nitro-glycerine (1866) attempts were made to reduce the freezing point by the addition of nitro-compounds of benzenic derivatives (nitro-benzene, nitro-toluene, &c).

The employment of mono and dinitro-glycerine in admixture with nitro-glycerine proper has been proposed. These nitrates are, however, hygroscopic and even soluble in water, and so objectionable.

The employment or poly-glycerine nitrates has also been suggested. Poly-glycerine or di-glycerine is made by heating glycerine for some time to about 290° C. in a flask with long neck. Water is formed and driven off, and two or more molecules of glycerine unite or condense, probably thus:—

$$2\{C_3H_5(OH)_3\} - H_2O = C_3H_5(OH)_2OC_3H_5(OH)_2$$

The di-glycerine (or poly-glycerine) formed is of very high boiling-point, and, although a very thick and viscous liquid at ordinary temperatures, does not seem to freeze. On nitration with the mixed acids in the ordinary way, a tetra-nitrate,

$$C_6H_{10}O(NO_3)_4,$$

is formed. This nitrate is stated to be less sensitive, and, at the same time, nearly equally as powerful as nitro-glycerine in explosive power. It does not freeze, and is insoluble in water. Recent experiments seem to indicate that nitrated mono-chlorhydrin is nearly as powerful as nitro-glycerine, and has the advantage of remaining liquid even at -25° C.

Mono-chlorhydrin, $C_3H_5(OH)_2Cl$, results from the action of hydrogen chloride on glycerine. It is easily nitrated by the mixed acids, and the dinitro-chlorhydrine,

$$CH_2Cl.CHNO_3CH_2NO_3,$$

is less soluble in acids or water than nitro-glycerine, its manufacture and purification are easy. Its specific gravity = 1·54 at 15° C.; on heating to about 180° C., red vapours appear, and at 190° C. it boils without exploding. It is very volatile under diminished pressure, distilling at about 120° under 15 mm. pressure.

It is comparatively safe against percussion or friction, but can be easily detonated by a fulminate detonator, and thus gives results differing but little from ordinary nitro-glycerine.

An addition of 20 per cent. of this dinitro-chlorhydrine to dynamite is said to prevent freezing in ordinary winter temperatures. This substance gelatinises nitrated celluloses.

In its explosion hydrochloric acid gas is evolved.

Aceto nitro-glycerine is said to be a slight improvement on the ordinary nitro-glycerine in the matter of non-liability to freezing, and at the same time produce almost the same effect on explosion.

It can be made by converting the glycerine into the mono acetate by the action of glacial acetic acid and subsequent treatment with the mixed acids in the ordinary way.

Its composition is represented by the formula

$$C_3H_5(NO_3)_2C_2H_3O_2.$$

Explosives of this type are often compared by exploding a weighed amount inside a lead cylinder. The increase in capacity, or widening out of the bore of the cylinder, is then ascertained and compared with a standard explosive.

CHAPTER IX.

HISTORY, PROPERTIES, ETC., OF SMOKELESS POWDERS AND CORDITE.
MANUFACTURE OF CORDITE.

ALTHOUGH smokeless, or semi-smokeless explosives have for some time been in use for sporting purposes, it is only within comparatively recent years that serious attention has been paid to the production of a smokeless powder for military purposes.

Immediately after the discovery of guncotton attempts were made, notably in Austria, to suit it for this purpose; but the extreme difficulty of controlling with certainty and uniformity its rate of combustion in guns and small-arms, prevented its adoption.

France, about the year 1885, was the first country to adopt a smokeless powder for the ammunition for use with the Lebel magazine rifle. It was known as "Vieille" powder, or "Poudre B," and was simply a mixture of soluble and insoluble cellulose nitrates, somewhat hardened by digestion with ether and alcohol. Since that date several preparations, giving little or no smoke, consisting essentially of guncottons, or nitrated celluloses, or of mixtures of them with other substances, specially treated to render them slower burning, have been proposed to take the place of black powder. The general nature of treatment, for which many patents have been taken out, consists in dissolving or gelatinizing the guncotton by the use of liquids, such as acetic ether and acetone, by which process the fibrous character of the original substance is more or less destroyed, and a horny material produced, the rate of combustion of which is slower than that of the substance in its fibrous condition, the reduction in the rate of combustion being entirely due to the physical condition of the resulting product. Heating compressed blocks or granules of these substances with camphor, instead of treating them with liquid solvents, also has the effect of hardening their surfaces, and of reducing the rate of combustion, and has been applied with some success to the production of semi-smokeless powders.

The solvents above mentioned (except camphor) do not enter into the composition of the finished material; the gelatinous mass obtained by their action is in this condition rolled out into sheets, or pressed through suitable dies, into cords, ribbons, or tubes, which on complete evaporation of the solvent, remain as homogeneous horn-like materials. The sheets, cords, or ribbons thus produced are cut up into small tablets, cakes, or cylinders, suitable for the charges of cartridges.

To Mr. Alfred Nobel, the inventor of dynamite, is due the combination of nitro-glycerine with soluble cellulose nitrates for the production of a smokeless explosive. Soluble guncottons absorb nitro-glycerine, and when this mixture is kneaded together at a moderate temperature the fibrous character of the cellulose compounds is lost, a more or less completely gelatinized product resulting. This has been known for some time as blasting gelatine. Camphor was employed by Mr. Nobel as a further agent for promoting the union of the two explosives as well as for reducing the rapidity of the explosion of the product. This explosive was known as Ballistite.

The camphor, however, does not remain a constant ingredient, and its evaporation, even at ordinary temperatures, leads in course of time to alterations in the ballistic properties of the material. This would be a grave defect in any explosive, especially when it has to stand exposure in various climates, and the defect was eventually recognised. It was with the view to remove the defect in question, and also to employ guncotton instead of soluble collodion cotton, in order to obtain an explosive of uniform composition and high ballistic qualities, that the Explosives Committee, of which Sir Frederick Abel was President, carried out a long series of exhaustive experiments. The final result of their labours was the production of a smokeless explosive, consisting essentially of nitro-glycerine and guncotton, incorporated and gelatinized by the aid of a solvent. This material is incorporated without the aid of heat, which is essential for the production of ballistite, and which makes the manufacture of the latter explosive not wholly unattended with danger. A small proportion of a mineral hydro-carbon is incorporated with this preparation.

This smokeless explosive is known by the name of "Cordite," owing to the cord-like form it finally assumes in manufacture.

Before describing the manufacture of cordite, the principal properties which all smokeless powders should, as far as possible, combine, will be briefly referred to.

Smokelessness.—Smoke is due to the presence of solid products of combustion in a very fine state of division. Substances which on explosion could produce nothing but non-condensible gases would be perfectly smokeless; as, however, the explosion of practically all modern powders gives rise to water vapour, they all show a little smoke, which varies according to the atmospheric conditions. Products of combustion of organic substances containing hydrogen, added as moderants, increase this. These substances also are not always completely consumed. Some quantity vapourises, and is recondensed on escaping from the gun.

Freedom from Objectionable Combustion Products.—The gases given off should not be such as will injuriously affect the firer. This, however, is not a great objection, as the gases are projected a considerable distance from the muzzle of the piece and are mixed by interpenetration almost instantly with a great volume of air.

Carbon-monoxide is produced in quantity from most smokeless powders, but much is burnt to carbon dioxide on issuing from the barrel. Other gases are oxides of nitrogen, but these are partly destroyed by the carbon-monoxide at the high temperature and partly condensed along with the water from the steam on contact with the atmosphere. [It should be noted that at the moment the gases escape from a gun there is a great change in temperature, pressure, and volume. Whenever gases expand heat is absorbed or used up and cooling results.]

The metal of the gun should not be affected, chemically or physically. This can, however, not be quite avoided. Oxides of nitrogen are probably without effect at the moment of their formation, but if allowed a very short time in contact with a moist atmosphere, nitrous and nitric acids result, and these set up a corrosive action on metals. The high temperature of the gases from most smokeless explosives, combined with the velocity or rush of the gases, is answerable for much of the erosion or wearing away of the metal.

Stability.—Stability, both chemical and ballistic, under all climatic and storage conditions, is one of the most important properties of any explosive. With black powders, so long as they were kept dry, there was no question on the score of stability.

As the manufacture and purification of guncotton, becomes better understood, there is less difficulty in making those used for smokeless powders very stable, and the experience of some years has proved that these powders can withstand severe climatic changes without serious deterioration, chemical or ballistic.

High velocities with moderate pressures.—The introduction of magazine rifles and quick-firing guns necessitated, not only the employment of a powder producing little if any smoke, but also, to enable them to develop their full effect, one giving much higher velocities than those obtainable with the old black powder, without exceeding the permissible limits of pressure in the bore. These improved ballistics became possible with the new powders, owing mainly to their colloidal or gelatine-like form. Ignition having taken place on the surface of the flake, tube, &c., combustion can only proceed by layer after layer burning away, with the result that although a much larger total volume of gas, and therefore greater velocity of the projectile is now developed than formerly, the gas production takes place gradually during the whole time of the passage of the projectile down the bore, with a correspondingly more uniform distribution of pressure. The total propelling force is greater, but as it is more regularly sustained the maximum pressure is not correspondingly increased. It follows therefore that for equal velocities much smaller charges are required than when black powder was used, and the chamber pressures are lower, and also that for the same or even lower chamber pressures higher velocities are obtained. In the old powders almost complete combustion of the explosive took place before the projectile had time to move far down the bore of the gun, high pressures were in consequence set up in the chamber, necessitating a massive breech. As the development of the gas and therefore of the pressure fell off rapidly, the gun thinned down considerably towards the muzzle, and was comparatively short. For smokeless powders the guns are more uniform in outline to suit the more uniform distribution of pressure, and they are longer, to enable the full effects to be obtained from the comparatively slow burning explosive. It is obvious that the property of burning in successive layers affords a ready means of adapting the new explosives to the various calibres of small arms and ordnance for which they are used. By increasing the thickness of the flakes or cubes, or the diameters of the cords or cylinders, the surface of ignition for a given weight is decreased, with a corresponding decrease of initial development of gas and consequently of initial pressure, and the time for total combustion is increased. The thicker the flake, cube, or cord, the slower will the powder burn, and the gun in which it can be advantageously used must be larger.

It may be here repeated that the main physical property on which the employment of this class of powders depends is the colloidal state.

Ease and safety of manufacture.—The manufacture of smokeless powders consists in, firstly, the production of the nitrated compounds; and secondly, their treatment with suitable solvents to give them the required colloidal condition.

All the operations in the manufacture of guncotton are as a rule perfectly safe up to the final drying. As stated (*ante*), dry guncotton is sensitive to friction and percussion, and in most of the processes and methods of smokeless powder making it must be at least moderately dry before being submitted to the gelatinizing agent or process.

Nitro-glycerine is much more dangerous to make or keep. When, however, the solvent or gelatinizing agent has been added to the guncotton and nitro-glycerine, the liability of accident is much diminished. There is no dust at any stage after addition of the solvent, as is the case with ordinary gunpowder, and although the solvents are highly volatile and combustible substances, the vapours of which form explosive mixtures with air, the risk of explosion is not great. In cases where the vapour of the solvent has become ignited and fire communicated to the gelatinized charge, it has simply burned away, rapidly and fiercely, without real explosion. It is thought that even if confined, as in the press cylinders, an explosion would be quite local and would not spread to the bulk of material under treatment.

Physical properties.—Most service smokeless powders are in the form of flakes, cubes, cords, ribbons, or cylinders, either solid or with one or more perforations; sporting powders are required to be quicker burning, and are often granular like the old gunpowders, or in the form of very thin flakes.

Some cord powders have one or more axial perforations. Flat strips with and without perforations are also made. The colours vary considerably, and depend to a great extent on the added non-explosive ingredients. Pure guncotton powders are, as a rule, greyish or yellow; those in which nitro-glycerine is present, vary in colour from light yellow to deep brown. Sporting powders sometimes contain colouring matters, and are frequently coated with graphite, which gives them a silvery-grey appearance. The surface of the flake, cube, and cord powders is usually smooth and hard, and in texture they are horn-like if made from guncottons, but softer and more of the consistency of indiarubber if containing nitro-glycerine. Their density varies according to the ingredients and method of manufacture. Unless they contain ingredients soluble in water, such as metallic nitrates, they are unaffected by damp, and they do not absorb any appreciable amount of moisture. They are more difficult to ignite than black powders, and, in the case of small-arm powders, require a stronger cap; cannon cartridges require a priming of fine-grain gunpowder or of guncotton.

Experiments carried out with cordite on several occasions, have shown that when packed in the service stout wood boxes with screwed-down lids, the boxes may be subjected to a fierce fire, which only ignites the cordite without explosion when the flames reach it, and that the cordite in a box may be ignited and burnt away without exploding or even setting fire to boxes packed round it. As far as experiments have hitherto shown, most smokeless powders are fairly insensitive to shock and are not exploded by the impact or passage through them of rifle bullets, even when made up in small-arm cartridges packed in boxes.

The composition of cordite for small arms and for all natures of ordnance, is the same, the required rate of combustion being obtained by varying the diameter of the die through which it is pressed in manufacture. Its density is constant (specific gravity 1·56), and it contains practically no moisture, nor is it affected in any way by damp, as it is non-absorbent. It is poisonous.

The composition of cordites are as follows :—

Nitro-glycerine	58 per cent.
Guncotton	37 ,,
Mineral jelly	5 ,,
	100

Cordite, M.D. :—

Guncotton	58 per cent.
Nitro-glycerine	37 ,,
Vaseline	5 ,,

Vaseline is obtained at a particular stage in the distillation of petroleum. The mineral or rock oils known as petroleums are mixture of, for the most part, hydro-carbons of the family or group known as paraffins, of which marsh gas or methane (CH_4) is the simplest member. A very large number of these hydro-carbons is known. They may all be represented by a "general" chemical formula, viz., C_nH_{2n+2}. Some are gaseous, some liquid, and some solid at ordinary temperatures, and all are characterised by what may be termed chemical indifference, or resistance to the action of re-agents. The melting and boiling points of the members of this series rises regularly for every addition of CH_2, and the whole series may be theoretically *considered* to be derived from methane (CH_4) by the addition of CH_2, thus $CH_4 + CH_2 = C_2H_6$ and $C_{10}H_{22} + CH_2 = C_{11}H_{24}$, &c. They are somewhat difficult to separate from each other by distillation. The sticky semi-solid substances known as vaseline or mineral jelly are mixtures of several of these hydro-carbons, and sometimes they contain small quantities of other hydro-carbons with less hydrogen content known as "olefines." These are rather objectionable compounds in connection with guncotton, as they are in chemical language unsaturated (represented by $C_n H_{2n}$), and are by no means so inert as the paraffins or $C_n H_{2n+2}$ series. They can become oxidised by substances like guncotton, &c.* The vaseline used in cordite should not "flash" below 204·5° C. (400° F.), nor melt completely below 30° C. (80° F.). It should be free from acidity and mineral substances, and have a specific gravity when fully melted at 38° C. of not less than 0·87.

In this country acetone is very generally employed as the solvent or gelatinizing agent in the manufacture of smokeless propellants.

It is a volatile, colourless liquid of somewhat aromatic odour of boiling point 56° C. miscible in all proportions with water or alcohol and many other organic liquids. It is an excellent solvent for many organic and mineral compounds. When pure it evaporates rapidly without the least residue. It is neither acid nor alkaline in reaction. Almost all the metallic acetates, when strongly heated in a dry state, decompose, giving acetone as one product. Calcium acetate is most generally used for this purpose, as it can be easily and cheaply prepared from the action of wood vinegar, obtained as a by-product of the distillation of wood, on chalk. Dry calcium acetate has the composition $Ca\begin{subarray}{l}OOCCH_3\\OOCCH_3\end{subarray}$ and, on heating, splits up into

$\underset{\text{Chalk}}{CaCO_3}$ and $\underset{\text{Acetone.}}{CH_3{-}CO{-}CH_3}$

---

* It has been mentioned that aniline and several other substances decompose guncotton, &c. Many "unsaturated" carbon compounds, hydro-carbons, acids, aldehydes, esters, &c., will also, but more slowly, act as deoxidizers of guncotton and that class of substance. Fungus of various kinds will also live upon and "reduce" it.

This formula shows the constitution of the substance. When heated a little above its boiling point a slight decomposition takes places, a little water is formed, and heavier substances of higher boiling point are left. These are objectionable to have in contact with guncotton. Sulphuric acid and other dehydrating substances abstract pretty easily the elements of water (H + O) from acetone producing these objectionable substances (phorones) and finally a benzene derivative (C_9H_{12}).

As used for cordite it should have a specific gravity of 0·8, and not more than 0·005 per cent. of acidity, and when mixed with a 0·1 per cent. potassium permanganate solution should not decolourise the latter in less than 30 minutes at 15° C. (or 60° F.). Acetone can also be made in other ways somewhat more directly from acetic acid.

Acetic ether or ethyl acetate is sometimes and in some places employed as the solvent. It is prepared by heating together alcohol, acetic acid, and sulphuric acid, the latter to absorb water.

The reactions are $CH_3COOH + C_2H_5OH = CH_3COOC_2H_5 + H_2O$. The sulphuric acid then combines with the water retaining it.

There are some advantages in the employment of acetic ether over that of acetone, but it is a little more costly than the latter, and it does not evaporate so rapidly.

The various processes in the manufacture of cordite are as follows :—

(A) Drying the guncotton.
(B) Weighing out, and mixing the guncotton and nitroglycerine.
(C) Incorporating.
(D) Pressing, and reeling or cutting.
(E) Drying.
(F) Blending and packing.

The guncotton after pulping, is compressed into cylinders, 5 inches diameter and 4½ inches high, of sufficient consistency to enable them to be handled with ease. It contains from 40 to 45 per cent. of moisture. In this form it is placed on trays with copper wire gauze bottoms, arranged on racks in the drying stoves. The drying is effected by means of warm air blown into the stove by an ordinary circular fan run at a fairly high speed, the air being warmed by passing it through a series of pipes surrounded by steam and contained in a cylindrical chamber or "heater," the whole arrangement resembling a small horizontal multitubular boiler. The warm air enters the stove through branches which project into it a few inches above the floor level, these branches being set at right angles to, and at intervals along the main air pipe, which is kept outside the stove. The openings in the branches are so arranged that the air impinges directly on to the floor of the stove. A clear space is left all round between the walls of the stove, and the racks for the trays. The only outlets for the air are two small windows covered with fine wire gauze, one at either end of the stove. The temperature in the stove is kept as nearly as possible at 40° C. (104° F.). The guncotton is dried down to under 0·5 per cent. of moisture; this takes under ordinary circumstances from 90 to 100 hours.

When dry and cool the guncotton is weighed out in the porch of the stove into brass-lined wooden boxes, $27\frac{3}{4}$ lb. to each box, and sent over in these boxes to the nitro-glycerine washing house. The corresponding quantity of nitro-glycerine for a $27\frac{3}{4}$ lb. charge of guncotton, namely, $43\frac{1}{2}$ lb.,* is weighed out from the filter tank into gutta-percha jugs and poured over the guncotton in the brass-lined boxes. On an average there are about 24 weighings of $43\frac{1}{2}$ lb. each in every charge of nitro-glycerine, and as soon as the charge has been weighed out and transferred to the boxes they are taken over to the "mixing houses," and the contents of each box is mixed by rubbing it through a $\frac{1}{2}$-inch mesh copper wire sieve into a barrel, so as to break up the guncotton and make it absorb the nitro-glycerine; in this condition the mixture of guncotton and nitro-glycerine is not nearly so sensitive or dangerous to handle and transport, as either the dry guncotton or the liquid nitro-glycerine alone. The guncotton and nitro-glycerine in this roughly mixed condition, is known as "cordite paste."

The cordite paste is next taken to the "incorporating houses." The incorporating machines in use at Waltham Abbey are of two sizes, one for incorporating 75 lb., the other for incorporating twice this quantity, viz., 150 lb., both machines are exactly similar in principle and construction. The incorporating machine, *see* Plates XXII, XXIII, is an iron box, on suitable supports, open at the top, and with a bottom shaped to form two semicircular troughs, in each of which a spindle, with propeller-shaped blades, revolves. The spindles turn in opposite directions, one moving at about twice the rate of the other. They are driven by cog-wheels on a third spindle running underneath the machine. This driving spindle has two pulleys on it, either of which can be put into gear by means of a friction cone. Both pulleys are driven from an overhead shaft, and as one has an open and the other a cross belt, the blades can be made to revolve inwards or outwards as desired. At the back is an arrangement for tilting the body of the machine to facilitate the removal of its contents. The lower or trough portion has an iron jacket, through which cold water circulates to keep down the temperature during incorporation: 40° C. (104° F.) is the maximum temperature allowed.

When at work, the blades revolve in close proximity to the bottom of the machine, and the paste is continually being squeezed between the blades and the bottom, and between the blades themselves as they approach each other along the centre line. The action is in fact a kneading one, and the machine is very similar to those used for making biscuit dough, and many other like purposes.

The details of the process are shortly as follows:—A portion of the charge of 15 lb. 10 oz. of the bottle of acetone having been poured into the machine, the blades are started to revolve

---

* For M.D. these quantities are different.

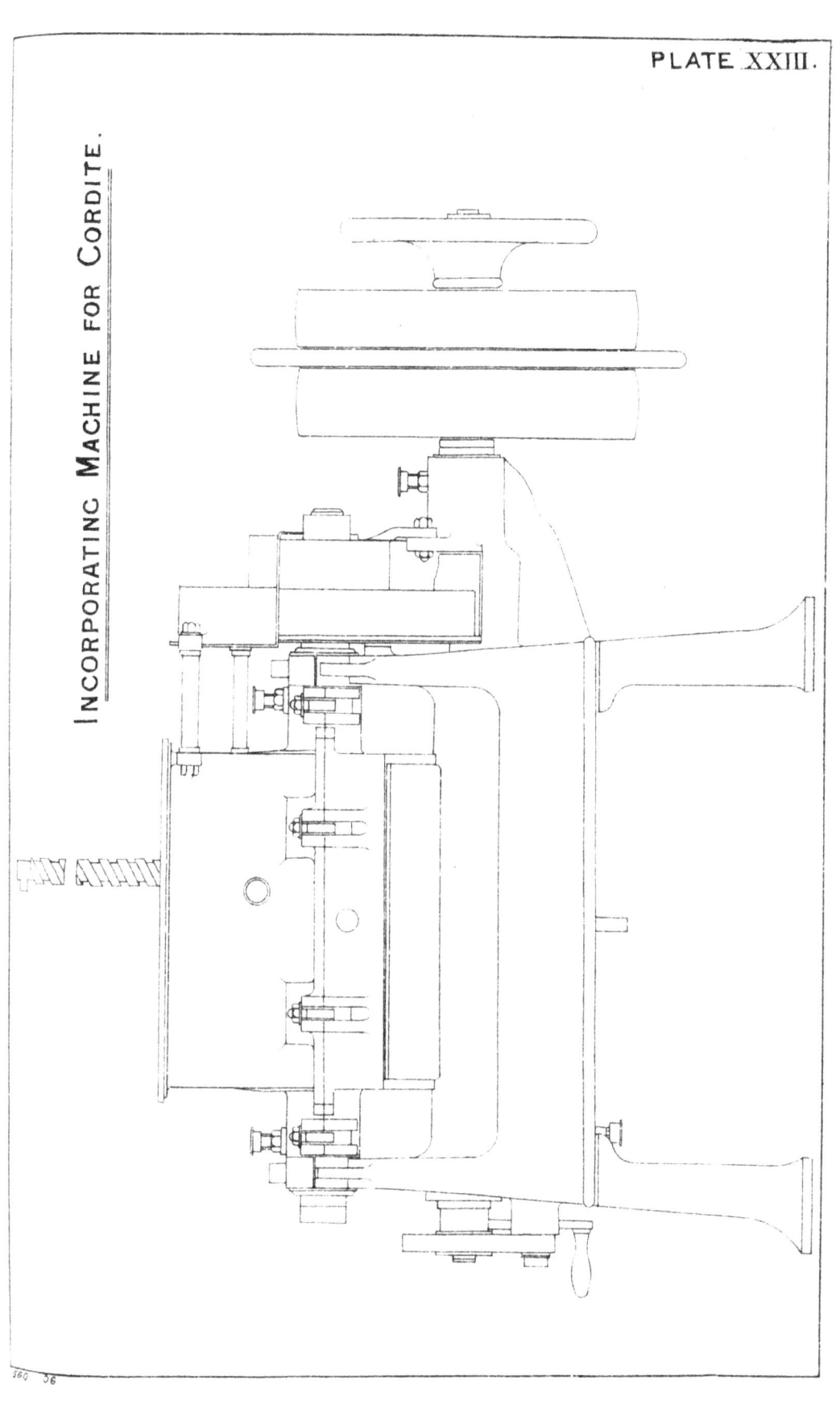

PLATE XXIII.

INCORPORATING MACHINE FOR CORDITE.

inwards, that is towards one another, and the cordite paste put in with a wooden scoop, the remainder of the acetone being poured in as the paste is being added. For the larger incorporators the contents of two boxes of paste, and of two acetone bottles, that is 31 lb. 4 oz. of acetone, are used. The operation of charging only takes a few minutes. The top of the machine is closed by means of a wooden cover to prevent the loss of acetone by evaporation, and the machine allowed to run for $3\frac{1}{2}$ hours. At the end of this time the mineral jelly, viz.—$3\frac{3}{4}$ lb. for the small, and $7\frac{1}{2}$ lb. for the large incorporators—is added, and the machine set to work for another $3\frac{1}{2}$ hours. For about the last quarter of an hour of the run, the motion of the blades is reversed, that is they are made to revolve away from one another; this has the effect of breaking up the "cordite dough," as it is now termed, in which condition it is more easily filled into the press cylinders. At the end of the seven hours the gelatinization of the guncotton and its admixture with the nitro-glycerine by the aid of the common solvent, acetone, is complete, and the mineral jelly is also uniformly distributed throughout the mass. The blades are now stopped, and the cordite dough removed from the machine and placed in barrels for conveyance to the press houses.

Waste cordite dough returned from the press houses, which has become partially dry owing to evaporation of the acetone, is put back into an incorporator, some fresh acetone added, and the incorporator run for about one hour, by which time the dough is again fit for pressing. Waste finished cordite is similarly treated, but for each charge of 75 lb., 15 lb. 10 oz. of acetone are required, and the incorporation proceeds until the dough has been brought to the proper consistency.

There are three natures of presses in use at Waltham Abbey for pressing or "squirting" cordite, viz., screw, screw and hydraulic combined, and hydraulic. The screw presses are used for the manufacture of the smaller sizes of cordite, and are combined with an automatic reeling arrangement for winding the cordite on to reels as it issues from the die. The screw and hydraulic combined, and the hydraulic presses, are for producing the large natures of cordite, and are provided with cutting gear for cutting the cordite to the required lengths, as it is pressed. The general construction of the screw press for small-arm cordite is shown on Plate XXVI. The plunger, the upper portion of which is screwed, passes up through the centre of a worm wheel worked by a worm on a horizontal shaft, to which the driving pulleys are attached. By means of automatic striking gear, the motion of the worm is reversed when the plunger comes to the bottom of its stroke, the speed of the return stroke being increased. On the completion of the up-stroke the automatic striking gear again comes into play and stops the machine altogether.

The reeling gear is shown on Plates XXIV and XXV. The reel, the body of which is of sheet brass, with skeleton brass ends, is mounted in front of the press, on a horizontal spindle with a cone pulley fixed to one end, and is driven by another cone pulley on the worm shaft; this latter pulley is made to revolve by means of a friction cone, worked by a lever on the right side of the machine. The object of the cone pulleys is to enable the speed of the reel to be adjusted to suit the rate at which the cordite is issuing from the die. The cordite is guided automatically from side to side of the reel as it is wound upon it.

The press cylinders are closed at the bottom by a plug, provided with handles for screwing it in and out, in the centre of which is the die. Resting on the plug is a steel plate with a number of holes in it. This plate supports a fine wire gauze disc, which acts as a sieve to prevent small particles of foreign substances from getting into and blocking up the die.

The press cylinders are filled by hand ramming. The full cylinder is placed in the press under the plunger, and the machine started and worked as above described. On completion of the up-stroke the empty cylinder is removed from the press and another full one inserted. Each cylinder contains a little over 1 lb. of cordite dough, which is pressed out into a length of about 1,800 feet in the case of rifle cordite, and wound on the reel. The reels as filled are taken to a truck for conveyance to the drying stove.

The combined screw and hydraulic presses for the larger natures of cordite are, as far as the actual pressing is concerned, on practically the same principle as the screw press just described. The press cylinders, however, are an integral part of the machine, and are not removed for filling, the filling being done from a hopper attached to the cylinder, which latter is deep enough to contain the whole charge in an uncompressed condition.

In one pattern of press the plunger screw is attached to a ram working in a small hydraulic cylinder. When the press cylinder is charged, the valve leading to the hydraulic cylinder is opened, and the pressure, acting on the ram and plunger, forces it down, and it compresses the material into the actual press cylinder. The valve is then closed, the screw gear started, and the material pressed out through the die. The arrangement of perforated plate and wire gauze strainer is the same as in the small press cylinder. The number of dies in the plug, that is, the number of cords that can be pressed at one time, depends on the diameter of the press cylinder, and on the size of the cordite which is being pressed.

The smaller sizes of cordite, that is, sizes $\frac{5}{12}$, $\frac{7\frac{1}{2}}{12}$, $\frac{10}{12}$, and $\frac{10}{7}$, are reeled by hand as they issue from the die, on reels of similar materials to those used for small-arm cordite. As soon as a pressing is completed, the reels are taken to a cutting machine, consisting of two horizontal steel blades, mounted on a stand opposite one another, and in the same plane. The reel is supported in the stand so that the cordite lies at right angles to, and between the two blades, which are then brought

PLATE XXIV.

REELING GEAR FOR RIFLE CORDITE.

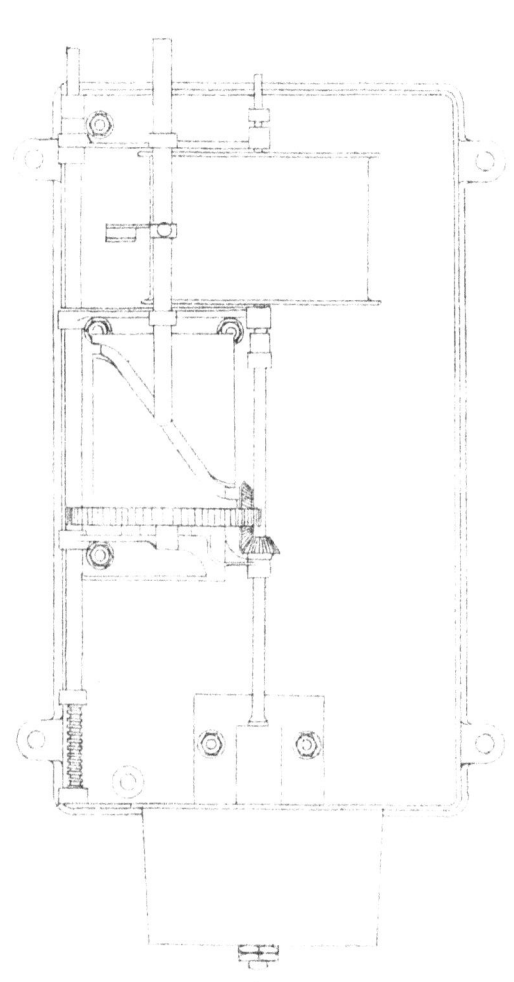

together, cutting through the cordite and dividing it into a number of strands of equal, or nearly equal length, this length being regulated by the diameter of the reel. Cutting is also done by hand on a board. The cordite is then laid out flat on shallow wooden trays, the bottoms of which are formed of narrow battens with open spaces between them.

The larger natures of cordite, viz., size $\frac{5}{4}$ and above, are led as they issue from the die, on to an endless leather band travelling at the same rate as the issuing cordite. This band has steel blades on its surface, fixed at right angles to the direction of its motion. The band passes under a roller adjusted so as to press the cordite on to the blades, and in this way it is cut to length, the length being regulated by the distance apart of the blades on the band. As they are cut, the strands are picked off the band by hand and arranged on trays, as described above in the case of the smaller natures.

The hydraulic press, is on the usual principle of such presses. The plunger is fixed and the cylinder is supported on a table which is secured to the ram. As the ram ascends, the cordite is pressed out, and reeled, or cut on the endless band, as already described.

All cordite, after pressing, is dried in stoves, heated by means of steam pipes or hot-air blast, to a temperature not exceeding 43·3° C. (110° F.). The reels or trays are arranged on open racks. The period of drying varies from two working days for size $\frac{1}{05}$, to fifteen days for size $\frac{50}{17}$.

The object of the drying is to remove the acetone from the cordite, a considerable amount, about 15 per cent., still remaining, even after the pressing, and also other volatile matter present.

After drying, small-arm cordite is blended as follows:— 10 single-strand reels are mounted on a frame and wound off simultaneously on to a larger reel. The winding is done by a small machine in which the single large reel is made to revolve and draw the strands from the 10 single-strand reels; a lever, through which the 10 strands pass, guides them from side to side of the larger reel as they are wound on it. The lever is worked by means of a pin and roller attached to it, which is pressed up against a revolving cam by a weighted rope passing over a pulley.

Six of the full 10-strand reels are next taken, mounted on a stand, and the 60 strands wound off on to a drum in the same way as the 10 single strands were wound on to the 10-strand reel. When the reeling is completed, the ends are all secured by a band of stout tape wound round the drum, and the drum is packed in a box or barrel for transport.

Larger natures of cordite, which have been cut into lengths, are blended as follows:—As the trays come from the stove, their contents are packed into boxes, each containing about 100 lb. of cordite. These boxes are divided into batches, the number of boxes in a batch varying with the size of cordite, and the cordite in each batch of boxes is blended by taking a few sticks from each box of the batch and packing them into another set of boxes, filling one box at a time, until the whole of the original boxes have been emptied. A box of the blended material is then taken from each blend, and the contents of these boxes again blended, as above described, so as to form, when completed, a uniform lot, the number of boxes forming a lot varying with the nature of the cordite and the capacity of the boxes, which hold from 55 to 115 lb., according to the size of the box and the nature of the cordite. When "lotting" sizes $\frac{5}{1\cdot2}$, $\frac{7\frac{1}{2}}{1\cdot2}$, and $\frac{10}{\cdot7}$, they are tied up with string into bundles weighing about $2\frac{1}{2}$ lb. each; this is to prevent the strands getting entangled.

Cordite is packed in wooden boxes lined with non-absorbent paper, except in the case of cordite on drums; these boxes are painted stone colour, to distinguish them from prismatic powder cases.

The usual information is stencilled in red on the lid and sides.

Cordite for Webley Pistol Cartridges, Short Range Practice Ammunition, and for Blank Ammunition.

Cordite for the Webley pistol is prepared by slicing size 1 cordite in a machine similar in principle to the one used for making $\frac{20}{SC}$. After slicing, it is sieved through a 40 and a 24-mesh sieve, to remove fine dust and large pieces; blended, and issued 80 lb. in an ordinary cordite case; it is designated $\frac{1}{\cdot 05}$.

Cordite for the ·303-inch short range practice ammunition is in the form of tape, 1·4 inch ± ·05 inch wide and ·01 inch ± ·002 inch thick. A length is cut, rolled up, and inserted into the cartridge case.

Cordite for blank ammunition is prepared from size 20 cordite. After the cordite has been dried, it is wound on reels. These reels are mounted on a stand in front of a machine which automatically feeds about 50 strands at a time through rows of holes in a fixed plate, in front of which, and close up against it, a disc revolves at a very high rate of speed. Attached to this disc are four knives set at right angles to one another, which cut thin slices off the strands as they are fed through the plate; the principle of the machine much resembling that of a chaff-cutter. The flakes vary in thickness between $0''\cdot 008$ and $0''\cdot 003$. After cutting, the flakes are first sieved through a 14-mesh wire gauze sieve to remove dust, and then through a 4-mesh wire gauze sieve to remove any large pieces, &c. It is blended into uniform lots of 50 cases, each case holding 50 lb. It is designated $\frac{20}{SC}$.

PLATE XXV.

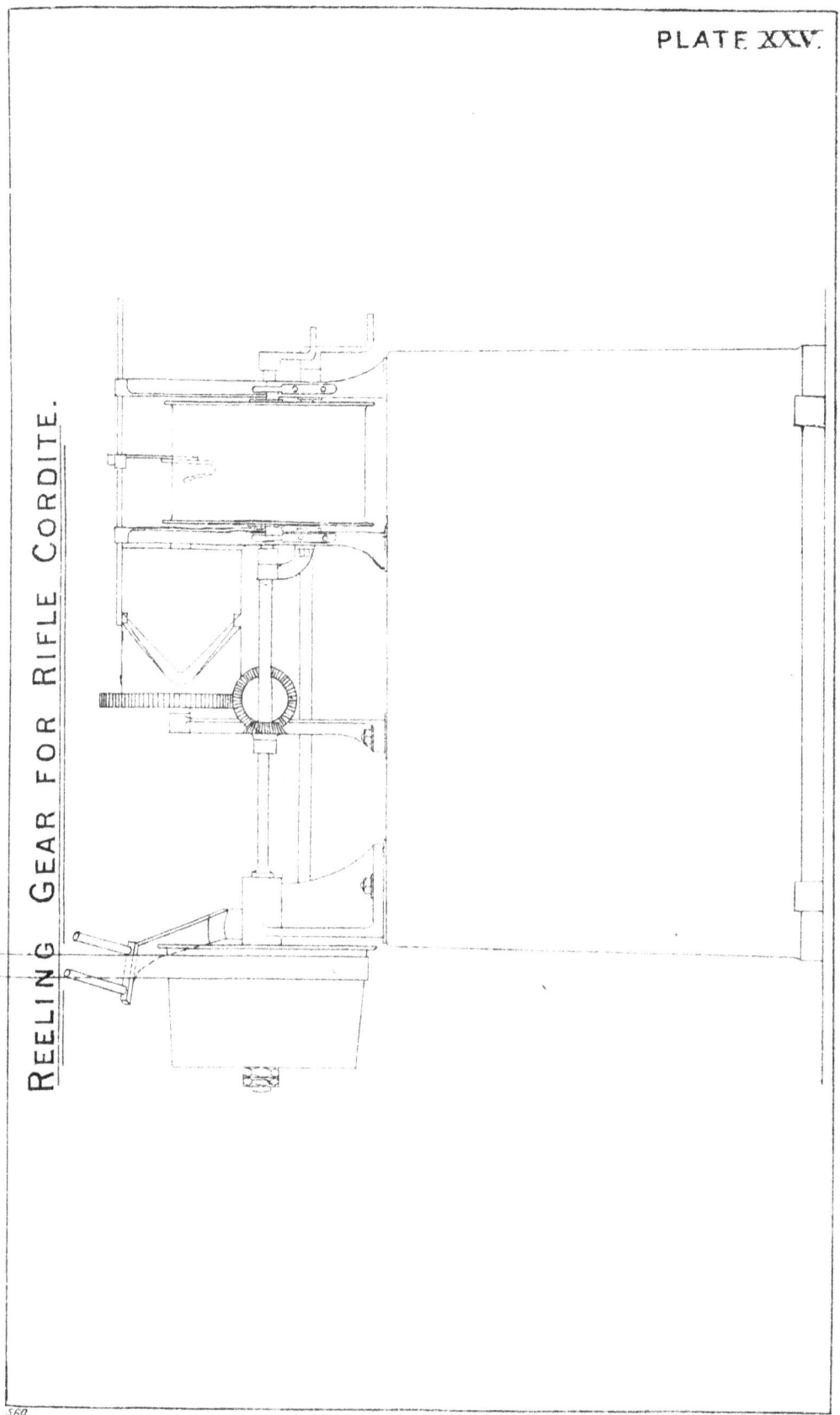

REELING GEAR FOR RIFLE CORDITE.

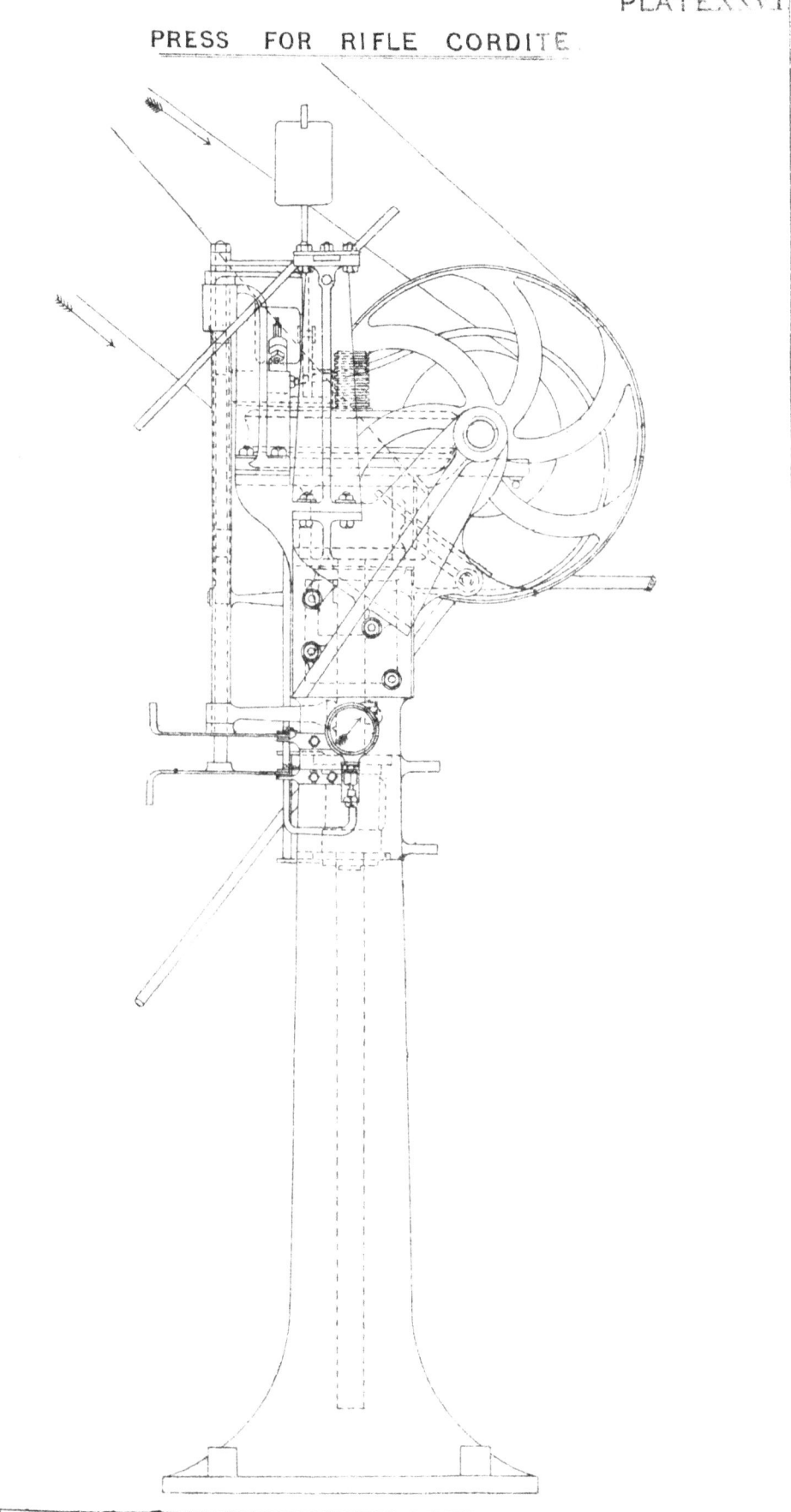

PLATE XXVII.

PRESS FOR RIFLE CORDITE.

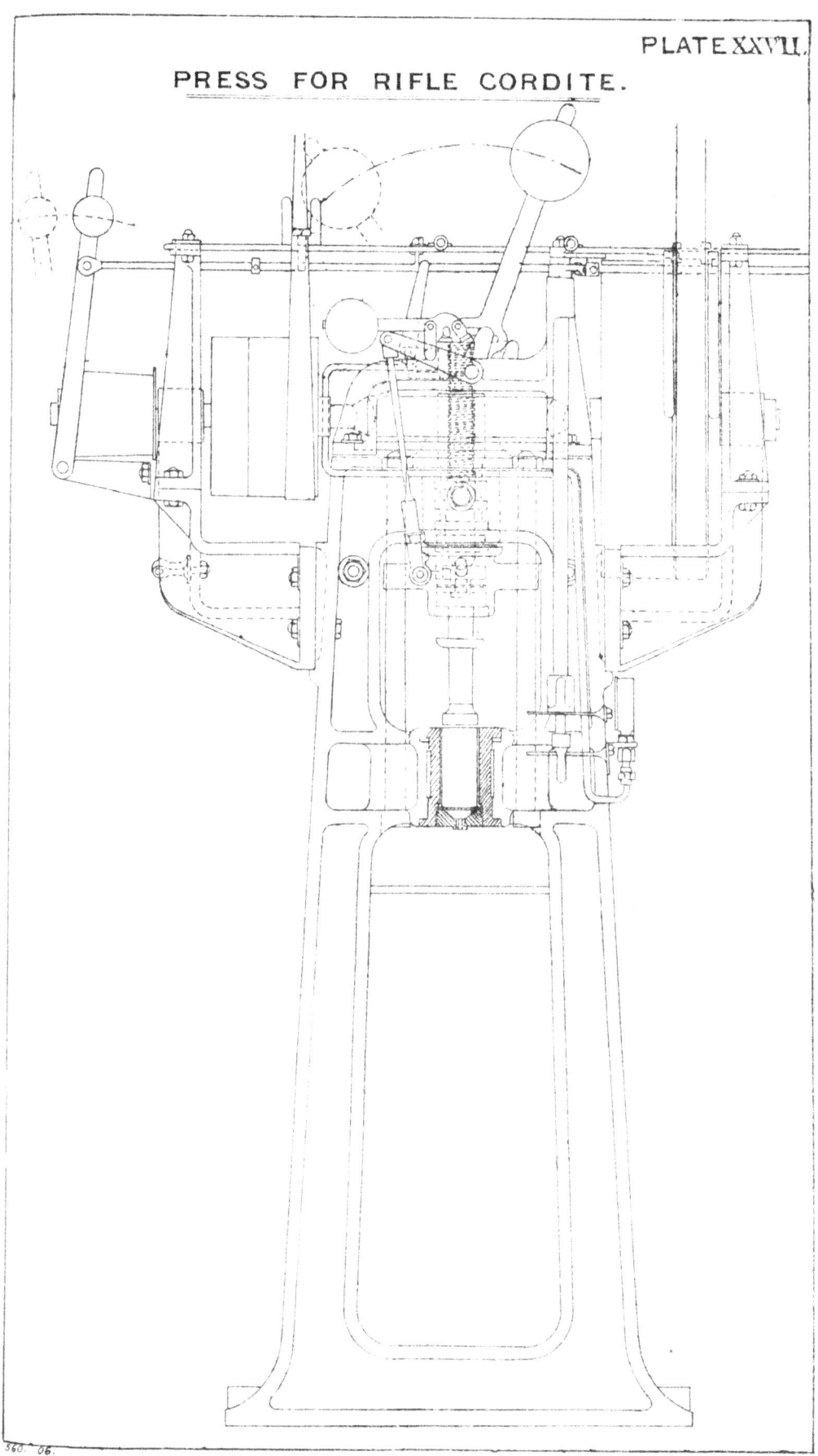

PART III.—MISCELLANEOUS EXPLOSIVES.

Under this heading is comprised a number of compounds and mixtures not exactly of the propellant class, although some of them might under certain circumstances be employed as such. Generally the substances, here included, are employed either alone or in admixture for blasting or detonating purposes. The designation "high explosive" is not an inappropriate one, and is frequently used for substances which tend to detonate rather than explode.

Some of the most important "high explosives" are derived from the hydro-carbon benzene, C_6H_6, one of the constituents of the coal tar of the gas works, from which it is obtained technically on a large scale by a series of fractional distillation processes.

Benzene is a peculiar hydro-carbon, very different in its internal constitution to the paraffins (mentioned under vaseline). It is a colourless liquid of slight aromatic odour, highly refractive, lighter than, and insoluble in, water. When cooled to about $0°C$ it freezes to a clear ice-like solid which melts again at $4·6°C$ and it boils at $80°C$. Between these temperatures it evaporates very rapidly and its vapour when mixed with air in certain proportions will on ignition explode very violently. The vapour can be ignited as it escapes from a containing vessel, and then burns quietly with a luminous and very smoky flame. Mixed with oxygen the vapour explodes very violently when ignited by a spark or flame. The complete reaction is $2(C_6H_6) + 15O_2 = 12CO_2 + 6H_2O$.

More heat is produced in this reaction than indicated by the equation, as benzene is endothermic.

This means also that 2 volumes of the vapour require 15 volumes of oxygen, or 75 of air, for complete combustion.

Benzene may be considered as derived from acetylene* (C_2H_2) by a peculiar condensative action in which 3 volumes of acetylene combine to form 1 of benzene vapour.

From the evidence of the known reactions of benzene the formula C_6H_6 may be expanded into

$$\begin{array}{c} H \\ C \\ HC \diagup \diagdown CH \\ | \quad \quad | \\ HC \diagdown \diagup CH \\ C \\ H \end{array}$$

which is intended to indicate that the atoms of carbon and hydrogen

---

* Acetylene is best produced by the action of calcium carbide on water (see later).

are in some way symmetrically arranged about each other in three dimensional space. Compared to the paraffins it is an unsaturated hydro-carbon, but it does not show this property so easily as other known unsaturated hydrocarbons no doubt on account of its internal structure.

Benzene is proof against most re-agents. Ammonia and the alkalis, hydrochloric acid and dilute nitric and sulphuric, have no action. Very strong nitric and sulphuric acids do act upon it.

Nitric acid of specific gravity 1·5 acts at the ordinary temperature somewhat violently; the products being nitro-benzene and water.

$$C_6H_6 + HNO_3 = H_2O + C_6H_5NO_2.$$

(These products of the action of nitric acid on benzene and benzenic compounds are a distinct class of substances, and are not identical with nitrites or nitrates, although they may sometimes contain the same relative amounts of oxygen and nitrogen. Their peculiarity depends on the fact that in them the nitrogen apparently is united to carbon directly, which is probably not the case in nitrites or nitrates).

Acid of less than 1·5 specific gravity will act at a higher temperature in the same way on benzene, only one product resulting. Technically, nitric of 1·2 specific gravity is employed, and the operation conducted in closed iron vessels.

Nitro-benzene is an oily liquid with an odour like bitter almonds; it boils at 206° C; its vapour burns with a smoky flame. It is insoluble in water, but volatile in steam. It can be exploded, but not easily, requiring a very powerful detonator. Mixed with substances like potassium chlorate, very powerful blasting explosives are obtained. It is used to a small extent in a few explosives, or as a solvent.

Rack-a-Rock and similar substances consist of nitro-benzene mixed with chlorates or nitrates and some inert porous material. Separately the substances are scarcely explosive. But when nitro-benzene, for instance, is soaked into a porous mixture of potassium chlorate and brick dust it forms a material of the nature of dynamite, which is easily detonated by a fulminate primer. Many other nitro-derivatives can be used in a similar way.

When benzene or nitro-benzene is heated with a mixture of sulphuric and nitric acids, to complete solution a further stage of nitration known as di-nitro-benzene is obtained. When the acid solution is poured into cold water the product separates as a yellow solid, which is but slightly soluble in water. In this acid mixture one function of the sulphuric acid is to absorb water, but probably it does more than this. The equation

$$C_6H_6 + 2HNO_3 + H_2SO_4 = C_6H_4(NO_2)_2 + 2H_2O + H_2SO_4$$

represents the end result only.

Di-nitro-benzene may be washed free from acid by cold water or solutions of alkalies. It dissolves in alcohol and some other liquids, and from these solutions it is easy to separate, by fractional crystallization of the crude product from the action of the acids, three different physical forms known as modifications or isomerides. They are all of the same composition, but differ in melting point, solubility, and other physical properties, so that their internal constitution or the relative arrangement of the atoms or groups of atoms in the molecule must be different. They are all explosive under certain conditions, but one modification is more easily exploded than the others. The differences in their physical properties is attempted to be expresed by the formulæ:—

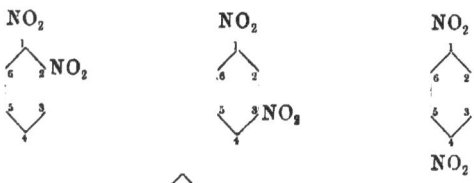

in which the hexagon is taken to represent benzene, each corner denoting a carbon atom with a hydrogen atom attached, and in the di-nitro-benzene two hydrogen atoms have been removed and their places taken by the residues or groups NO_2 from the nitric acid. Assuming the benzene molecule itself to be symmetrical when one hydrogen is removed and replaced by something else—and hydrogen only is removed in any action on benzene short of utter destruction—one kind of disturbance only is produced, or is theoretically possible, and only one kind of product results. But when two or more atoms of the benzenic hydrogen are replaced there starts the possibility of more than one arrangement of these replacing substances with regard to each other. The result is, in the case of two hydrogen atoms being replaced, three physically differing substances; their physical and some slight chemical differences being due to a different internal arrangement of the molecule.

This formula does not suggest the actual shape, but more the relative arrangement of the atoms of the molecule.

These varieties of di-nitro-benzene are often spoken of as the ortho, meta and para derivatives, or neighbouring, unsymmetrical and symmetrical:

$(1:1)$. $(1:3 = 1:5)$. $(1:4)$.

Di-nitro-benzene enters into the composition of a number of explosives, employed mostly for blasting purposes. When so employed it is generally mixed with ammonium nitrate or other nitrates, guncotton, &c. They are fired by detonators, and give, as a rule, only a small flame. Some sporting and nearly smokeless powders have been made with small amounts of di-nitro-benzene as a constituent, the main portion being a nitrated cellulose mixture.

Benzene by drastic treatment with the mixed acids will yield a tri-nitro and even a tetra-nitrated product. Both are more easily exploded than the di-nitro, but have not yet found employment in practical explosives.

Another very valuable constituent of coal tar is the substance phenol or carbolic acid. This substance contains oxygen as well as carbon and hydrogen. It is, however, a benzenic substance or derivative of benzene from which it may be made and to which it may be reduced by simple means. Its composition is represented by C_6H_5OH, in which the OH is to be understood as occupying the place of a hydrogen atom in a benzene molecule. The formula indicates that it is a hydrate, but owing to some peculiar influence of the benzene group or ring it is more like a feeble acid than a hydrate of the alcohol class, or of the carbohydrate or cellulose class. It can form definite compounds with metals which may be expressed generally by C_6H_5OM, in which M represents a metal, as sodium, &c. In fact, some metals will actually displace this hydrogen from it on contact, either in a fused state or in water solution. Nitric and sulphuric acids do not combine with it in the same manner as they do with alcohol or glycerine or cellulose. Nitric acid reacts with peculiar ease on phenol. When very dilute (10 per cent.) a mono-nitro product results, $C_6H_5OH + HNO_3 = H_2O + C_6H_4OHNO_2$, which exists also in three modifications (see dinitro-benzene). These substances are known as nitro-phenols; they act as acids. Their potassium salts—as $C_6H_4NO_2OK$—are explosive when dry and respond to percussion, but not easily. Stronger nitric acid acting on phenol produces di-nitro phenols, and finally tri-nitro phenols as the final result. When strong nitric acid (1·5 specific gravity) comes in contact with phenol the action is very violent, and in addition to the formation of tri-nitro phenol, there is some loss owing to oxidation. After the action has died down and the liquids cooled a yellow crystalline precipitate of a particular form of tri-nitro phenol, known as picric acid, $C_6H_2OH(NO_2)_3$, forms.

Of several known modifications it is the most symmetrically consituted and is probably in consequence of that the most stable. The symmetrical idea is shown by the structural formula

$$\underset{NO_2}{\overset{OH}{\underset{H \quad H}{\bigcirc}}} NO_2$$

A number of other substances besides phenol yield picric acid as one end product of the action of nitric acid. It was first obtained from indigo, later from certain resins, silk, &c.

Picric acid is a pale yellow crystalline solid, melting at 122·5° without change. Its specific gravity = 1·813. It may be sublimed by very careful heating, but generally fires and puffs off when rapidly heated to above its melting point. 100 parts of water at 15° C. dissolve 1·16 ; at 20° C., 1·225 at 77° 4 parts, and *considerably* more at 100°. It is very soluble in alcohol, ether, acetone, and similar liquids. It is not volatile in steam.

A hot concentrated aqueous solution on being cooled to about 70° deposits most of the picric acid in very small crystals. Strong nitric acid dissolves a little more than water at the same temperature, but has no chemical action. Strong sulphuric acid decomposes picric when heated, but scarcely affects it at ordinary temperatures.

Picric acid solidifies from the melted condition in a closer or denser form than from water solution, the crystals interlacing in all directions and thus producing a somewhat tough mass, especially just before it is quite cold. In this "solidified from fusion" form it is much more completely and easily detonated than in the form of loose crystals. It requires in any case a very powerful detonator. When confined in a strong vessel and rapidly heated to considerably above its melting point detonation generally occurs, but as a rule some quantity even then undergoes quiet decomposition.

Picric acid when dry and unconfined may be ignited by a flame, and then burns quietly with production of much black smoke. Mercury fulminate will act as a detonator for picric acid, but some substances chemically related to it are more effective in this respect.

The name lyddite is applied to the melted and solidified picric acid.

Picric acid is not made on the manufacturing scale by the direct action of nitric acid, it would be far too dangerous as well as wasteful.

The first step is the formation of phenol-sulphonic acid $C_6H_4OHSO_3H$. When phenol is warmed to about 120° with a little more than its own weight of strong sulphuric acid, the reaction $C_6H_5OH + H_2SO_4 = H_2O + C_6H_4OHSO_3H$ quietly takes place. This substance is phenal sulphonic acid.

The sulphonic acid is then boiled with dilute nitric acid (10 per cent. acid), very little more than the theoretical amount of nitric acid being employed. The reaction

$$C_6H_4\,OHSO_3H + 3HNO_3 = C_6H_2OH\,(NO_2)_3 + H_2SO_4 + 2H_2O$$

takes place. Both these operations should be conducted in stoneware or porcelain vessels, but leaden ones are sometimes used. The heating is generally effected by means of coils of pipe through which superheated steam can be passed. As the liquid cools picric acid separates out in crystals, which are drained and washed with cold water to free them from most of the adhering sulphuric acid, and recrystallized from boiling water to finally eliminate this acid. It is very important that every trace of sulphuric acid should be removed from picric acid intended to be used as lyddite. A better plan of purifying picric acid required for lyddite is to make the crude acid into the sodium salt by dissolving in strong, hot sodium carbonate solution. Any sulphuric or nitric acids are by this means converted into sodium salts also. On cooling, almost chemically pure sodium picrate crystallizes out, and may be filtered from impurities which remain in solution, then redissolved in boiling water and decomposed by hydrochloric acid. The crystals of picric acid this time are only contaminated by traces of sodium chloride and hydrochloric acid, the latter of which is volatile. Picric acid may be stored with perfect safety when moist. It should, however, not be in contact with metals, metallic oxides, or salts, as it acts as a real acid, dissolving some metals, as zinc or iron, with evolution of hydrogen and production of salts known as picrates.

Picric acid forms compounds with ammonia and amine bases and almost all the metals. They are generally yellow crystalline substances, more or less soluble in water. Many are extremely sensitive, when dry, to friction or percussion, and all decompose in an explosive manner when heated.

Ammonium picrate, $C_6H_2(NO_2)_3ONH_4$, is easily formed by adding ammonium hydroxide to picric acid, either solid or in solution. It is readily soluble in water but very slightly so in alcohol, and can be precipitated from a strong aqueous solution by addition of alcohol. It is employed in Bengal fire (25 parts ammonium picrate, 8 sulphur, 67 barium nitrate), and in some fuze compositions.

Sodium picrate, $C_6H_2(NO_2)_3ON$, can be formed by contact of picric acid with sodium carbonate, either air dry or in solution in water, better by the addition of sodium hydroxide to a hot picric acid solution. It then crystallizes out on cooling; one part water at 15° dissolves 10 parts of the salt. When dry this salt explodes by friction or percussion as well as on heating.

The potassium salt can be formed in a similar manner. It is, however, much less soluble in cold water, 1 part of the salt requiring, at 15°, 228 parts water. It is more sensitive when dry than the sodium salt.

Small quantities of these salts are liable to be formed on contact of picric acid with almost any sodium or potassium compound. Either of these compounds can be employed as detonators for picric acid. The picrates of the heavier metals are considerably more sensitive to friction when dry than the sodium, potassium or ammonium salts.

Lead picrate $(C_6H_2(NO_2)_3O)_2Pb$, can be made in a pure state and most easily by mixing hot solutions of sodium or ammonia picrate with lead acetate or nitrate. The lead compound then crystallizes out on cooling the liquid. Some lead salt is also formed on contact of picric acid with ordinary dirty metallic lead, with lead oxides, white lead, or in fact almost any substance, as ordinary paint, which contains that metal. Lead picrate also combines with lead oxide in several proportions, for instance $(C_6H_2(NO_2)_3O)_2Pb + 4PbO$, &c., and also with lead salts as the acetate and nitrate. All these are very dangerous compounds when in a dry state. Metallic hydroxides and most carbonates dissolve in hot solutions of picric acid and yield crystalline picrates. Some can be obtained only by double decomposition, from a nitrate of a metal for instance, and sodium picrate.

Although picric acid is quite safe to melt in a clean vessel and even to set fire to when pure it is not so when in contact with rusty metals or metallic oxides or carbonates. When melted in contact with a very little red lead, Pb_2O_3, or almost any heavy metallic oxide, it generally detonates very sharply and this detonation is responded to by free picric acid.

The solid hydroxides of sodium or potassium, and especially some peroxides as BaO_2, Na_2O_2 &c., will generally inflame even wet picric acid on contact. Contact with nitrates, chlorates, chromates, permanganates or persulphates is also particularly to be avoided.

Pure picric acid should dissolve completely in hot water giving a clear yellow solution, on adding a little hydrochloric acid and barium chloride no appreciable cloudiness should be produced. A white precipitate indicates sulphuric acid. A little of the solid acid heated on a piece of clean porcelain or platinum foil should burn quickly, or evaporate, without leaving any appreciable residue after burning off the carbon first deposited.

Sulphuric acid is a dangerous impurity when the picric acid is melted to make lyddite, &c., and also if the acid come in contact with any metal. Any residue left on evaporation of the picric acid indicates the presence of metals or metallic oxides, which may be extremely dangerous.

Volatile acids, as nitric or hydrochloric acid, if present in the picric are destroyed or expelled, if in small amount, during the melting into lyddite.

A considerable number of compositions have been proposed or tried in which picrates, ammonium picrate and others, are essential materials. They are mostly eminently dangerous to store or use.

Designolle's powder contains potassium picrate, charcoal and potassium nitrate in varying proportions, depending on the purpose of the powder.

Brugère's powder consisted of ammonium picrate 54 parts and potassium nitrate 46 parts.

None of these powders are smokeless.

Turpin's melinite consisted of picric acid made into a colloidal state by mixing with from 3 to 5 per cent. of collodion or soluble guncotton, on melting at about 140° it could be cast in a mould. In this form it is so far insensitive that it can be detonated only when confined.

An *Emulsion* of picric acid in strong nitric acid is somewhat easily detonated.

Like all nitro compounds, picric acid can be reduced by the action of nascent hydrogen. The first stage of this action results in the production of picramic acid, $C_6H_2(NO_2)_2OHNH_2$, a substance possessing both acid and basic characters MP. 169° C. It is generally obtained by the action of ammonium hydro-sulphide on a hot alcoholic solution of picric acid.

Picramic acid is a mild explosive. It is employed in some explosive compositions. With picric acid it forms a molecular compound which also possesses mild explosive properties.

Coal tar oils contains several substances of the same class

as phenol. One of these, cresol, $C_6H_4CH_3OH$, yields by treatment similar to that employed for the formation of picric acid, a tri-nitro cresol, $C_6H\ CH_3OH(NO_2)_3$. This substance closely resembles picric acid in its properties. It was known as "ecrasite," and employed in a similar manner to lyddite. It explodes under the same conditions and is a little more vigorous than the latter. It also forms similar compounds with metals which explode on heating or by percussion.

Xylenol, naphtol, and generally all the substances of similar phenolic type yield nitro derivatives of more or less explosive power, and their salts with metals are also sensitive to heat or percussion, particularly when dry.

An interesting explosive is produced by the action of a solution of potassium cyanide on picric acid. It has the composition $C_8H_5N_5O_6$. It explodes in a peculiarly sharp manner on heating, producing much black smoke.

Toluene, $C_6H_5CH_3$, is a liquid hydrocarbon obtained along with benzene from coal tar; various nitro products are obtained by the action of nitric acid alone upon it, and when heated for some time with a mixture of nitric and sulphuric acid, a trinitro-toluene $C_6H_2CH_3(NO_2)_3$ is produced. This substance melts at about 80° C., is nearly insoluble in water, and only slightly so in cold alcohol; it burns quietly with a very smoky flame under ordinary circumstances, but can be detonated by mercury fulminate and some other detonators. It does not form metallic salts as picric acid does. This nitro product, as ordinarily made, may contain several modifications, but is mostly that represented by

$$\underset{NO_2}{\underset{|}{\overset{CH_3}{\overset{|}{\bigcirc}}}}\begin{smallmatrix}NO_2\\ \\NO_2\end{smallmatrix}$$

Ammonium nitrate or nitrite are types of amino self-contained explosives. The former is largely employed in some blasting powders. The latter is not practically employed. Its products of decomposition when gently heated either dry or in solution in water are, however, interesting. Its internal combustion is of the simplest type, thus: $NH_4NO_2 = 2\ H_2O + N_2$.

Nearly all amino compounds, that is, substances containing the group NH_2, can form nitrates, and in all these cases, more or less complete, internal combustion is possible at some more or less elevated temperatures. For instance, urea forms $NH_2CONH_2HNO_3$, urea nitrate, which gives water nitrogen and carbon monoxide when heated to a moderate temperature. It is, however, deliquescent, and otherwise impractical as a propellant.

Amino acetic acid, CH_2NH_2COOH, forms a nitrate which, theoretically, decomposes, as shown by

$$CH_2NH_2HNO_3COOH = 3H_2O + 2CO + N_2$$

and good results are said to have been obtained from it practically as a propellant.

Amino derivatives from benzenic compounds such as aniline $C_6H_5NH_2$, contain too much carbon for anything approaching complete combustion. A partial combustion takes place with deposition of much carbon when their nitrates are heated.

All substances of the amino type can be converted by the action of nitrous acid into diazo derivatives.

All the known members of this class of substance are explosive, not from internal combustion, but evidently owing to the peculiar form of combination of their contained nitrogen. The first compound of this nature was obtained by the action of nitrous acid on aniline. It is known as diazobenzene. Its preparation may be indicated by the equation—

$$C_6H_5NH_2HNO_3 + HNO_2 = C_6H_5N:N \cdot NO_3 + 2H_2O$$
aniline nitrate $\qquad\qquad$ diazo benzene nitrate

This substance decomposes very easily, undergoing hydrolysis in contact with water with formation of phenol and liberation of nitrogen gas. In a dry state all the diazo compounds are very sensitive to heat or friction.

All diazo compounds seem capable of uniting with acids to form crystalline salts. The nature of the acid has some effect on the character of the compounds, chromic acid, for instance, forming exceedingly dangerous compounds with diazo derivatives.

A diazo compound can be obtained from picramic acid; it has the composition $C_6H_2N_4O_5$. When dry this detonates on heating to about 150° or on percussion. It is scarcely soluble in water, and may be kept in a moist state for years unchanged. Generally, however, the diazo compounds are too sensitive for practical employment.

The discovery of a method by which the substance hydrazine, N_2H_4, could be prepared and isolated, led in turn to the discovery of the substance N_3H or $\overset{N}{\underset{N}{\cdot\cdot}}NH$, which may be looked upon as a diazo derivative from ammonia. It is known as azoimide or hydrazoic acid, the latter name because of its marked acid properties. In a free state it is a very volatile liquid, and is the most powerful explosive known up to date. Its vapour detonates on contact with a flame. It is soluble in water, and the solution dissolves some metals and forms salts, such as $Zn\genfrac{}{}{0pt}{}{N_3}{N_3}$; NaN_3; AgN_3, &c. All these metallic salts are frightfully explosive.

The most interesting compound is that with ammonia. It has the composition $N_3H\ NH_3$ or N_4H_4. It is a white crystalline solid, which burns after the quick manner of loose guncotton when ignited in the open and in small amount. Under percussion or heating in a closed vessel it is resolved into nitrogen and hydrogen, 60 grams of the salt yielding 88,000 cubic centimetres of gases, or, roughly, 1,400 times its volume.

Fulminates are compounds of a peculiar acid, the so-called fulminic with metals. Several are known, but one only, that of mercury, is sufficiently stable to allow of its being practically employed. Fulminic acid is probably the result of the oxidation of alcohol by nitrous anhydride or nitrous acid, and the action might be represented

$$C_2H_5OH + N_2O_3 = 2H_2O + C_2H_2N_2O_2.*$$

Although many formulæ have been proposed, the constitution of this substance has not been satisfactorily made out. The mercury compound is largely used as an igniting and detonating substance.

Mercury fulminate, $HgC_2N_2O_2$, was obtained by Howard in 1800 by mixing a solution of mercuric nitrate in nitric acid with alcohol. It is prepared by dissolving 3 parts of mercury in 36 of nitric acid (specific gravity 1·34), keeping at a low temperature until dissolved, when 17 parts of 90 per cent. alcohol are added. A somewhat violent reaction commences after a short time, whereupon another 17 parts of alcohol are gradually added. The mercury salt precipitates as a white or grey crystalline powder, which may be washed with cold water. It may be purified by recrystallization from boiling water or alcohol, but this is seldom required for ordinary purposes. The specific gravity of mercury fulminate is 4·42. It explodes by heating, friction, or gentle percussion, or by contact with strong sulphuric acid. When quite unconfined, moderately small quantities may be ignited, when it burns extremely rapidly with a bright flash, and neighbouring cold surfaces are coated with mercury. If enclosed in a very slight degree, even between sheets of paper, it is inclined to detonate violently when ignited. The products of its burning in a closed space are mercury, nitrogen, and carbon monoxide. One molecule (284 grammes) gives 116,000 calories on burning. Mercury fulminate can be stored wet, water having no decomposing action. It is decomposed on contact with sulphuretted hydrogen, ammonium sulphide, and other soluble sulphides. The sulphides produce sulphide of mercury, and the other part of the compound undergoes a very thorough change. Contact with some metals, as zinc, when damp, also decomposes it. Strong alkalis and bases as aniline, hydrochloric acid, and the solutions of some salts also decompose it. Mercury fulminate is the active ingredient of cap composition and many forms of exploders, and is so used because of the ease with which it can be exploded by percussion or friction. It is, generally, for use in cap compositions and the like, diluted with an inert powder such as ground glass, so that its explosion is sufficiently delayed to allow of its flame igniting some other more strongly flaming mixture. Such a "flaming" mixture is native sulphide of antimony (stibnite) and potassium chlorate or nitrate.

---

* See also Berlin Berichte $\frac{40}{2}$ p. 418.

Mercury fulminate alone burns or explodes much too rapidly to ignite gunpowder or cordite.

When partially enclosed, as, for instance, in a metal tube with open ends, it detonates on firing with a hot wire or a flame. Many forms of detonators, electric or otherwise, depend on the action of undiluted fulminate. Mercury fulminate is extremely poisonous. Silver fulminate (and other metallic fulminates) may be obtained by means similar to those for the mercury compound, or from mercury fulminate. The silver compound is much too sensitive to friction for practical employment. It explodes also with greater violence.

Acetylene is a gaseous hydrocarbon, of very peculiar nature, produced by the action of water on calcium carbide. This carbide is formed by heating together, in an electric furnace, coke and limestone. Its composition is expressed by the formula CaC_2, and it is undoubtedly a highly endothermic substance, from the manner in which it decomposes water, and from the nature of the acetylene itself. The reaction seems to be $CaC_2 + 2H_2O = Ca(HO)_2 + C_2H_2$ (acetylene).

It is a gaseous substance at all ordinary temperatures, and burns in air with the production of an exceedingly hot and brilliant flame. A mixture of the gas and air explodes with much force. A mixture with pure oxygen is still more violent. Contact of the gas with chlorine, fuming nitric acid, or hot metallic oxides, may bring about inflammation or explosion. The gas can be made to explode or detonate by heating under pressure. It then breaks up into carbon and hydrogen.

Acetylene unites with a number of metallic oxides or salts forming solid compounds which in a dry state explode or detonate by heat or friction in a manner closely resembling fulminates. Its compounds, with some silver and mercury salts, are particularly violent explosives, and very sensitive to friction when in a dry state.

Some compounds of copper, when in solution, or even when suspended in water or exposed in a moist state to acetylene, also absorb and combine with it. Cuprous oxide and chloride, either solid, or better in solution in ammonia, give a red, insoluble compound, which can be decomposed by strong hydrochloric acid, acetylene being reproduced. When dry the copper compounds explode, on moderate heating or the application of a screwing-motion pressure, in a feeble manner, liberating carbon and copper.

Many, but not all, silver salts in ammonia solution give white insoluble acetylene compounds, which become black on drying and exposure to light. They are moderately sensitive to friction when dry, and detonate very violently when heated to about $200°$ C. In nearly all cases silver and carbon are deposited as two of the products of decomposition.

The bichromate, persulphate, and other silver salts form complex compounds with acetylene, and many of them are exceedingly powerful explosives of the detonating type, but much too sensitive to slight friction or sudden rise of temperature, when dry, for practical employment, excepting in some very special cases.

Chlorates are compounds containing much oxygen, nearly all of which is in a state available for supporting combustion.* Most metals are capable of forming chlorates, but practically very few are made technically or employed.

The chlorates of sodium, potassium, and barium are non-deliquescent crystalline substances which decompose when heated to moderate but still pretty safe temperatures (such as 200° C. to 350° C.). As a rule they give up the whole of the contained oxygen thus:—

$$BaCl_2O_6 = BaCl_2 + 3O_2 \text{ and } 2NaClO_3 = 2NaCl + 3O_2.$$

Most other chlorates are either deliquescent or contain crystal water or hydrolyse in water solution.

When *very rapidly heated* chlorates decompose undoubtedly in a manner approaching that of a detonation.

When in contact with any kind of organic (carbon) compound, sulphur, metallic sulphides, some finely-powdered metals as magnesium and aluminium, and especially phosphorus, either white or red, chlorates give up some or all their oxygen and either burn or detonate—the former on heating and, as a rule, the latter on percussion or friction. Hydrocarbons, for instance, and especially compounds of the benzenic type, may be either fired or detonated with more or less ease depending to some extent on the carbon compound. Nitro-benzene, dinitro-benzene, naphtaline, &c., mixed with potassium chlorate may be detonated by pretty strong friction, or easily by a fulminate detonator. Rack-a-Rock consists of nitro-benzene soaked into a mixture of chlorate and a powder, as brick-dust. These mixtures burn, as a rule, when simply ignited. The most sensitive mixture is a chlorate and phosphorus. Ordinary phosphorus will burn under water by gentle friction with crystals of a chlorate or the addition of sulphuric acid. Red phosphorus is used as the basis of some friction-tube compositions, because of the ease with which it can be started burning on contact with a chlorate.

Mixtures of chlorates with organic substances can also be fired by contact with strong sulphuric acid.†

Sugar, starch, or wood-pulp mixed with a chlorate in about the quantity necessary to supply sufficient oxygen for combustion form very good blasting powders. They all, however, require most careful handling when dry, and are not superior to other detonators. As propellants they are impossible.

---

* Some of this oxygen, perhaps all, is combined with the halogen, and their peculiar nature may be represented by the structural formula—

$$M-Cl\begin{smallmatrix} O \\ O \\ O \end{smallmatrix}$$

† Chlorates, when treated with an acid, give off a gaseous oxide of chlorine, ClO_2, which is also a very powerful oxidising substance.

Mixtures of finely-divided or powdered metals, especially magnesium and aluminium, with a chlorate as that of potassium, are used as flash-light powders for photographic purposes. They explode very violently on percussion, or when moderate quantities are heated.

Anthracene, $C_{14}H_{10}$, and similar dense hydrocarbons are somewhat difficult to burn or explode by means of chlorates unless the latter be in large amount. Some of these mixtures produce much smoke on being fired.

The Perchlorates are in some respects safer, and at the same time more energetic, than the chlorates as ingredients of explosive or fiery compositions. Potassium perchlorate $KClO_4$ is almost the only one of this class that has been actually employed. The compound here named withstands a higher temperature before decomposing than the chlorate, and mixtures containing it are much less sensitive to percussion or friction. They explode better, however, because of their larger store of available oxygen.

The permanganates are as good providers of oxygen as the chlorates or perchlorates. Two only are in common use, those of potassium, $K_2Mn_2O_8$, and sodium, $Na_2Mn_2O_8$.

The substances mentioned in connection with chlorates, and especially the metals magnesium and aluminium, in a finely divided condition, when mixed with potassium permanganate, can be fired by a flame or by percussion or friction on a hard substance. Contact of strong sulphuric acid will also fire most permanganate mixtures, the reason being that an oxide of manganese, Mn_2O_7, is liberated by the action of the acid. This oxide decomposes at a very moderate temperature (about 100° C.), liberating four of its oxygen atoms. It is, therefore, a very powerful oxidising substance. Mn_2O_7 is a liquid which gives off a pink vapour at ordinary temperatures, and is very dangerous even in small quantity either alone or in contact with most carbon compounds.

The bichromates are suppliers of oxygen and can, under some limited conditions, serve as ingredients of explosive mixtures, but their activity is much less than that of the permanganates. Some match or friction compositions contain potassium or lead bichromates.

Ammonium bichromate is a self combustible of an exceedingly mild description. From the decomposition reaction:

$$(NH_4)_2Cr_2O_7 = Cr_2O_3 + N_2 + 4H_2O$$

it will be seen to be a perfect example of internal combustion.

The metals magnesium, and aluminium, and in a less degree zinc, when in a finely divided condition form fiery mixtures with a number of metallic oxides, particularly that class known as peroxides, as MnO_2, manganese dioxide, or BaO_2, barium dioxide, etc.

Some of these compositions—as, for example, one consisting of $3CuO + Al_2$,—may be ignited by a match flame and then burn quickly, producing an extremely high temperature. They are mostly responsive to friction and percussion, more especially to that produced by a "glancing blow" or when struck with a hammer on an anvil.

Mixtures of powdered aluminium and oxysalts as permanganates and chromates are extremely violent explosives, igniting either by a flame or by friction.

A mixture of aluminium powder and ferricoxide produces an extremely high temperature when the reaction is started. This mixture is known as "Thermite."

The metal calcium will undoubtedly take the place of aluminium and magnesium in some "heat" producing compositions.

APPENDIX I.
GRAVIMETRIC DENSITY TABLE.

Gravimetric density, when each pound of a powder charge occupies any of the undermentioned number of cubic inches. Gravimetric density = 1, when one pound of powder occupies 27·73 cubic inches.

Cubic Inches.	·0	0·1	0·2	0·3	0·4	0·5	0·6	0·7	0·8	0·9
22	1·260	1·255	1·249	1·243	1·238	1·232	1·227	1·222	1·216	1·211
23	1·206	1·200	1·195	1·190	1·185	1·180	1·175	1·170	1·165	1·160
24	1·155	1·151	1·146	1·141	1·136	1·132	1·127	1·123	1·118	1·114
25	1·109	1·105	1·100	1·096	1·092	1·087	1·083	1·079	1·075	1·071
26	1·066	1·062	1·058	1·054	1·050	1·046	1·042	1·039	1·035	1·031
27	1·027	1·023	1·019	1·016	1·012	1·008	1·005	1·001	0·997	0·994
28	0·990	0·987	0·983	0·980	0·976	0·973	0·970	0·966	0·963	0·959
29	0·956	0·953	0·959	0·946	0·943	0·940	0·937	0·934	0·930	0·927
30	0·924	0·921	0·918	0·915	0·912	0·909	0·906	0·903	0·900	0·897
31	0·894	0·892	0·889	0·886	0·883	0·880	0·877	0·875	0·872	0·869
32	0·867	0·864	0·861	0·858	0·856	0·853	0·851	0·848	0·845	0·843
33	0·840	0·838	0·835	0·833	0·830	0·828	0·825	0·823	0·820	0·818
34	0·815	0·813	0·811	0·808	0·806	0·804	0·801	0·799	0·797	0·795
35	0·792	0·790	0·788	0·785	0·783	0·781	0·779	0·777	0·775	0·772
36	0·770	0·768	0·766	0·764	0·762	0·760	0·758	0·756	0·753	0·751
37	0·749	0·747	0·745	0·743	0·741	0·739	0·737	0·735	0·734	0·732
38	0·730	0·728	0·726	0·724	0·722	0·720	0·718	0·716	0·715	0·713
39	0·711	0·709	0·707	0·706	0·704	0·702	0·700	0·698	0·697	0·695
40	0·693	0·691	0·690	0·688	0·686	0·685	0·683	0·681	0·680	0·678
41	0·676	0·675	0·673	0·671	0·670	0·668	0·666	0·665	0·663	0·662
42	0·660	0·659	0·657	0·655	0·654	0·652	0·651	0·649	0·648	0·646
43	0·645	0·643	0·642	0·640	0·639	0·637	0·636	0·634	0·633	0·632
44	0·630	0·629	0·627	0·626	0·624	0·623	0·622	0·620	0·619	0·618
45	0·616	0·615	0·613	0·612	0·611	0·609	0·608	0·607	0·605	0·604
46	0·603	0·601	0·600	0·599	0·598	0·596	0·595	0·594	0·592	0·591
47	0·590	0·589	0·587	0·586	0·585	0·584	0·582	0·581	0·580	0·579
48	0·578	0·576	0·575	0·574	0·573	0·572	0·570	0·569	0·568	0·567
49	0·566	0·565	0·564	0·562	0·561	0·560	0·559	0·558	0·557	0·556
50	0·555	0·553	0·552	0·551	0·550	0·549	0·548	0·547	0·546	0·545
51	0·544	0·543	0·542	0·540	0·539	0·538	0·537	0·536	0·535	0·534
52	0·533	0·532	0·531	0·530	0·529	0·528	0·527	0·526	0·525	0·524
53	0·523	0·522	0·521	0·520	0·519	0·518	0·517	0·516	0·515	0·514
54	0·513	0·512	0·511	0·510	0·510	0·509	0·508	0·507	0·506	0·505
55	0·504	0·503	0·502	0·501	0·500	0·500	0·499	0·498	0·497	0·496

EXPLANATION OF APPENDIX I.—Knowing the cubic contents of the chamber of a gun and the amount of powder in the charge, the number of cubic inches allotted to each pound of powder can be found; the table then indicates the corresponding gravimetric density (G.D.); thus the cubic content of the chamber of the 9·2 inch B.L. gun is 5,000 cubic inches, and the powder charge is 175 lbs. hence—
$$5,000 \div 175 = 28·57 \text{ cub. ins.},$$
are allotted to each lb. of the charge, and from the table, columns 1, 7 and 8, the G.D. = 0·973 − 0·7 (0·973 − 0·970)
= 0·971.

EXPLANATION OF APPENDIX II.—The theoretical amount of work capable of being performed on a projectile when a powder charge *of unit gravimetric density* expands to definite amounts in the bore of a gun is stated in the table: thus, suppose a charge of 5 lbs. G.D. = 1 expands four times, under these circumstances each pound of powder (see Table, columns 5 and 7), performs 82·107 ft.-tons of work, and as there are 5 lbs. of powder, the total is 82·107 × 5 = 410·535 ft.-tons; only a part, called the factor of effect, is however realised, owing to loss from heat given to the gun and other causes; suppose the factor is 0·8, the total work realised is 410·535 × 0·8 = 328·428 ft.-tons.

Practically, however, the gravimetric density is seldom or never unity, and deduction must be made for the work lost in expanding from a *supposed* G.D. of unity to a G.D. equal to a tabulated density of the products of explosion (see Table, columns 2, 6 and 10) for no work is practically performed on the projectile in this part of the expansion of the powder charge: thus, again taking the 9·2 inch B.L. gun, the length of the bore, less the length of the chamber, is 289·8 − 43·8 = 246 inches, hence—
the capacity of the bore 289 × ¼π(9·2)² = 19,212 cubic inches,
and the capacity of the chamber = 5,000 ,, ,,
∴ the total capacity = 24,212 ,, ,,
as a charge of 175 lbs. of unit gravimetric density occupies 175 × 27·73 = 4,853 ,, ,,
it must expand 24,212 ÷ 4,853 = 4·99 times.
Under these circumstances the amount of work performed (see Table) is
$$90·565 + 0·9 \times 0·820 = 91·303 \text{ ft.-tons};$$
from this a deduction must be made: we have seen above, in the explanation of Appendix I, that the G.D. of this charge is 0·971; if the products of explosion had been allowed to change from G.D. = 1·0 to G.D. = 0·971, while *the powder gas is pressing on the base of the projectile*, we see from Appendix II, columns 2 and 3, that 2·870 ft.-tons of work would have been performed; but as expansion has taken place to this extent, *without the performance of work*, this amount must be *deducted* from the total and thence the theoretical work is
$$91·303 − 2·870 = 88·433 \text{ ft.-tons per pound}$$
of charge: multiply this amount by the number (175) pounds of powder in the charge, and taking a factor of effect (judged from experience) of 0·726, the total energy realised is
$$88·433 \times 175 \times 0·726 = 11,240 \text{ ft.-tons}.$$

Now $\dfrac{wV^2}{2g \times 2240}$ ft.-tons is equal to this same amount; substitute the value 380 lbs. for w and we have—
$$\frac{380 V^2}{2 \times 32·19 \times 2240} = 11,240,$$
whence V = 2065 f.s.

APPENDIX II.

TABLE OF WORK CAPABLE OF BEING DONE BY EXPLODING GUNPOWDER.

Number of volumes of expansion.	Corresponding density of products of combustion.	Work that powder is capable of performing.		Number of volumes of expansion.	Corresponding density of products of combustion.	Work that powder is capable of performing.		Number of volumes of expansion.	Corresponding density of products of combustion.	Work that powder is capable of performing.	
		Per lb. burned in foot-tons.	Difference.			Per lb. burned in foot-tons.	Difference.			Per lb. burned in foot-tons.	Difference.
1·00	1·000	...	...	1·84	0·543	44·394	0·625	4·90	0·204	90·565	0·841
1·01	0·990	0·980	0·980	1·86	0·537	45·009	0·615	5·00	0·200	91·385	0·820
1·02	0·980	1·936	0·956	1·88	0·532	45·614	0·605	5·10	0·196	92·186	0·801
1·03	0·971	2·870	0·934	1·90	0·526	46·209	0·595	5·20	0·192	92·968	0·782
1·04	0·962	3·782	0·912	1·92	0·521	46·795	0·586	5·30	0·188	93·732	0·764
1·05	0·952	4·674	0·892	1·94	0·515	47·372	0·577	5·40	0·185	94·479	0·747
1·06	0·943	5·547	0·873	1·96	0·510	47·940	0·568	5·50	0·182	95·210	0·731
1·07	0·935	6·399	0·852	1·98	0·505	48·499	0·559	5·60	0·178	95·925	0·715
1·08	0·926	7·234	0·835	2·00	0·500	49·050	0·551	5·70	0·175	96·625	0·700
1·09	0·917	8·051	0·817	2·05	0·488	50·383	1·333	5·80	0·172	97·310	0·685
1·10	0·909	8·852	0·810	2·10	0·476	51·673	1·290	5·90	0·169	97·981	0·671
1·11	0·901	9·637	0·785	2·15	0·465	52·922	1·249	6·00	0·166	98·638	0·657
1·12	0·893	10·406	0·769	2·20	0·454	54·132	1·210	6·10	0·164	99·282	0·644
1·13	0·885	11·160	0·754	2·25	0·444	55·304	1·172	6·20	0·161	99·915	0·633
1·14	0·877	11·899	0·739	2·30	0·435	56·439	1·135	6·30	0·159	100·536	0·621
1·15	0·870	12·625	0·726	2·35	0·425	57·539	1·100	6·40	0·156	101·145	0·609
1·16	0·862	13·338	0·713	2·40	0·417	58·605	1·066	6·50	0·154	101·744	0·599
1·17	0·855	14·038	0·700	2·45	0·408	59·639	1·034	6·60	0·151	102·333	0·589
1·18	0·847	14·725	0·687	2·50	0·400	60·642	1·003	6·70	0·149	102·912	0·579
1·19	0·840	15·400	0·675	2·55	0·392	61·616	0·974	6·80	0·147	103·480	0·568
1·20	0·833	16·063	0·663	2·60	0·384	62·563	0·947	6·90	0·145	104·038	0·558
1·21	0·826	16·716	0·653	2·65	0·377	63·486	0·923	7·00	0·143	104·586	0·548
1·22	0·820	17·359	0·643	2·70	0·370	64·385	0·899	7·10	0·141	105·125	0·539
1·23	0·813	17·992	0·633	2·75	0·363	65·262	0·877	7·20	0·139	105·655	0·530
1·24	0·806	18·614	0·622	2·80	0·357	66·119	0·857	7·30	0·137	106·176	0·521
1·25	0·800	19·226	0·612	2·85	0·351	66·955	0·836	7·40	0·135	106·688	0·512
1·26	0·794	19·828	0·602	2·90	0·345	67·771	0·816	7·50	0·133	107·192	0·504
1·27	0·787	20·420	0·592	2·95	0·339	68·568	0·797	7·60	0·131	107·688	0·496
1·28	0·781	21·001	0·581	3·00	0·333	69·347	0·779	7·70	0·130	108·177	0·480
1·29	0·775	21·572	0·571	3·05	0·328	70·109	0·762	7·80	0·128	108·659	0·482
1·30	0·769	22·133	0·561	3·10	0·322	70·854	0·745	7·90	0·126	109·133	0·474
1·32	0·758	23·246	1·113	3·15	0·317	71·585	0·731	8·00	0·125	109·600	0·467
1·34	0·746	24·324	1·078	3·20	0·312	72·301	0·716	8·10	0·123	110·060	0·460
1·36	0·735	25·371	1·047	3·25	0·308	73·002	0·701	8·20	0·122	110·514	0·454
1·38	0·725	26·389	1·018	3·30	0·303	73·690	0·688	8·30	0·120	110·902	0·448
1·40	0·714	27·380	0·991	3·35	0·298	74·365	0·675	8·40	0·119	111·404	0·442
1·42	0·704	28·348	0·968	3·40	0·294	75·027	0·662	8·50	0·117	111·840	0·436
1·44	0·694	29·291	0·943	3·45	0·290	75·677	0·650	8·60	0·116	112·270	0·430
1·46	0·685	30·211	0·920	3·50	0·286	76·315	0·638	8·70	0·115	112·695	0·425
1·48	0·676	31·109	0·898	3·55	0·282	76·940	0·625	8·80	0·114	113·114	0·419
1·50	0·667	31·986	0·877	3·60	0·278	77·553	0·613	8·90	0·112	113·528	0·414
1·52	0·658	32·843	0·857	3·65	0·274	78·156	0·603	9·00	0·111	113·937	0·409
1·54	0·649	33·681	0·838	3·70	0·270	78·749	0·593	9·10	0·110	114·341	0·404
1·56	0·641	34·500	0·819	3·75	0·266	79·332	0·583	9·20	0·109	114·739	0·398
1·58	0·633	35·301	0·801	3·80	0·263	79·905	0·573	9·30	0·108	115·133	0·394
1·60	0·625	36·086	0·785	3·85	0·260	80·469	0·564	9·40	0·106	115·521	0·388
1·62	0·617	36·855	0·769	3·90	0·256	81·024	0·555	9·50	0·105	115·905	0·384
1·64	0·610	37·608	0·753	3·95	0·253	81·570	0·546	9·60	0·104	116·284	0·379
1·66	0·602	38·346	0·738	4·00	0·250	82·107	0·537	9·70	0·103	116·659	0·375
1·68	0·595	39·069	0·723	4·10	0·244	83·157	1·050	9·80	0·102	117·029	0·370
1·70	0·588	39·778	0·709	4·20	0·238	84·176	1·019	9·90	0·101	117·395	0·376
1·72	0·581	40·474	0·696	4·30	0·232	85·166	0·990	10·00	0·100	117·757	0·362
1·74	0·575	41·156	0·682	4·40	0·227	86·128	0·962	11·00	0·091	121·165	3·408
1·76	0·568	41·827	0·671	4·50	0·222	87·064	0·936	12·00	0·083	124·233	3·074
1·78	0·562	42·486	0·659	4·60	0·217	87·975	0·911	13·00	0·077	127·036	2·797
1·80	0·555	43·133	0·647	4·70	0·213	88·861	0·886	14·00	0·071	129·602	2·566
1·82	0·549	43·769	0·636	4·80	0·208	89·724	0·863	15·00	0·066	131·970	2·368

NOTE.—For further problems connected with the two tables in Appendices I and II, as well as for an explanation of the mode of obtaining the "factor of effect," see pp. 23, 24, "Text Book of Gunnery, 1887."

APPENDIX III.

Showing the Details of Manufacture of the Powders made at the Royal Gunpowder Factory.

Nature.	Size of grains or pieces.	Charcoal. Time of burning.	Charcoal. Material.	Incorporation under iron runners. Time.	Incorporation under iron runners. Moisture in mill-cake.	Dusting.	Glazing. Time.	Glazing. In what barrels.	Storing. Time.	Storing. Temperature.	Finishing.	Blending.	Remarks.
		Hours.		Hours.	Per cent.				Hours.	F.			
R.F.G.	Meshes to 1 inch 12 to 20	4	Dogwood	4	1·5	Through slope-reel before and after glazing.	5½	Large 6-feet drum	1	100°	2½ hours in horizontal reels covered with 18-mesh canvas	(1.) Four glazings are blended together in the 4-way hopper before stoving (2.) After stoving the four glazings are "finished" and blended into uniform batches of 50 barrels each (3.) Two or more of the above batches are blended in 4-way hopper into uniform lots of 100 or 200 barrels each	Packed in barrels of 100 lb. each.
R.F.G.[3]	12 to 20	8	do.	8	2·5		10	do.	2	100°			
M.G.[1]	7 to 14	4	do.	7	3·5		4	do.	2	110°			
*Q.F.[1]	⅜" × ⅜" × ⅜"												
B.L.G.[3]	3 to 6	3½	Alder and willow	3	2½		1½	do. (with graphite)	2	110°	45 minutes		Packed in barrels of 110 lb. each.
B.L.G.[4]	2 to 3	4	do.	3	4		3	do.	6	115°	1 hour in horizontal reels		
P.	⅜-inch cubes	4	Alder and willow	3	4 to 5		4	Ordinary glazing barrels	36	130°	1 hour in large skeleton reel with wooden reel with graphite	(1.) Eight glazings mixed in large skeleton reel to make 102 barrels of 125 lb. each (2.) Above divided into 2 batches of 51 barrels, and each batch *separately* blended in 4-way hopper to make it uniform (3.) One barrel from each batch of 51, to make uniform lot of 102 barrels of 125 lb. each	Packed in barrels of 125 lb. each.
P.[2]	1½-inch cubes	6	do.	4	do.			do.	120	130°			
*Prism[1] Black	Height ·976, diameter over sides 1·29, diameter of hole ·393.	4 hours	do.	4	5 to 6	The foul grain is run through a slope-reel before moulding			24 and 12	90° and 140°		By hand into lots of 100 cases of 100 lbs. each	Packed in cases of 100 lb. each.

* Not manufactured at Waltham Abbey.

N.B.—"Rifle pistol" powder is made from R.F.G. siftings, the size being from 20 to 36 meshes to the linear inch.   R.L.G. powder is still in the service, the size being 4 to 8 meshes.

APPENDIX IV.

TABLE SHOWING THE CONDITIONS OF ACCEPTANCE OF SERVICE POWDERS.

N.B.—*See* Appendix III, for Size of Grains or Pieces.

Nature.	Fired at Proof in	Charge of Powder.	Weight of Projectile.	Density.		Moisture.		Muzzle Velocity.		Pressure.	
				Min.	Max.	Min.	Max.	Min.	Max.	Max.	Mean.
						per cent.	per cent.	f.s.	f.s.	Tons per sq. in.	Tons per sq. in.
Rifle Pistol	Webley Pistol	18 grs.	265 grs.	1·58	1·65	0·9	1·2	670*	710*	—	—
B.F.G.	Snider Rifle	70 grs.	480 grs.	1·58	1·62	0·9	1·2	1250	1290	—	—
R.F.G.³	M.H. Rifle	85 grs.	480 grs.	1·72	1·75	0·9	1·2	1300†	1340†	—	—
	7-pr. R.M.L., 200 lb.	12 oz.	7 lb.					960	1000	8·0	7·5
M.G.¹	1-in. Nordenfelt	625 grs.	3,170 grs.	1·75	—	1·0	1·3	1460	1520	12·0	11·5
Q.F¹	6-pr. Hotchkiss Q.F. Gun	1 lb. 15 oz.	6 lb.	1·75	—	1·0	1·3	1800	1840	14·5	14·0
	6-pr. Nordenfelt Q.F. Gun	1 lb. 15 oz.	6 lb.	1·75	—	1·0	1·3	1820	1860	14·5	14·0
	3-pr. Hotchkiss Q.F. Gun	1 lb. 8 oz.	3 lb. 5 oz.	1·75	—	1·0	1·3	1820	1860	13·5	13·0
	3-pr. Nordenfelt Q.F. Gun	1 lb. 8 oz.	3 lb. 5 oz.	1·75	—	1·0	1·3	1900	1940	13·5	13·0
R.L.G.	9-pr. R.M.L. Gun.	1¾ lb.	9 lb.	1·67	1·69	—	—	1385	1435	—	—
B.L.G.³	13-pr. R.M.L. Gun	3 7/16 lb.	13 lb.	1·65	—	1·0	1·3	1540	1590	16·5	16·0
R.L.G.⁴	64-pr. R.M.L. Gun	11 lb.	67¼ lb.	1·65	—	1·0	1·3	1380	1420	17·0	16·5
P.	6-in. B.L. (80-pr.)	34 lb.	80 lb.	1·75	—	1·0	1·3	1890	1930	16·5	16·0
S.P.	12-pr. B.L.	4 lb.	12½ lb.	1·75	—	1·0	1·3	1690	1730	14·5	14·0
P².	12·5 in. R.M.L.	200 lb.	812 lb.	1·75	—	1·0	1·3	1540	—	22·0	21·0
Prism¹—Black	12·5-in. R.M.L.	210 lb.	812 lb.	1·76	—	1·0	1·3	1530	1570	20·0	19·0
Prism¹—Brown	11-in. B.L.	295 lb.	655 lb.	1·80	—	1·7	2·2	1980	2020	17·5	17·0
E.X.E.	6-in. B.L., IV.	48 lb.	100 lb.	1·80	—	1·5	2·0	1940	1980	17·0	16·5
S.B.C.	11-in. B.L.	360 lb.	655 lb.	1·85	—	1·7	2·2	2010	2050	16·5	16·0
S.B.C.	13·5-in. B.L.	630 lb.	1,250 lb.	1·85	—	1·7	2·2	1980	2020	17·0	16·5

* Observed velocity at 30 feet from muzzle.
† Should service solid case cartridges be employed for proof, the velocity to be 30 f.s. greater in each case.

APPENDIX V.

TABLE SHOWING THE CONDITIONS OF ACCEPTANCE OF SERVICE CORDITE.

*Nature of Cordite.	Dimensions.						Volatile Matter.	Gun.	Weight of Charge.	Gravi-metric Density.	Firing Proof.						
	Length.			Diameter.							Weight of Projectile.	Number of Rounds.	Muzzle Velocity.		Factor of Regularity.	Pressure.	
	Min.	Max.	Mean.	Min.	Max.	Mean.	Max.						Min.	Max.		Max. 1 round.	Mean.
	ins.	ins.	ins.	in.	in.	in.	per cent.		lb. oz.		lb. oz.		f.s.	f.s.		tons.	tons.
50/16	16	16·6	16·3	0·484	0·495	0·490	·6	12-inch B.L., VIII	167 8	—	850 0	3	2,350	2,400	The mean of the deviations of the muzzle velocities of the several rounds, from the mean muzzle velocity of all the rounds, not to exceed 10 f.s.	17	16·5
40	—	—	—	0·343	0·353	0·348	·6	9·2-inch B.L., Wire	63 0	—	380 0	3	—	—		—	—
30/14	13·2	13·8	13·5	0·258	0·268	0·263	·5	6-inch Q.F. ...	13 4	—	100 0	5	2,175	2,225		16	15·5
20/14	13·2	13·8	13·5	0·175	0·184	0·1795	·5	4·7-inch Q.F. ...	5 7	—	45 0	5	2,160	2,210		15·5	15
15/14	13·2	13·8	13·5	0·131	0·140	0·1355	·5	4-inch Q.F. 12-pr. Q.F., 12 cwt.	3 9 1 15	—	25 0 12 8	5 5	2,300 2,210	2,340 2,260		15·0 15·0	14·5 14·0
10	—	—	—	—	—	—	—	—	—	—	—	—	—	—		—	—
7¾/11	10·6	11·4	11·0	0·059	0·067	0·063	·4	5-inch B L., III, IV, V	4 7¼	113·18 / 0·24	50 0	5	1,745	1,795		15·5	15
5/11	10·7	11·3	11·0	0·042	0·046	0·044	·4	12-pr. B.L., I ...	1 0	114·5 / 0·242	12 8	10	1,660	1,700	Do. 5 f.s.	14·5	14
5	On drums.							6-inch B.L., Howitzer	1 13	126·4	118 8	3	770	790	Do.	11·0	—
3¾	On drums.			0·0303	0·0343	0·0323	·4	5-inch B L., Howitzer	C 11 7/4	0·219 / 104·34 / 0·266	50 0	5	760	780		11·0	—
								·303 Mag. Rifle	31 ± ·5 grs	Mean f. of m. of five targets, 20 rounds each at 500 yards, not to exceed 3 inches.	—	—	1,910 Obs. vely. at 90 ft.	1,990 Obs. vely. at 90 ft.	—	16	15
20 S.C.	Thickness of flakes, 0′ ·0053 ± 0″ ·0025.						—	·303 Mag. Rifle	10 grs.	50 rounds in service ·303 Mark V blank, to fire correctly.					To be dry, homogeneous, and free from fine dust.		

* The numerator gives, in hundredths of an inch, the nominal diameter of the die through which the cordite is pressed, the denominator, the length of the sticks in inches. S.C. means "Sliced Cordite."

APPENDIX VI.

TABLE SHOWING THE GUNS FOR WHICH THE VARIOUS SIZES OF CORDITE ARE INTENDED.

Nature of Ordnance.	50	40	30	20	15	10	7¼	5	3¾	3¾/S.C.
	lb. oz.	lb. oz.	lb. oz.	lb. oz.	lb. oz.	lb. oz.	lb. oz.	lb. oz.	lb. oz.	lb. oz.
B.L. Guns.										
12-inch, I, III, IV, V, VI, VII	167 8	—	—	—	—	—	—	—	—	—
12-inch, VIII, wire	—	—	88 8*	—	—	—	—	—	—	—
10-inch, I, II, III, IV	—	—	76 0*	—	—	—	—	—	—	—
9.2-inch, I-VII	—	—	50 8*	—	—	—	—	—	—	—
9.2-inch, wire	—	68 0*	—	—	—	—	—	—	—	—
8-inch, III	—	—	—	28 12*	—	—	—	—	—	—
8-inch, IV, VI	—	—	—	32 10*	—	—	—	—	—	—
6-inch, III, IV, V, VI	—	—	—	14 12	—	—	—	—	—	—
5-inch, II, III, IV, V	—	—	—	—	—	—	4 7¼	—	—	—
4-inch, II, III, IV, V, VII	—	—	—	—	—	2 6	—	3 1	—	—
30-pr., I	—	—	—	—	—	—	—	0 15¾	—	—
12-pr. 7 cwt., I	—	—	—	—	—	—	—	0 15¾	—	—
15-pr. 7 cwt., I	—	—	—	—	—	—	—	0 12 15⁄16	—	—
12-pr. 6 cwt., I	—	—	—	—	—	—	—	—	—	—
Q.F. Guns.										
6-inch, I, II, III	—	—	13 4	5 7	—	—	—	—	—	—
4.7-inch, I, II, III, IV	—	—	—	—	3 9	—	—	—	—	—
4-inch, I	—	—	—	—	1 15	1 9¼†	—	—	—	—
12-pr. 12 cwt., I	—	—	—	—	—	0 13¼*	—	—	—	—
12-pr. 8 cwt. I	—	—	—	—	—	—	—	—	—	—
6-pr. N. and H.	—	—	—	—	—	—	—	0 7¼	—	—
3-pr. N. and H.	—	—	—	—	—	—	—	0 6 15⁄16	—	—

* Provisional.   † Alternative.

APPENDIX VI.—continued.

Nature of Ordnance.	Size of Cordite and Weight of Charge.								
	50	40	30	20	15	10	7¼	5	3¾	3¾ S.G.
	lb. oz.	lb. oz.	lb. oz.	lb. oz.	lb. oz.	lb. oz.	lb. oz.	lb. oz.	lb. oz.	lb. oz.
B.L. HOWITZERS.										
8-inch	—	—	—	—	—	—	4 8*	—	—	—
6-inch 30 cwt.	—	—	—	—	—	—	—	1 13*	2 1*	—
6-inch 25 cwt., I	—	—	—	—	—	—	—	—	0 13½*	—
5·4-inch, I	—	—	—	—	—	—	—	—	0 11 7⁄16	—
5-inch, I	—	—	—	—	—	—	—	—	—	—
									grs.	grs.
SMALL ARMS AND MACHINE GUNS.										
M.-H. Rifle, rolled case	—	—	—	—	—	—	—	—	43½	—
M.-H. Rifle and Carbine, solid case	—	—	—	—	—	—	—	—	48¼	—
·303-inch, Mark II, Rifle and Machine Gun	—	—	—	—	—	—	—	—	31	9
·303-inch, Mark I, Short Range Practice	—	—	—	—	—	—	—	—	—	6¼
Pistol, Webley, Mark I	—	—	—	—	—	—	—	—	46	—
Machine Gun, M.-H. Chamber	—	—	—	—	—	—	—	—	—	—
Machine Gun, ·45-inch, G.G. Chamber	—	—	—	—	—	—	—	—	48½	—

* Provisional.

APPENDIX VII.

EXPLOSIVES ACT, 1875.

HEAT TEST AS APPLIED TO EXPLOSIVES OF THE NITRO-COMPOUND CLASS (as defined by Order in Council, No. 1, of 5th August, 1875).

GENERAL INSTRUCTIONS.

Apparatus Required.

1. A water bath, consisting of a spherical glass or copper vessel (*a*) Fig. I., of about 8 inches diameter, and with an aperture of about 5 inches; the bath is filled with water to within a quarter of an inch of the edge. It has a loose cover of sheet copper about 6 inches in diameter (*b*), and rests on a tripod stand about 14 inches high (*c*), which is covered with coarse iron wire gauze (*e*), and is surrounded with a screen of thin sheet tin or copper (*d*). Within the latter is placed an Argand burner (*f*), with glass chimney. The cover (*b*) has four holes arranged as seen in Fig. II., No. 4 to receive the regulator, No. 3 the thermometer, Nos. 1 and 2 the test-tubes containing the guncotton or other materials to be tested. Around holes 1 and 2 on the under side of the cover are soldered three pieces of brass wire with points slightly converging (Fig. III.); these act as springs and allow the test-tubes to be easily placed in position and removed.

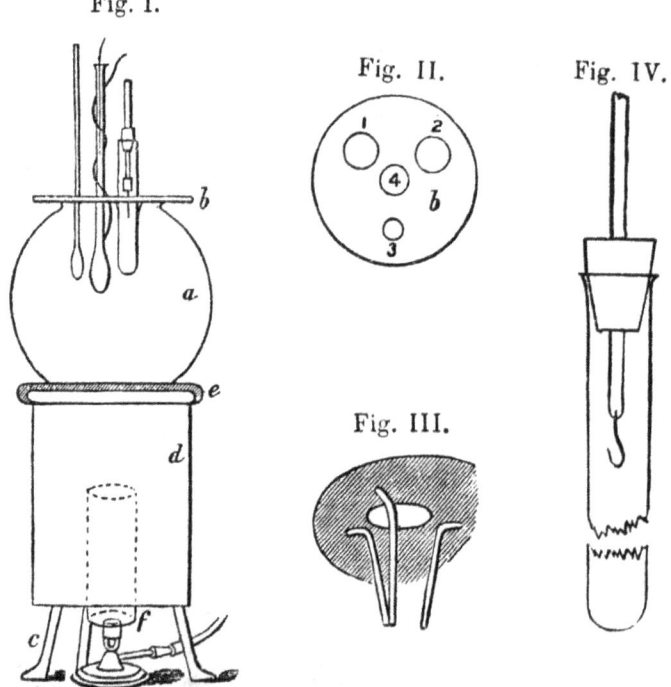

Fig. I.

Fig. II.

Fig. III.

Fig. IV.

*2. Scheibler's or Page's temperature regulator.
*3. Two cells of Le Clanché's battery No. 1 ⎫ if Scheibler's
*4. A few yards of insulated copper wire ⎭ regulator is used.

5. Test-tubes from $5\frac{1}{4}$ to $5\frac{1}{2}$ inches long, and of such diameter that they will hold from 20 to 22 cubic centimetres of water when filled to a height of 5 inches.

6. India-rubber stoppers, fitting the test-tubes and carrying an arrangement for holding the test-paper, viz., a narrow glass tube passing through the centre of the stopper, drawn out so as to form a hook, or terminating in a platinum wire hook (Fig. IV.).

7. A thermometer, with range not less than from 30° to 212° F.

8. A minute clock.

Materials required.

a. *Test-paper.*—The test-paper is prepared as follows:— 45 grains of white maize starch (cornflour), previously washed with cold water, are added to $8\frac{1}{2}$ ounces of distilled water, the mixture is stirred, heated to boiling, and kept gently boiling for 10 minutes; 15 grains of pure potassium iodide (*i.e.*, which has been re-crystallised from alcohol) are dissolved in $8\frac{1}{2}$ ounces of distilled water. The two solutions are thoroughly mixed and allowed to get cold. Strips, or sheets, of smooth white English filter paper, previously washed with water and re-dried, are dipped into the solution thus prepared, weighing, air dry, about 6·5 grams per 100 square inches, and allowed to remain in it for not less than 10 seconds; they are then allowed to drain and dry in a place free from laboratory fumes and dust. The upper and lower margins of the strips, or sheets, are cut off and the paper is preserved in well stoppered or cork bottles *and in the dark.*† The dimensions of the pieces of test-paper used are about $\frac{4}{10}$ inch by $\frac{8}{10}$ inch (10 mm. by 20 mm.).

b. *Standard tint-paper.*—A solution of caramel in water is made of such concentration that when diluted one hundred times (10 cc. made up to 1 litre) the tint of this diluted solution equals the tint produced by the Nessler test in 100 cc. water containing 0·00075 grm. of ammonia or 0·00023505 grm.

---

* This is not absolutely required, as the temperature of the bath can be kept constant by proper attention to the heating flame.

† When a paper is freshly prepared, and as long as it remains in good condition, a drop of dilute acetic acid, put on the paper with a glass rod, produces no colouration. In process of time, however, the stronger the light to which the paper is exposed the sooner a drop of acid produces a brown or bluish coloration (a single hour of direct sunlight produces a marked effect), and whenever this is the case the paper should be rejected. After preparation the paper should be kept in the dark for a month before being taken into use. After that, if carefully kept in the dark, it will remain good for six months or more, but should be tested from time to time, as above.

of chloride of ammonium. With this caramel solution lines are drawn on strips of white filter paper* by means of a clean quill pen. When the marks thus produced are dry, the paper is cut into pieces of the same size as the test-paper previously described, in such a way that each piece has a brown line across it near the middle of its length, and only such strips are preserved in which the brown line has a breadth varying from ½ mm. to 1 mm. ($\frac{1}{50}$ of an inch to $\frac{1}{25}$ of an inch).

I.—Testing Dynamite, Blasting Gelatine, and Other Explosives of the First Division of the Nitro-compound Class.

A.—Dynamite, &c., &c.

Nitro-glycerine preparations, from which the nitro-glycerine can be extracted in the manner described below, *must* satisfy the following test.

This test, however, though at present looked upon as the most important, as far as testing the purity of the nitro-glycerine is concerned, is only one of several which any given sample of nitro-glycerine preparation has to satisfy in order to establish its compliance with the definition in the Authorised List.

Apparatus required.

A funnel 2 inches across (*d*), a cylindrical measure divided into grains (*e*). (*See* sketch.)

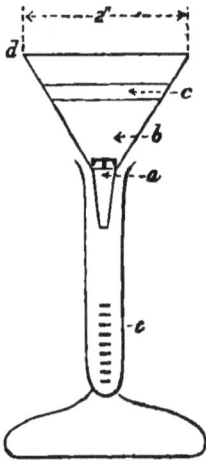

---

* This paper must be carefully washed with distilled water in the first instance, to remove any traces of bleaching matter, and dried.

Mode of operation.

About 300 to 400 grains of dynamite (*b*) finely divided, are placed into the funnel, which has previously been loosely plugged by some freshly ignited asbestos (*a*).

The surface is smoothed by means of a flat-headed glass rod or stopper, and some clean washed and dried Kieselguhr (*c*) is spread over it to the depth of about $\frac{1}{8}$ inch.

Water is next carefully dropped from a wash bottle upon this Kieselguhr, and when the first portion has been soaked up, more is added; this is repeated until sufficient nitro-glycerine has been collected in the graduated measure (*e*) below.

If any water should have passed through with the nitro-glycerine, it should be removed with a piece of blotting-paper, and the nitro-glycerine, if necessary, filtered through a dry paper filter.*

Application of the Test.

The thermometer is fixed so as to be inserted through the lid of the water bath described under 1, page 1, into the water (which is to be steadily maintained at a temperature of 160° F.†) to a depth of $2\frac{3}{4}$ inches. Fifty grains of nitro-glycerine, to be tested, are weighed into a test-tube in such a way as not to soil the sides of the tube. A test-paper is fixed on the hook of the glass rod so that when inserted into the tube it will be in a vertical position. A sufficient amount of a mixture of half distilled water and half glycerine to moisten the upper half of the paper is now applied to the upper edge of the test-paper, by means of a camel's hair pencil, the cork carrying the rod and paper is fixed into the test-tube and the position of the paper adjusted so that its lower edge is about half way down the tube; the latter is then inserted through one of the perforations of the cover to such a depth that the lower margin of the moistened part of the paper is about five-eighths of an inch above the surface of the cover. The test is complete when the faint brown line which after a time makes its appearance is at the line of boundary between the dry and moist part of the paper equals in tint the brown line of the standard tint paper.

The nitro glycerine under examination will not be considered to have satisfied the test unless the time necessary to produce the standard tint as above described is at *least* 15 minutes.

---

* A filter suction pump is very useful for this.
† For explosives supplied for His Majesty's Military and Naval Services the temperature is fixed by the War Office at 180°.

B.—BLASTING GELATINE, GELATINE DYNAMITE, AND ANALOGOUS PREPARATIONS.

Fifty (50) grains of blasting gelatine are to be intimately incorporated with one hundred (100) grains of French chalk.* The mixture is to be gradually introduced into a test-tube of the dimensions prescribed above for the dynamite heat test, with the aid of gentle tapping upon the table, between the introduction of successive portions of the mixture into the tube, so that when the tube contains all the mixture it shall be filled to the extent of 1¾ inches (one inch and three quarters) of its height. The test-paper is then to be inserted and the heat is to be applied in the manner prescribed above for the dynamite heat test, and the sample tested is to withstand exposure to 160° Fahr. for a period of ten (10) minutes, before producing a discolouration of the test-papers corresponding in tint to the standard colour test which is employed for governing the results of the dynamite heat test.

(For Exudation and Liquefaction tests for Blasting Gelatine, &c., &c., see Appendix).

N.B. Non-gelatinized nitro-glycerine preparations, from which the nitro-glycerine cannot be expelled by water, are tested without any previous separation of the ingredients, the temperature being as above (160° Fahr.) and the time being seven (7) minutes.

C.—CORDITE AND BALLISTITE.

1. *Apparatus required.*

The apparatus necessary for the application of the heat test to cordite is identical with that described above (*see* page 128) for Explosives of the nitro-compound class generally† with the addition of a mill and a nest of sieves‡ similar to those used at Waltham Abbey for preparing the cordite for testing (*see* instructions below).

---

* This can be readily affected by carefully working the two materials together with a wooden pestle in a wooden mortar.

The French chalk should be of good commercial quality, and, after being carefully washed with distilled water and dried in a water oven, it should be exposed under a bell jar to moist air until it has taken up about 0·5 per cent. of moisture. It should then be bottled for use: and with ordinary care the limits of 0·5 per cent. can be maintained in keeping.

† In the Waltham Abbey apparatus the cover (Fig. II.) has all the holes around the circumference instead of having one in the centre and three around the circumference.

‡ A nest of two sieves with holes drilled in sheet copper. The holes in the top sieve have a diameter = 14 B.W.G.; those in the second = 21 B.W.G.

If too hard for the mill, it may be softened by exposure to the vapour of acetone, or reduced to the necessary degree of sub-division by means of a sharp moderately coarse rasp, or better by "scraping" with a sharp knife, the edge being held perpendicularly to the side of the rod of cordite. Should it have become too soft in the acetone vapour for the mill, it should be cut up into small pieces which may be brought to any desired degree of hardness by simple exposure to air.

Explosives which consist partly of gelatinized collodion cotton and partly of ungelatinized guncotton are best reduced to powder by a rasp, or softened by exposure to mixed ether and alcohol vapour at a temperature of 90° to 100° Fahr.

2. Preparation of the Sample to be Tested.

Pieces half an inch long are cut from one end of every stick selected for the test; in the case of the thicker cordites, each piece so cut is further subdivided into about four portions. These cut pieces are then passed once through the mill, the first portion of material which passes through being rejected on account of the possible presence of foreign matter from the mill. The ground material is put on the top sieve of the nest of sieves, and sifted. That portion which has passed through the top sieve, and been stopped by the second, is taken for the test. If the mill is properly set, the greater portion of the ground material will be of the proper size.

If the volatile matter in the explosive exceeds 0·5 per cent. the sifted material should be dried at a temperature not exceeding 140° F. until the proportion does not exceed 0·5 per cent.

After each sample has been ground, the mill must be taken to pieces and carefully cleaned.

3. Application of the Test.

The thermometer is fixed so as to be inserted through the lid of the water bath, described under 1, page 128, so as to be immersed in the water to a depth of $2\frac{3}{4}$ inches. The water is maintained at a constant temperature of 180° F. When this temperature is reached 25 grains of the sifted cordite are put into one of the test-tubes, and collected at the bottom by gentle tapping. A test-paper is fixed on to the hook of the glass rod, so that when inserted into the tube it will be in a vertical position. A mixture of equal parts of distilled water and pure glycerine (Price's) is now applied to the upper edge of the test-paper by means of a camel's hair pencil, in sufficient amount to moisten the upper half; the stopper carrying the rod and paper is fixed into the test-tube, and the position of the paper adjusted so that its lower edge is about half-way down the tube; the latter is then inserted through one of the perforations of the cover to the same depth as the thermometer. The lower margin of the moistened part of the paper should then be about five-eighths of an inch above the surface of the cover. The test is completed when the faint brown line, which after a time makes its appearance at the margin between the wet and dry portions of the test-paper, equals in depth of tint the brown line drawn on the standard tint paper.

4. The time which elapses between the insertion of the test-tube and the completion of the test must not be less than 15 minutes.

N.B. In the case of ballistite the treatment is the same, except that when it is in a very finely granulated condition it need not be cut up.

II.—Testing Guncotton, Schultze Gunpowder, E.C. Powder, and other Explosives of the 2nd Division of the Nitro-Compound Class.

A.—Compressed Nitro-Cellulose, Tonite, &c., &c.

Sufficient material to serve for two or more tests is removed from the centre of the cartridge by gentle scraping, and, if necessary, further reduced by rubbing through a sieve with a clean hard brush.

The fine powder thus produced is spread out in a thin layer upon a paper tray 6 inches by $4\frac{1}{2}$ inches which is then placed inside a water oven, kept, as nearly as possible, at 120° F.

The wire gauze shelves in the oven should be about 3 inches apart. The sample is allowed to remain at rest for 15 minutes in the oven, the door of which is left wide open.

After the lapse of 15 minutes the tray is removed and exposed to the air of the room for two hours, the sample being at some point within that time rubbed upon the tray with a brush, in order to reduce it to a fine and uniform state of division.

Application of the Test.

The cover of the water bath is fitted with the gas regulator, which is inserted through the centre hole (No. 4). The thermometer is fixed into hole No. 3. The water in the bath is then heated to 170° F., and the regulator set to maintain that temperature. Twenty grains of the sample to be tested are weighed out, placed in the test-tube, and gently pressed down until the specimen occupies a space of not more than $1\frac{5}{16}$ inches in a test-tube of the dimensions specified. A test-paper is affixed to the hook of the glass rod or tube, and moistened by touching the upper edge with a drop of distilled water containing 50 per cent. of Price's glycerine. The quantity of liquid used must be only sufficient to moisten about half of the paper. The cork carrying the rod and test-paper is then fixed into the test-tube, and the latter inserted into the bath to a depth of $2\frac{1}{2}$ inches, measured from the cover, the regulator and thermometer being inserted to the same depth. The test-paper is to be kept near the top of the test-tube, but clear of the cork, until the tube has been immersed for about five minutes. A ring of moisture will about this time be deposited upon the sides of the test-tube a little above the cover of the bath; the glass rod must then be lowered until the lower margin of the moistened part of the paper is on a level with the bottom of the ring of moisture in the tube; the paper is now closely watched. The test is complete when the faint brown line which makes its appearance at the line of boundary between the dry and moist parts of the paper equals in tint the brown line of the standard tint paper.

The interval of time between the first insertion of the tube containing the sample of guncotton in the water at 170° and the production of the standard tint constitutes the test, and this interval of time must be *not less* than ten minutes, or the sample will not be considered to have satisfied the test.

B.—Gelatinized and Semi-Gelatinized Nitro-cellulose Preparations.*

Twenty-five grains introduced into the test-tube* of the dimensions prescribed for the dynamite heat test, then proceed as for Blasting Gelatine, &c., taking the temperature at 180° F., and the time as 15 minutes.

C.—Nitro-cellulose not included in A. or B., Schultze Powder, E.C. Powder, &c., &c.

Sufficient of the sample, without further mechanical division, is dried in the oven as above, and then exposed for two hours to the air. The test as directed above for compressed nitro-cellulose, &c., is then applied, the minimum duration of test being the same, viz., 10 minutes.

D.—Picric Acid.

(1.) The material shall contain not more than 0·3 part of mineral or non-combustible matter in 100 parts by weight of the material dried at 160° F.

(2.) It should not contain more than a minute trace of lead.

(3.) One hundred parts of the dry material shall not contain more than 0·3 part of *total* (free and combined) sulphuric acid, of which not more than 0·1 part shall be *free* sulphuric acid.

(4.) Its melting point should be between 248° and 253° F.

E.—Ammonite, Bellite, Roburite and Explosives of Similar Composition.

These are required to stand the same heat test as compressed Nitro-cellulose (*see ante* p. 134).

III.—Testing Chlorate Mixtures.

The material must not be too sensitive† and must show no tendency to increase in sensitiveness on keeping.

The material must contain nothing liable to reduce the chlorate.

---

* If in a compressed form it should be broken up in the same manner as cordite and ballistite.

† They will be considered too sensitive if they can be exploded however partially by means of a glancing blow with a broomstick on soft wood (such as deal).

Chlorides calculated as potassium chloride must not exceed 0·25 per cent.

The material must contain no free acid, or substance liable to produce free acid.

Explosives of this class containing nitro-compounds will be subject to the heat test as if they belonged to Class III.

J. H. THOMSON,
Captain,
H.M. Chief Inspector of Explosives.

Home Office, Whitehall, S.W.
1st January, 1906.

APPENDIX VIII.

EXUDATION AND LIQUEFACTION TEST FOR BLASTING GELATINE, GELATINE DYNAMITE, AND ANALOGOUS PREPARATIONS.

TEST FOR LIQUEFACTION.

A cylinder of blasting gelatine is to be cut from the cartridge to be tested, the length of the cylinder to be about equal to its diameter and the ends being cut flat.

The cylinder is to be placed on end on a flat surface without any wrapper, and secured by a pin passing vertically through its centre.

In this condition the cylinder is to be exposed for one hundred and forty-four (144) consecutive hours (six days and nights to a temperature ranging from 85° to 90° F. (inclusive), and during such exposure the cylinder shall not diminish in height by more than one-fourth of its original height, and the upper cut surface shall retain its flatness and the sharpness of its edge.

Note.—If the blasting gelatine and the gelatine dynamite to be tested be not made up in a cylindrical form, the above test is to be applied with the necessary modifications.

TEST FOR LIABILITY TO EXUDATION.

There shall be no separation from the general mass of the blasting gelatine or gelatine dynamite of a substance of less consistency than the bulk of the remaining portion of the materials under any conditions of storage, transport, or use, or when the material is subjected three times in succession to alternate freezing and thawing, or when subjected to the liquefaction test hereinbefore described.

Fig. I.

Apparatus for Extraction with Ether

*Soxhlet's Circular Water Bath,
with stand extractors and condensers*

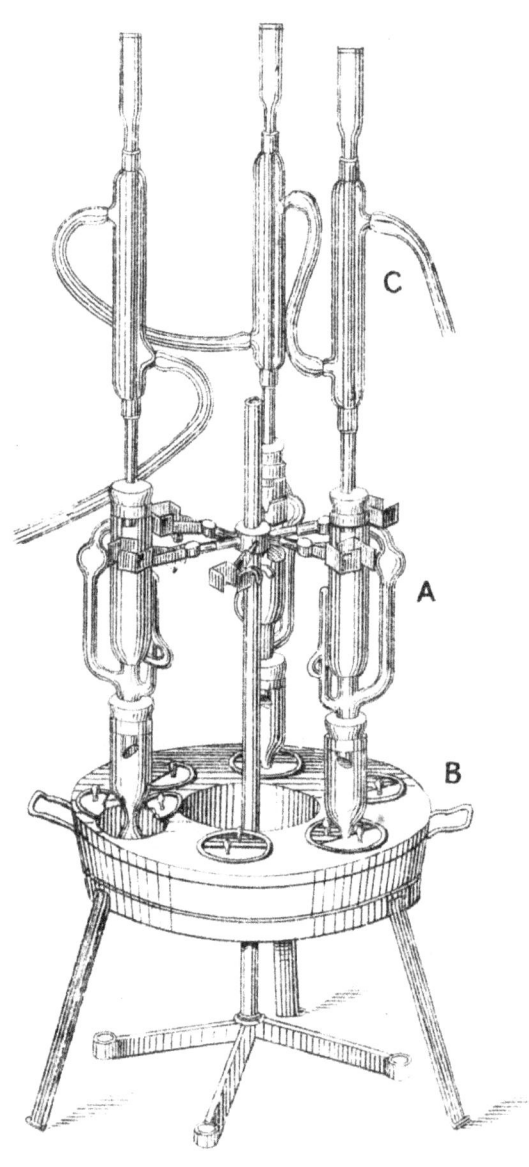

APPENDIX IX.

STABILITY TEST.

QUANTITATIVE.

General Instructions.

I.—APPLICATION OF STABILITY TEST AT 70° C.

The chief advantage of working under these conditions is that cordite can be examined directly.

Preparation of Bath.

The bath (Fig. 2) is first filled to within two inches of the lid with commercial methyl alcohol, which boils somewhat below 70° C. The condenser is fitted to the bath and the lower opening of its jacket connected to the water supply by means of a piece of rubber tubing. The other tube of the condenser is led to the sink, and a gentle current of water is allowed to flow through the condenser. The copper tubes in the cover of the bath are then filled with heavy mineral oil (cylinder oil), so much being added that the well in the bath is about half filled. The thermometer is allowed to rest in one of the large holes in the bath. The bath is now heated to boiling by means of a Bunsen burner or lamp, and the temperature read as soon as it becomes constant. The alcohol must not boil too vigorously, otherwise the condensation may not be complete. The temperature will be found to lie somewhat below 70° C. A little water is added and the temperature again allowed to become constant. It will be found to be somewhat higher than before. The addition of water is continued until the resultant mixture keeps the bath at a constant temperature of 70° C. when allowed to boil gently. Care should be taken not to add too much water, as a considerable quantity of methyl alcohol will be required to reduce the boiling point to 70° C if excess of water be added. The deviation of the temperature from 70° C. should not exceed 0·2° to 0·3°. It is advisable to protect the flame from draughts by a screen in order to ensure constancy of boiling. The liquid in the bath should not be within 1 inch of the lid when the bath is in use.

Preparation of the Glass Apparatus.

This must be carefully cleaned and dried. The capillary tubes are best dried by allowing them to stand in a warm place, and drawing a current of air through them. (In default of any mechanical apparatus for passing air through the tubes, this may be done by suction with the mouth; blowing through the tubes must, of course, be avoided.

Application of the Test at 70° C.

For the introduction of the mercury into the manometer, a small measuring tube is provided, which holds the required amount when filled up to the mark. This quantity is measured out, and poured into the cup at the top of the manometer tube. The mercury should form an unbroken column in the tube, containing no air bubbles, and should fill the vertical tubes to about half their height. Air bubbles in the open limb of the manometer are best removed by passing a thin iron wire down the tube; wire of other metals must not be used, since most of these amalgamate with mercury. Any bubbles introduced into the closed limb should be removed by tapping. The scale is then fitted to the manometer.

The powder is not ground, but is cut into lengths of approximately 8·5 centimetres ($3\frac{1}{4}$ inches). Fifty grammes of the powder are introduced into the heating vessel. Five grammes of the granulated calcium chloride are weighed into the drying vessel, which is then fitted into the hollow stopper, and the latter lubricated with a mixture of beeswax and adeps lanae.

The heating vessel containing the powder is then inverted and fitted on to the stopper, a gentle pressure being applied to ensure that the connection is perfectly gas-tight. The stopper is made tight with the help of the spring clip, the tap D being allowed to remain open.

The heating tube is now introduced into one of the large holes in the bath, the manometer being supported by allowing the glass rod F to rest upon the horizontal rod of the retort stand. The thermometer is placed beside the vessel in the same orifice.

The time is noted at which the heating commences, and the tap is closed after four hours. The manometer tube is now tapped gently to allow the mercury to adjust itself accurately, and the level of the mercury is read in the two tubes with the help of a lens. The mercury should stand at the same height in the two tubes. If this is not the case, the difference is probably due to enclosed air bubbles, which should be searched for and removed by careful tapping. The corrected barometric height and the temperature of the bath are noted at the same time. Three readings are taken on each following day, at the beginning, middle, and end of the working day respectively, until the test is complete, as indicated below. The reading consists in measuring the difference between the heights of the mercury columns in the two tubes (after gentle tapping) by means of the millimetre scale provided; the barometer reading

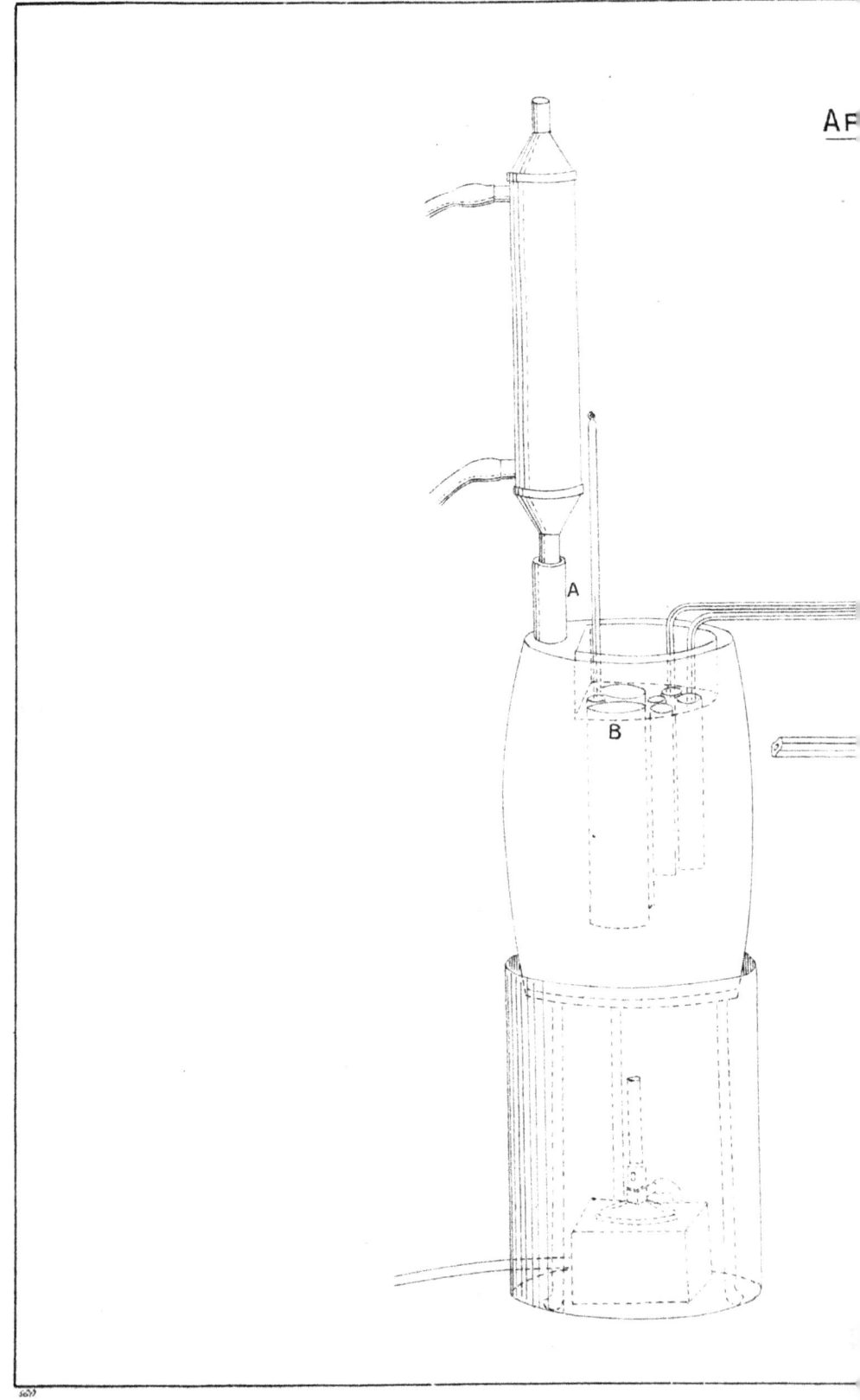

Fig. 2.
us for Stability Determination.

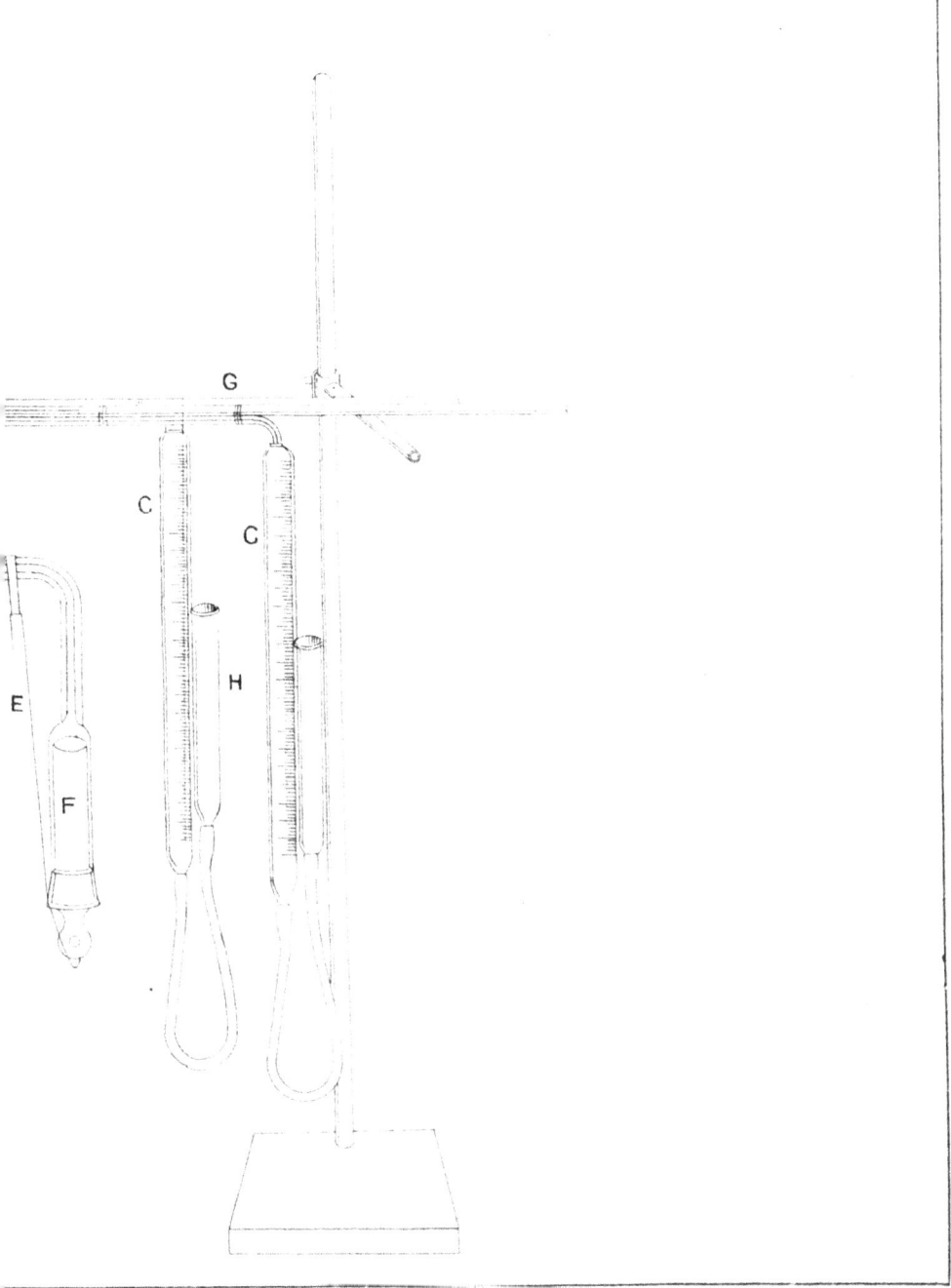

(corrected for temperature) and temperature of the bath being noted at the same time. The manometer readings should be accurate to the nearest 0·5 millimetre, care being taken to avoid errors due to parallax.

After the experiment, the mercury is filtered and returned to the bottle, a filter funnel being provided for this purpose. A sheet of paper about 5 inches square is folded twice at right angles and opened out into a cone, the apex of which is then pierced with a pin. The cone is fitted into the filter funnel, and the mercury allowed to pass through the hole. Care must be taken that the mercury does not come in contact with any metal with which it might amalgamate.

Calculation of Results.

From the readings of the pressure, the alterations in volume are calculated as follows:—The total capacity of the vessel is known (90 cubic centimetres). This must first be corrected for the volume of the powder and of the drying vessel. The volume of 50 grammes of Cordite Mark I or M.D. may be taken as approximately 31·5 cubic centimetres. That of the drying vessel filled with calcium chloride may be taken as 3·0 cubic centimetres. Thus the corrected capacity of the vessel is 55·5 cubic centimetres. It may be assumed that this volume undergoes no alteration, when the height of the column of mercury in the capillary tube changes by a few centimetres.

The variations in the specific gravity of Cordite are insufficient to cause any material alteration in the results. In applying the test to nitro-cellulose, the volume of 50 grammes should be calculated from the specific gravity of the powder under investigation.

The pressure under which this volume of gas exists at the time of reading is ascertained by correcting the barometric reading by the difference in height of the mercury columns in the two limbs of the capillary tube. Thus, if the mercury column in the open tube be higher than in the closed tube of the manometer, the difference is added to the barometric reading. If the height in the closed tube be greater, the difference is subtracted from the barometric reading. If the barometer be graduated in inches, the readings may be converted to millimetres by multiplying by 25·400. Since the temperature t of the heated vessel is known, the corrected volume can be calculated from the formula:—

$$\text{Corr. Vol.} = V \times \frac{273}{273 + t} \times \frac{P}{760}$$

where V and P are the volume and pressure respectively.

It is convenient to plot the results in curves, the times being taken as abscissæ, and the corrected volumes as ordinates.

Nitro-celluloses give a gradual evolution of gas, the rapidity of which forms a measure of the degree of instability of the powder. A powder which gives an evolution exceeding 5 cubic centimetres per 24 hours should be condemned as unsafe for storage. (This limit is liable to further modification.)

In examining cordites by this method it is found that a gradual absorption of gas (oxygen) occurs at first. After some time a minimum is reached, and then a gradual expansion is observed. The experiment should be proceeded with, until two successive readings show that the minimum has been passed, and that an expansion is occurring.

The stability of cordites is judged of by the initial velocity of gas absorption, and by the time required to reach the minimum absorption. The initial velocity of absorption is found by determining the time necessary for the absorption of approximately 5 cubic centimetres of gas, and calculating from it the number of cubic centimetres absorbed per 10 hours. The time required to reach the minimum is estimated directly from the curve.

The limits which indicate the safety of the powder for storage are as follows:—

Safety limits at 70 degrees.

	Initial Velocity (cubic centimetres absorbed per 10 hours).	Duration of Contraction (hours from time of closing tap).
Cordite Mark I	4	20
,, M.D.	4	20

If a greater initial velocity be observed, or if the minimum be reached in less than the prescribed time, the powder is to be considered unsafe for storage. (These limits are liable to further modification.)

If the minimum be passed during the first night, as indicated by an increase of volume during the second morning, no deduction can, of course, be drawn as to the initial velocity. In this case, however, the rapidity with which the minimum is reached is in itself sufficient to show the instability of the powder.

If the corrected contraction does not reach 5 cubic centimetres during the second day, the experiment may be discontinued and the cordite regarded as safe for storage.

The temperature should not be allowed to deviate more than $0.5°$ from that specified ($70°$ C.). For small differences of temperature, a correction may be applied. A rise in temperature of $1°$ increases the velocity by approximately 8 per cent., and reduces the duration of the contraction in about the same ratio.

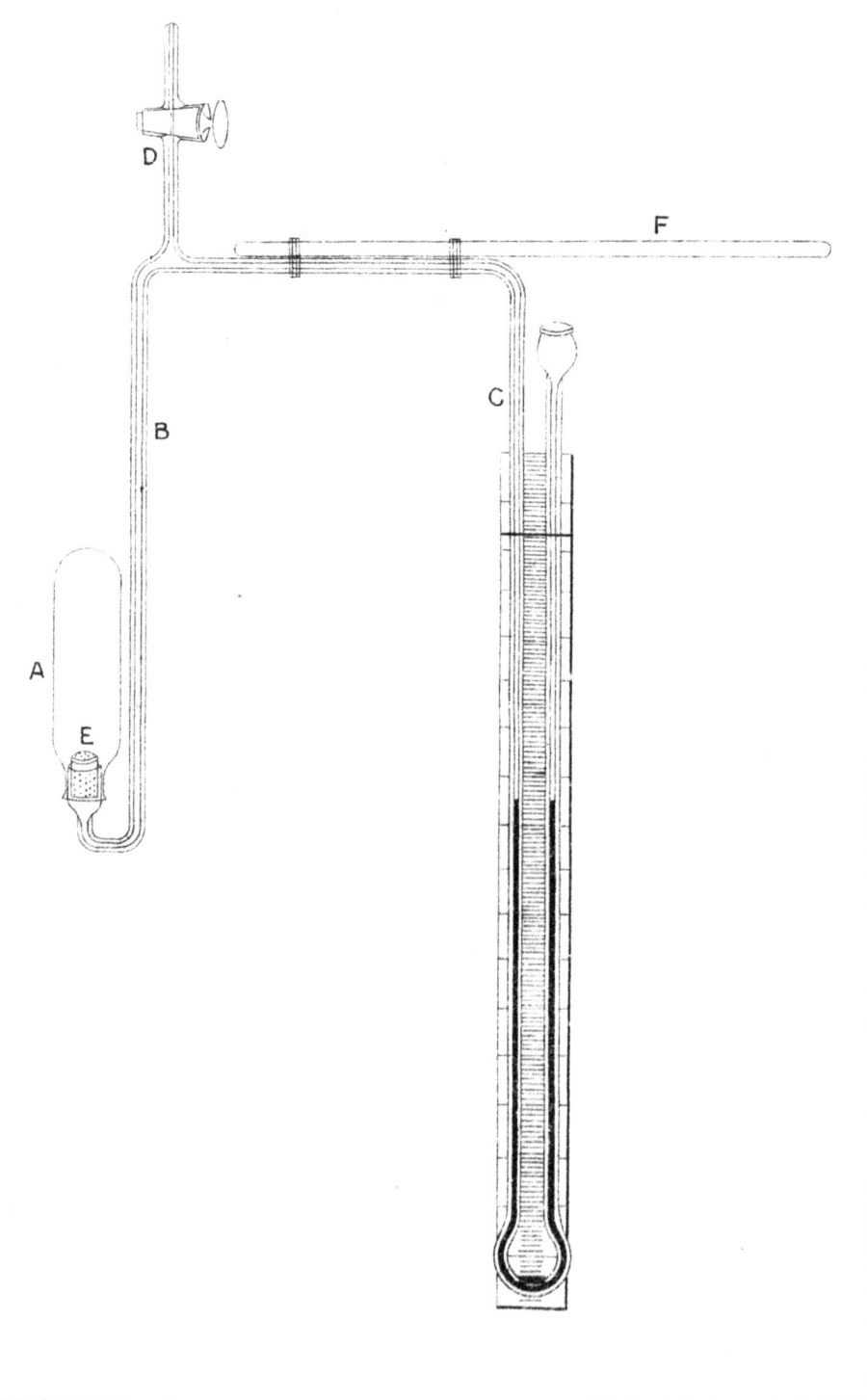

Example.—Stability of Cordite Mark I :—

Quantity = 50 grammes.
Capacity of vessel, and portion of capillary tube
(as indicated) .. .. 90·5 cc.
Volume of 50 grammes Cordite Mark I . .. 31·2 „
Volume of drying vessel and calcium chloride.. 2·2 „
Available space for gases.. .. .. .. 57·1 „
Introduced into bath, 29.11.04. 10.0 A.M.
Closed tap, 29.11.04. 2.0 P.M.

Date and Time.	No. of Hours from commencement.	Difference in height of mercury columns (mm).	Temperature of Bath (degrees C).	Barometer pressure (corr.) mm.	Corrected Volume ccm.	Alteration in Volume ccm.
29.11.04 2.0 P.M.	0	— 1·0	70·0	764·8	45·7	0
30.11.04 10.0 A.M.	20	— 83·5	70·2	765·0	40·7	—5·0
„ 1.0 P.M.	23	— 87·5	70·0	764·0	40·5	—5·2
„ 5.0 P.M.	27	— 95·0	70·1	763·4	40·0	—5·7
1.12.04 9.0 A.M.	43	—115·0	70·0	765·1	38·9	—6·8
„ 1.0 P.M.	47	—115·0	70·1	763·9	38·8	—6·9
„ 5.0 P.M.	51	—114·5	70·1	763·0	38·8	—6·9
2.12.04 9.0 A.M.	67	— 98·0	70·5	759·8	39·5	—6·2
„ 2.0 P.M.	72	— 95·0	69·9	757·7	39·6	—6·1

Initial velocity = 2·5 cubic centimetres per 10 hours.
Minimum reached 48 hours after closing tap.
Hence the cordite is safe for storage.

II.—APPLICATION OF STABILITY TEST AT 115 DEGREES C.

The chief use of this modification is the examination of nitro-cellulose powders and the residual nitro-cellulose from cordite, &c.

Preparation of Bath.

If the bath has been previously used for the test at 70° C., the methyl alcohol should be emptied out and preserved for future use. The bath (Fig. 2) is now filled to within 1½ inches of the lid with a mixture of three parts by volume of glycerine and one part of water. (This solution boils slightly above the temperature required for the test, viz., 115° C., at sea level.) The condenser is fitted to the bath and to the water supply as before. The copper tubes in the bath are filled with heavy mineral oil until the well is about half filled, and the thermometer is fitted into the small hole by means of a cork, so as to reach nearly to the bottom. The bath is now heated to boiling with a large Bunsen burner or lamp, and the temperature read as soon as it becomes constant.

Should the temperature be found to lie above 115° C., as will generally be the case except at high altitudes, a little more water should be added, and the temperature again allowed to become constant. If the boiling point be below 115° C., more glycerine must be added. The addition of too much water is to be avoided, as a large quantity of glycerine is required to restore the boiling point to 115° C. if the solution be made too dilute. In this manner the temperature should be regulated until it is within about 0·2° to 0·3° of the required temperature. It is advisable to protect the flame from draughts by a screen in order to ensure constancy of boiling.

Preparation of Air Bath.

The water-jacketted air-bath is provided with a thermometer and thermoregulator; its temperature is regulated to 60° C., and the temperature should not fluctuate more than 3° on either side of this.

Extraction of Cordite with Ether.

Soxhlet's extraction apparatus.—This is shown in Fig. 1. The cordite to be extracted is put into a "thimble" of filter paper, as manufactured for this purpose. This is introduced into the extractor, A, which is then adapted, by means of a cork, to the flask, B, containing the ether. A condenser, C, is attached to the upper end of the extractor, and kept cool by means of a current of water, whose temperature must not be more than 12° C., unless more effective condensers are used (as, for instance, Allihn's). The ether is kept gently boiling on a water bath. The ether vapour passes through the bye-pass from the flask to the condenser, where it is condensed and drops back on to the Cordite. When the ether reaches the level of the top of the syphon it flows over and passes back into the lower flask. The same process is repeated automatically, and in this manner very perfect extraction may be attained with a limited quantity of ether. The amount of ether must be about twice as much as will fill the extractor to the level of the top of the syphon. The residual ether containing nitro-glycerine should be destroyed after each experiment by pouring it into a flat vessel and burning it. The ether burns very vigorously, and so should not be destroyed in large quantities.

Preparation of the Glass Apparatus.

This must, of course, be thoroughly cleansed from all traces of matter from the previous experiment. It is necessary to emphasise the importance of drying the apparatus thoroughly before use; if it has stood for some time, a film of moisture may be present on the glass. It is, therefore desirable to place the burettes and heating tubes in a hot atmosphere for some hours before use, as for instance, by placing them on the top of the heated air bath. The fittings are all arranged as indicated in Appendix C, and the stopper is lubricated with a mixture of beeswax and adeps lanae. The burette is then almost filled with a saturated solution of common salt, the reservoir being fixed so that the brine can be retained at this level whilst the powder is being introduced into the apparatus. It is well to renew the salt solution for each test.

Preparation of Nitro-cellulose Powders for the Test at $115°$ C.

The nitro-cellulose is ground and sifted though sieves containing 30 and 60 meshes to the inch respectively, and the portion retained between the two sieves is used for the test. For this purpose 2 grammes (30·9 grains) of the ground powder are weighed out on to a watch glass. This is laid on a glass tripod in a flat-bottomed glass dish, containing a layer of calcium chloride (granular), which must be renewed for each experiment. The glass dish is covered with a watch-glass and placed in an air oven, regulated to $60°$ C., as above. It is allowed to remain at this temperature for 20 hours, after which the nitro-cellulose can be introduced into the stability apparatus.

Caution.—In so doing, great care must be exercised to avoid the introduction of moisture. The following procedure is to be recommended:—The small flat-bottomed heating tubes and a copper scoop are put into the hot-air oven at the same time as the powder, so that they may be perfectly dry. At the expiration of 20 hours drying, the previously-weighed powder is taken straight from the oven and quickly transferred from the watch-glass by means of the copper scoop to the small glass tube, which must be absolutely dry and warm, and this introduced without delay into the inverted-stoppered tube of the apparatus in the position shown in Fig. 2 (F).

The powder introduced into each burette is noted, and the burette should be provided with an easily visible number to facilitate the subsequent readings.

The tubes are now ready to be introduced into the hot glycerine bath.

Preparation of Cordite for the Test at 115° C.

In the case of cordite it is necessary to extract the nitro-glycerine with ether, and to test the residual nitro-cellulose. For this purpose, sufficient of the ground cordite should be taken to yield about 3 grammes of nitro-cellulose (Mark I, about 8 grammes, M.D., about $4\frac{1}{2}$ grammes). This is extracted with ether in a Soxhlet extractor for 5 hours (as, for instance, from 9.30 a.m. to 2.30 p.m.); then the "thimble" containing the residual nitro-cellulose is placed in a warm aluminium dish, laid on top of an air oven at 60° C., and left for about half an hour (3 p.m.), to drive off the ether. Care must be taken to avoid the condensation of moisture on the residual nitro-cellulose as much as possible. The contents of the "thimble" are then emptied on to a warm weighed watch-glass, and placed in the oven for an hour (4 p.m.). After allowing them to cool, they are placed, one by one, on the scale of the balance, and nitro-cellulose is removed, little by little, until exactly 2 grammes (30·9 grains) remain on each watch-glass.

The watch-glass and contents are laid on a small glass tripod in a flat-bottomed dish containing granular calcium chloride (fresh for each experiment). The dish is covered with a watch-glass and introduced into the air oven at 60° C., together with the small flat-bottomed tubes and a copper scoop, for 20 hours, after which the nitro-cellulose is introduced with the aid of the copper scoop into the small tubes, and these into the apparatus as described under Nitro-cellulose.

Caution.—In the case of cordite, it is particularly important that moisture should be completely excluded from the residue during the introduction of the substance into the apparatus. It is, therefore, highly important that no time be lost in the transference from the watch-glass to the heating-tubes, and that all the apparatus be thoroughly dried and warm. For this reason, the test at 70° C. will, in general, be found preferable in testing cordites.

Application of the Test at 115° C.

The nitro-cellulose having been introduced into the stability apparatus, the test may be commenced. The glass apparatus is introduced into the glycerine bath in such a way that the inverted-stoppered tube rests in one of the narrow copper tubes of the bath, and is completely submerged beneath the thick lubricant oil, and the burette is supported by the glass rod resting on the stand provided for this purpose.

When supported in this way, the burette has no tendency to alter its position during the test. Any movement of the heating tube in the bath is to be avoided, as this might lead to fluctuations in the gas volumes.

The reservoir hangs in the position shown in Fig. 2, being supported by a string from the top of the burette. The time is noted at which the commencement of the heating takes place. After the expiration of 2 hours the first reading of the burette is taken. This is done by raising the reservoir until the level of the salt solution is the same in the burette and in the reservoir, and reading the height of the column of liquid as indicated by the graduated marks on the burette. The temperature of the bath is at the same time noted. The heating is continued over-night, and requires no attention during this time. After 20 hours from the commencement, the volume of gas and the temperature are again read off in the same manner. The increase of volume during this 18 hours is to be taken as a criterion of the stability.

Correction for the temperature of the glycerine bath.—The rate of evolution of gas is very much affected by slight differences of temperature in the bath; hence, if the temperature of the bath, as indicated by the mean of the readings taken before and after the heating, be not exactly 115° C., a correction must be applied to the volume of gas evolved. A rise of temperature of 1° C. increases the volume of gas evolved by 17 per cent. of its amount.

It occasionally happens that traces of moisture find access to the nitro-cellulose in conveying it from the drying oven to the stability apparatus. If this occurs, an increased evolution will be obtained from the tube containing moisture; hence, if deviations are found in the evolution on repeating the experiment with the same powder, the lowest volume should be taken as the correct evolution.

Moreover, it is advisable, when the safety limit is exceeded, to check the result by a repetition of the determination, with precise observance of the precautions laid down for the exclusion of moisture. Errors in the manipulation (resulting in the presence of moisture) can generally be detected by the altogether abnormal results obtained, since, if a wet decomposition sets in, it undergoes such a rapid acceleration that the burette becomes nearly filled with the gases evolved.

Limits of Safety.—The following provisional limits may be given:—If the volume evolved during the interval of 18 hours, at 115° C., be less than 14 cc., the nitro-cellulose may be considered as safe, if more than 16 cc., as unsafe, for storage. Should the volume of gas evolved lie between these limits it must be corrected for temperature and pressure. It is, therefore, necessary in this case to note the temperature of the air and the barometric pressure at the time of reading.

Thus, if the increase of volume measured be V, the temperature (centigrade) t, and the pressure (in millimetres of mercury) p, the corrected volume is—

$$V \times \frac{273}{273 + t} \times \frac{p}{760}.$$

After reduction of the volume of gas to 0° C. and 760 mm. pressure, the safety limit becomes 14 cc.

Example.—Stability of a modified cordite—

- 30th July, 1903, 12 noon.—4·5 grammes of cordite, M.D. were introduced into a Soxhlet extractor and extracted with ether for 5 hours.

- 30th July, 5 p.m.—The " thimble " containing the residual nitro-cellulose was placed in a warm aluminium dish on a hot-air oven, and left for half an hour; the nitro-cellulose was then tipped on to a weighed watch glass, and dried in the oven until 6.30 p.m.

- 30th July, 6.30 p.m.—The watch glass was allowed to cool until 6.45 p.m. So much powder was taken off the watch glass that the weight of the remainder was just two grammes.

- 30th July, 7 p.m.—Watch glass and contents were returned to oven.

- 31st July, 3 p.m.—Nitro-cellulose was quickly transferred from the watch glass to the heating tube whilst still warm, and the latter introduced into the apparatus.

- 31st July, 3.15 p.m.—Apparatus was introduced into the bath.

- 31st July, 5.15 p.m.—First reading: Volume = 3·8 cc.; temperature of bath = 114·95°.

- 1st August, 11.15 a.m.—Final reading: Volume = 14·4 cc.; temperature of bath = 115·10°. Increase during 18 hours (uncorrected) = 10·6 cc. at 115·0°. This is within the limit, and hence need not be corrected for temperature and barometric pressure.

For the sake of example, however, the correction is here appended. The air temperature was 18° C, and the barometric pressure 764·5 millimetres.

$$\text{Corr. Vol.} = 10\cdot6 \times \frac{273}{273 + 18} \times \frac{764\cdot5}{760} = 10\cdot0 \text{ ccm.}$$

LIST OF APPARATUS REQUIRED TO CARRY OUT THE STABILITY TEST AT 70° C.

Description.	Number required.
1 Water bath, copper, with seven orifices and tripod stand, to take the burettes, with Habermann's condenser and screen for burner, according to the pattern. (Fig. 2 and Appendix B)	1
2 Bunsen gas burner, diameter $\frac{5}{8}$ inch (external), or one lamp capable of burning for 24 hours	1
3 Thermometer (accurate), with range from 50 degrees to 105 degrees centigrade, divided into $\frac{1}{5}$ degrees ...	1
4 Glass apparatus, with aluminium drying vessel, detachable scale, measuring tube for mercury, and spring clip, according to the pattern. (Fig. 3 and Appendix B)	6
5 Retort stand, with clamp to support apparatus whilst filling, &c. Length of rod, 36 inches, base 6 inches by 12 inches	1
6 Retort stand, to support the apparatus while being heated in the bath; 36-inch rod. Base 6 inches by 12 inches, with adjustable horizontal rod 12 inches long	1
7 { Rubber tubing for gas burner	2 yards
" " condenser	2 yards
8 Box of weights, 50 grammes to 1 milligramme	1
9 Flask fitted with boiling tube, with steam jacket, for standardising thermometer	1
10 Scales (these are included in the Abel Test Apparatus)	...
11 Filter funnel (diameter $2\frac{1}{2}$ inches)	1
12 Small lens	1
13 Logarithmic table, to four decimal places	1
14 Squared paper, for plotting curves, with 10 divisions per inch, in sheets about foolscap size	3 dozen
Chemicals—	
Methyl alcohol (crude commercial, free from acid)	2 gals.
Special tin	...
Mercury	1 lb.
Calcium chloride (granular, for drying gases, sifted between sieves containing holes $\frac{1}{4}$ inch and $\frac{3}{16}$ inch diameter respectively), in 1-lb. bottles ...	4 lbs.
Heavy mineral oil (Vocabulary Store)	1 quart
Lubricant (prepared by melting together equal parts of beeswax and adeps lanae)	2 ozs.

Additional Apparatus Required to Carry Out the Stability Test at 115° C.

	Description.	Number required.
1	Water oven, copper, 9 inches by 9 inches, with gauge, two holes in top, and stand complete	1
2	Burette fitted with stoppered heating tube and reservoir, according to the pattern. (Fig. 2 and Appendix C)	6
3	Soxhlet's water bath, copper, six holes and covers, mounted on stand, with circular gas burner or spirit lamp and iron support for condensers. (See Fig. 1)	1
4	Extraction tubes, 60 ccs. with condensers and corked flasks for above. (See Fig. 1)	4
5	Fat extraction thimbles, for use with the Soxhlet's apparatus. Size, 22 by 80 mm.	One box of 25.
6	Flat-bottomed aluminium dishes, diameter, $3\frac{1}{2}$ inches; depth, $1\frac{1}{4}$ inches	
7	Accurate thermometer, with range from 90 degrees to 125 degrees centigrade, divided into 10ths of a degree	1
8	Thermometers, with range from 0 degrees to 100 degrees centigrade, divided in whole degrees	2
9	Bunsen gas burner, external diameter $\frac{7}{16}$ inch, or one lamp capable of burning for 24 hours	1
10	Watch glasses, $2\frac{1}{4}$ inches diameter	1 dozen.
	" $4\frac{1}{2}$ "	6
11	Flat-bottomed glass dishes, diameter 4 inches, height 2 inches	4
12	Glass tripods, height 1 inch, length of side 3 inches	4
13	Indiarubber bands	6 dozen.
14	Thermoregulator (for drying bath)	1
15	Rubber tubing for gas burners	3 yards.
	" " condensers	6 yards.
	" " burettes, $\frac{3}{16}$ inch internal diameter, walls $\frac{1}{16}$ inch	6 yards.
16	Flat iron dish or burning waste ether containing nitroglycerine	1
	Chemicals—	
	Ether, methylated, specific gravity ·720, to be supplied in 1-lb. bottles	6 lb.
	Common salt	14 lb.
	Glycerine (commercial)	20 lb.
	The following apparatus is also required, but is included in the Abel Test apparatus:—	
	Grinding mill	...
	Sieves—Nest of two, containing 30 and 60 meshes per inch	...
	Small scoop of thin sheet copper	...

DESCRIPTION OF APPARATUS FOR TEST AT 70° C.

The bath is about 7 inches in diameter and $10\frac{1}{2}$ inches in depth, and is of the form shown in Fig. 2. It is closed by a steam-tight cover, in which is a well 2 inches deep extending to within $\frac{3}{4}$ inch of the edge for nearly three-quarters of the circumference of the cover. This well contains a number of orifices which are fitted with copper tubes dipping into the bath and closed at their lower ends. The dimensions of these tubes are as follows:—Two tubes 2 inches diameter and $6\frac{1}{2}$ inches deep, four tubes 1 inch diameter and 5 inches deep, and one tube $\frac{1}{2}$ inch diameter and 5 inches deep.

The cover is also fitted with a copper tube, A, which rises to a height of about 4 inches above the surface of the bath, and can be connected by means of a well-fitting conical brass joint with a Habermann's condenser.

A screen is provided to protect the flame under the bath from draughts.

The glass apparatus is shown in Fig. 3; the heating vessel, A, has a total length of 5 inches, and is somewhat constricted at the neck, whose internal diameter is 1 inch. The stopper, which must be very well ground, is hollow, and is joined by a capillary tube, B, of 2 mm. bore, to the manometer, C. A tap, D, is fitted on to the capillary tube in the position shown.

The capacity of the vessel, including the hollow stopper, and the capillary tube to a point half way down the manometer tube should lie between 89·5 and 90·5 cubic centimetres.

The open tube of the manometer terminates in a small cup of about 5 cubic centimetres capacity, for the purpose of filling in the mercury. The manometer is fitted with a detachable scale divided into millimetres. The drying vessel, E, consists of a small cylindrical aluminium box, 1 inch in depth, with a detachable lid. The box is perforated at both ends and at the sides, and fits into the hollow stopper. It is filled with calcium chloride during the experiment.

A spring clip is provided for the purpose of holding the stopper firmly in place.

APPARATUS FOR TEST AT 115 DEGREES.

(For description of bath, *see* page 144.)

The burette, C (Fig. 2), is about 10 inches long, and has a capacity of 50 cc. Each burette should be numbered for the sake of identification. The burette is joined by means of a horizontal tube, D, of about 2 mm. bore, and 14 inches in length, with the heating tube, an inverted stoppered tube, which dips into the bath. This is shown on an enlarged scale in the supplementary sketch, E. It has a capacity of approximately 9 cc., which must be nearly the same in each apparatus. The stopper must be numbered in order to indicate to which tube it belongs. The stopper is fitted with a piece of brass wire terminating in a hook. This is connected by a rubber band with the horizontal tube, and thus the stopper is held firmly in position. F is a small flat-bottomed tube which contains the explosive to be tested, and is placed upright in the inverted stoppered tube.

A glass rod, G, is bound on to the horizontal tube, D, and is supported on a stand to hold the burette in position.

The reservoir, H, is connected to the burette with a piece of indiarubber tubing about 15 inches long. It is most conveniently supported by hooking it to a loop in a short length of string affixed to the top of the burette.

Standardization of Thermometers.

As the accuracy of the temperature measurements is of great importance, it is occasionally necessary to restandardize the thermometers used in the glycerine or methyl alcohol baths. For this purpose the range has been so chosen that the restandardization may be carried out by means of the boiling point of water at atmospheric pressure. For convenience the following table is appended:—

Boiling point of water under varying pressure.

Barometric pressure (corrected).		Boiling point of water (degrees C.).	Barometric pressure (corrected).		Boiling point of water (degrees C.).
Millimetres.	Inches.		Millimetres.	Inches.	
633·7	24·95	95·0	707·1	27·84	98·0
636·0	25·04	95·1	709·7	27·94	98·1
638·3	25·13	95·2	712·3	28·04	98·2
640·7	25·23	95·3	714·9	28·15	98·3
643·1	25·32	95·4	717·5	28·25	98·4
645·4	25·42	95·5	720·1	28·35	98·5
647·8	22·51	95·6	722·7	28·45	98·6
650·2	25·60	95·7	725·3	28·56	98·7
652·6	25·70	95·8	727·9	28·66	98·8
655·0	25·79	95·9	730·5	28·76	98·9
657·4	25·88	96·0	733·2	28·87	99·0
659·8	25·98	96·1	735·8	28·97	99·1
662·2	26·07	96·2	738·5	29·08	99·2
664·7	26·17	96·3	741·1	29·18	99·3
667·1	26·26	96·4	743·8	29·28	99·4
669·5	26·36	96·5	746·5	29·39	99·5
672·0	26·46	96·6	749·2	29·49	99·6
674·5	26·55	96·7	751·9	29·60	99·7
676·9	26·65	96·8	754·6	29·70	99·8
679·4	26·75	96·9	757·3	29·81	99·9
681·9	26·85	97·0	760·0	29·92	100·0
684·4	26·94	97·1	762·7	30·03	100·1
686·9	27·04	97·2	765·5	30·14	100·2
689·4	27·14	97·3	768·2	30·25	100·3
691·9	27·24	97·4	771·0	30·36	100·4
694·4	27·34	97·5	773·7	30·47	100·5
696·9	27·44	97·6	776·5	30·57	100·6
699·5	27·54	97·7	779·3	30·68	100·7
702·0	27·64	97·8	782·1	30·79	100·8
704·6	27·79	97·9	784·9	30·90	100·9

A flask and jacketed boiling tube are provided for the calibration of the thermometer.

Addendum I.—Heat Tests.

A considerable number of methods have been devised and proposed for testing the stability of guncotton and powders, such as cordite, of which it is the base or fundamental ingredient.

These explosives must be kept in store for some time, and it is very desirable, of course, that they should not deteriorate on keeping, it may be, for a number of years.

Guncotton, when made on a large scale, is always liable to contain some impurity, derived either from the original cellulosic material, or owing to imperfections in the mode of manufacture.

Nitro-glycerine is less liable to either of these faults, as it is, to begin with, a perfectly definite material, or chemical entity, and its stability depends almost entirely on the care expended on its manufacture.

Vaseline, and substances of that kind, would, if they consisted entirely of paraffinoid compounds, be absolutely inert, and remain unchanged for an indefinite time.

As a matter of observation, commercial guncottons and many of the powders containing them do undergo slow changes on keeping at the ordinary temperature of 15° C., and more quickly when exposed to higher temperatures, especially when in closed or only partially ventilated vessels.

It is probable that all kinds of powders containing guncotton and nitro-glycerine would keep for an indefinite time under water with little or no change.

As ordinary guncottons are observed to deteriorate in hot climates more quickly than in temperate, a number of methods of testing stability against climatic changes have been tried. One method, proposed by Professor Will, consists essentially in heating a definite small quantity (2·5 grammes or so) of the guncotton to a temperature of 135° C. in an atmosphere of pure carbon-dioxide, in such manner that a current of this gas passes continuously over the heated guncotton so as to carry away any gases produced by its decomposition, and after passing over some metallic copper heated to redness in order to decompose oxides of nitrogen, is received in a graduated vessel containing strong potassium hydroxide solution.

Here the carbon-dioxide—the carrier—is absorbed, and the nitrogen resulting from the destruction of any oxides of nitrogen collected and measured.

The operation is carried on so that the nitrogen gas can be measured at definite time intervals, the time and volumes of gas in cubic centimetres being then plotted out.

Generally speaking, a good product will give little gas during the first period—say, 15 minutes—of heating, and the amount will increase but little during successive equal time periods. The reverse of this—viz., rapidly increasing gas volumes in equal times—should indicate instability.

The diagram opposite p. 153 shows another arrangement

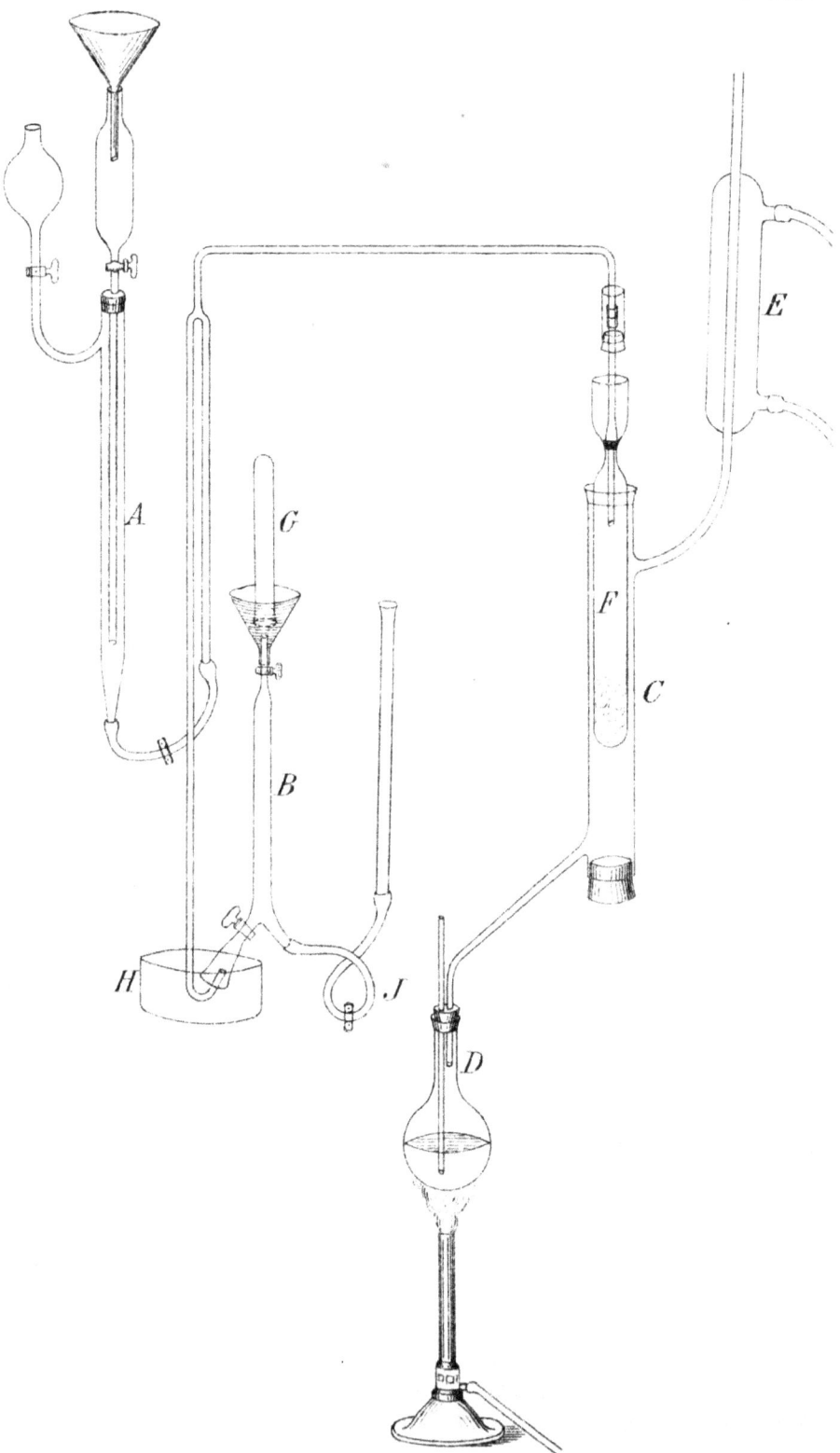

PLATE XXVIII.

devised by Dr. Hodgkinson, by which an explosive or other substance may be heated to some definite temperature in a vacuum vessel, and the gases evolved collected and measured at any time interval, and, if desired, removed and submitted to analysis.

The weighed amount of substance is contained in the test-tube (F). This has been melted in and narrowed in the neck so as to fit with a rubber ring air-tight on the end of the Sprengel pump tube (A).

The test-tube then sits in the copper tube (C), the fitting being secured either by a cork ring or a little cement.

After a vacuum has been obtained, the liquid in D is boiled, and its vapour passing through C into the condenser E heats up the substance.

The whole of B being filled with mercury and the clamp closed, the gas collects in B, and can be brought to atmospheric pressure and read off as desired.

The gases from guncotton are nitrogen, nitric oxide (NO), carbon-dioxide, and nitrogen peroxide (NO_2).

Liquids of definite boiling point are infinitely superior to mechanical mixtures as baths for heating, and toluene, a liquid boiling at 111° C., is very convenient for guncotton.

As nitro-glycerine evaporates somewhat freely in a vacuum of 100° C., a considerably lower temperature, such as that of boiling acetone at 56° C., is sufficient in the case of cordites.

Remarks.

The ordinary heat test employed for guncotton and smokeless powders generally depends on the liberation of iodine from an iodide, such as potassium or cadmium iodide, by the action of nitrous acid. The iodine so liberated then combines with starch, producing a highly coloured compound sometimes spoken of as starch iodide.

Many substances of the amine class (*see* 114) when brought into contact with nitrous acid form highly coloured diazo compounds—for instance, *a* naphtylamine, $C_{10}H_7NH_2$, diphenylamine $(C_6H_5)_2NH$, and others.

Diphenylamine has been proposed as a test for nitrous acid, as it gives an intense blue colour with very small quantities.

The *a* naphtylamine has been similarly employed.

An excellent form of the test consists of molecular proportions of the amine and sulphanilic acid, dissolved in hydrochloric or acetic acid and used either soaked on filter paper or in solution.

One proposed method consists in having the explosive to be tested in a wide U-tube standing in a bath of the required temperature, and passing a stream of purified air over it, and then through a solution of the naphtylamine and sulphanilic acid, noting the time of first appearance of a pink colour and the final depth of pink tint after standing for 20 minutes.

The pink tint can then be compared with a standard colour produced from known quantities of nitrous acid. These tests are, however, if anything, too delicate for common use.

In the Will process of heating guncotton to 130° C. in carbon dioxide, some oxides of nitrogen other than (NO) are given off. This has also been observed when guncotton has been heated to 111° C. (boiling toluene) in a vacuum tube. These other oxides of nitrogen attack the mercury of the pump.

Messrs. Robertson and Napper, of Waltham Abbey, have recently described—Jour. Chem. Soc., April, 1907, 761—a process for estimating the amount of (NO_2) produced in the decomposition of guncotton heated to 135° C., which consists essentially in observing the absorption spectrum of the (NO_2) at low pressures, either in the presence of air or carbon dioxide.

The absorption bands are then photographed, and their intensity compared with standards prepared by mixing NO_2 with air or CO_2 at different dilutions and pressures. This method of examination has been applied also as an adjunct to the ordinary Will process, the gases being caught and examined with the spectroscope on their way from the decomposition tube to the heating arrangement, where they pass over red-hot copper.

Description of the two main processes, with diagram, are taken from Chem. Soc. Jour.

Process 1.

Two grammes of well-dried guncotton are introduced into the decomposition tube, which is then connected to the observation tube by means of a mercury joint, the apparatus is evacuated, and the decomposition tube containing the guncotton is lowered into the bath at 135°. For half-an-hour the apparatus is kept connected to the pump and evacuated continuously to abstract water and air from the guncotton. The cock to the pump is then closed, and the fall in pressure is observed, whilst photographs of the absorption spectrum of the nitrogen peroxide evolved are taken at intervals.

Process 2.

When the total nitrogen evolved is estimated, in addition to the nitrogen as nitrogen peroxide, the procedure is as follows:—

The whole apparatus, except the combustion tube, is thoroughly evacuated; carbon dioxide is admitted, evacuated, and again admitted and evacuated; the guncotton is heated in the bath at 135° for ten minutes, carbon dioxide is admitted and passed through the whole apparatus, including the combustion tube, at a measured rate into an absorption burette. The apparatus, now quite free from air and filled with carbon dioxide, is shut off from the combustion tube and evacuated; the decomposition tube containing the guncotton being now surrounded by the bath at 135°, after half-an-hour of continuous evacuation the pump is shut off, the actual experiment begins.

At intervals the spectrum of nitrogen peroxide is observed, photographs are taken, and the fall in the level of the mercury in the manometer is noted every quarter of an hour during the course of the experiment, which is usually continued for four hours.

At the end of the experiment the gaseous products of decomposition are swept out of the apparatus by a stream of carbon dioxide and led through the combustion tube, after which the gases, now consisting of carbon dioxide and nitrogen, pass into the absorption burette, containing caustic potash, where the latter is measured, a small correction being made for the unabsorbed residue in the carbon dioxide used.

The concentration of the nitrogen peroxide was obtained by direct comparison with the standard photographs described in the previous paper. The weight of nitrogen peroxide was then calculated from the concentration and the volume of the apparatus, and thus the weight of nitrogen existing as nitrogen peroxide was arrived at. The figures obtained in this way are compared with the total weight of nitrogen given by the combustion just described.

Addendum II.—Silvered Vessel Test.

Waltham Abbey Silvered Vessel Test to be applied to Cordite.

General Instructions.

1. *Apparatus Required.*

(a) A copper water bath, consisting of a cylindrical vessel about 38 cm. in diameter and 40 cm. in height, fitted with a fixed cover of copper pierced with seven holes from which cylindrical copper tubes, closed at their lower ends, dip into the bath. The bath rests on a stand about 15 cm. high, and below it is placed a Bunsen burner. *See* Figure.

(b) Silvered vacuum jacketed vessels, fitted with side tubes, of the pattern shown in the Figure.

(c) Thermometers for the silvered vessels. These are of a range of $0°$ to $100°$ C. and pass through a cork in the neck of the vessel. The scale should be of such a length that when the bulb of the thermometer is in the centre of the vessel, at least $78°$ C. should be indicated at the level of the top of the cork.

(*d*) Discs of asbestos cardboard to fit round the neck of the flasks and lie over the cylindrical holes in the bath; also discs fitting the bottom of the cylindrical holes of the bath.

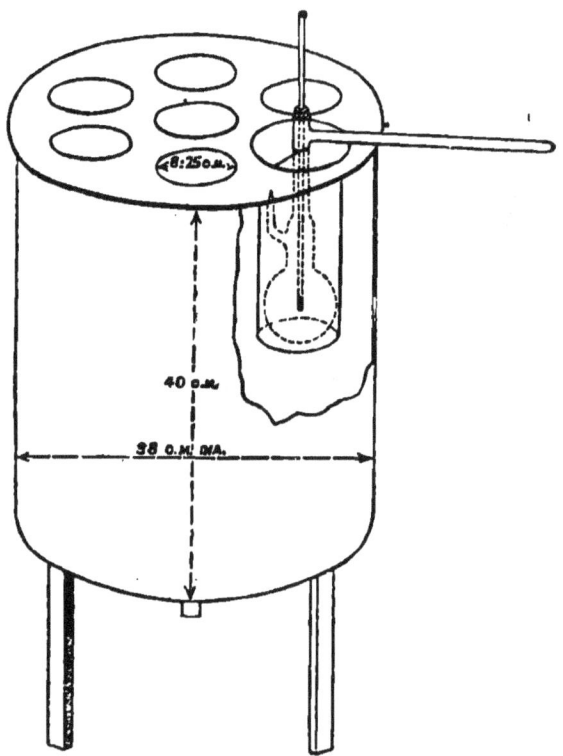

(*e*) A mill as for the Abel heat test.
(*f*) A nest of sieves as for the Abel heat test.

2. *Preparation of the Sample of Cordite to be tested.*

About 50 grams of the cordite ground as for the Abel heat test are required.

3. *Application of the Test.*

The ground cordite is put into the bulb of the silvered vessel so that the spherical portion remains full after gentle tapping. The thermometer is then passed through the cork fitting into the neck of the vessel, and is so adjusted that its bulb is situated at the centre of the spherical portion of the vessel.

The bath, full of water up to one inch from the top, is regulated by means of a suitable regulator so that the temperature of the explosive is at 80° C.

The silvered vessel containing the cordite, and fitted with its asbestos cardboard disc, is then lowered into one of the cylindrical holes of the bath, and arranged so that the side tube points towards the front.

It will be found that the cordite remains for a period at a temperature of 80° C., but ultimately the thermometer records a rise in temperature. When this rise in temperature reaches 2° C. above the normal temperature, the time in hours from the start is noted and the vessel removed from the bath.

This period of time is the measure of the stability of the cordite.

An indication of the approach of rise in temperature is usually obtained by the column of gas in the side tube of the silvered vessel becoming orange coloured.

Results—Royal Gunpowder Factory.

The results of the test are expressed in hours and refer to the time which elapses before the rise in temperature, indicating that internal oxidation is proceeding, reaches 2° C. above the normal temperature of 80° C. This in the case of newly-made cordites (Mark I.) is from 500–600 hours.

After this vessel had proved itself capable of discriminating between N/C powders and placing them in what was regarded as their true relative position of stability, its use was extended to cordites, when results equally satisfactory were returned at the Royal Gunpowder Factory. A few of these may be quoted here, the figures given being the time in hours before decomposition in the silvered vessel at 80° C. took place.

Good Cordites.		Cordites Suspicious as Regards Stabling.					
		Suspicious on Account of Composition.		Suspicious on Account of Impure Materials.		Suspicious on Account of Deterioration on Storage.	
Nature of Sample.	Hours.	Nature of Sample.	Hours.	Nature of Sample.	Hours.	Nature of Sample.	Hours.
Current Manufacture. (5 per cent. M/J.)	621 527 502 543	Cordite without M/J.	83	Cordite made with "Z" G/C (G/C contained H_2SO_4 ester and spontaneously decomposed).	216	Cordite from other sources.	215 230 137 153 374
Do.	520	Cordite with 2 per cent. M/J. Cordite with 3 per cent. M/J.	263 335				

The results obtained with this test at the Royal Gunpowder Factory confirm the contention that it reflects the conditions obtaining in actual storage at moderately elevated temperatures, and are in agreement with the theoretical considerations set forth above.

Thus there is an obvious familiarity between the phenomena observed in the case of the silvered vessel and actual experience. A long, apparently quiescent period, during which only small changes in composition occur is succeeded in both cases by one of chemical activity when a rise in temperature sets in, culminating in an inflammation of the same order of violence in the case of the silvered vessel as those which have sometimes actually occurred.

Then the theory that mineral jelly acts in a chemical manner in preserving the cordite by limiting the abnormal acceleration that would set in if the nitric peroxide were not removed, is borne out by the above results, which show that the duration of resistance to heating is proportional to the active mass of the mineral jelly originally present. Deducting the time required for the reaction to take place when no mineral jelly is present (83 hours) from the time of resistance of cordite containing two, three and five per cent. of mineral jelly, the resulting figures 160, 232, and 437 are in practically the same proportion as the percentages, namely, 2, 3·1, and 5·4.

Again, the presence of impure materials in the cordite, such as unstable guncotton containing sulphuric esters, was pointed out by the low results obtained.

Apparatus for Estimation of NO_2 Evolved in Vacuo.

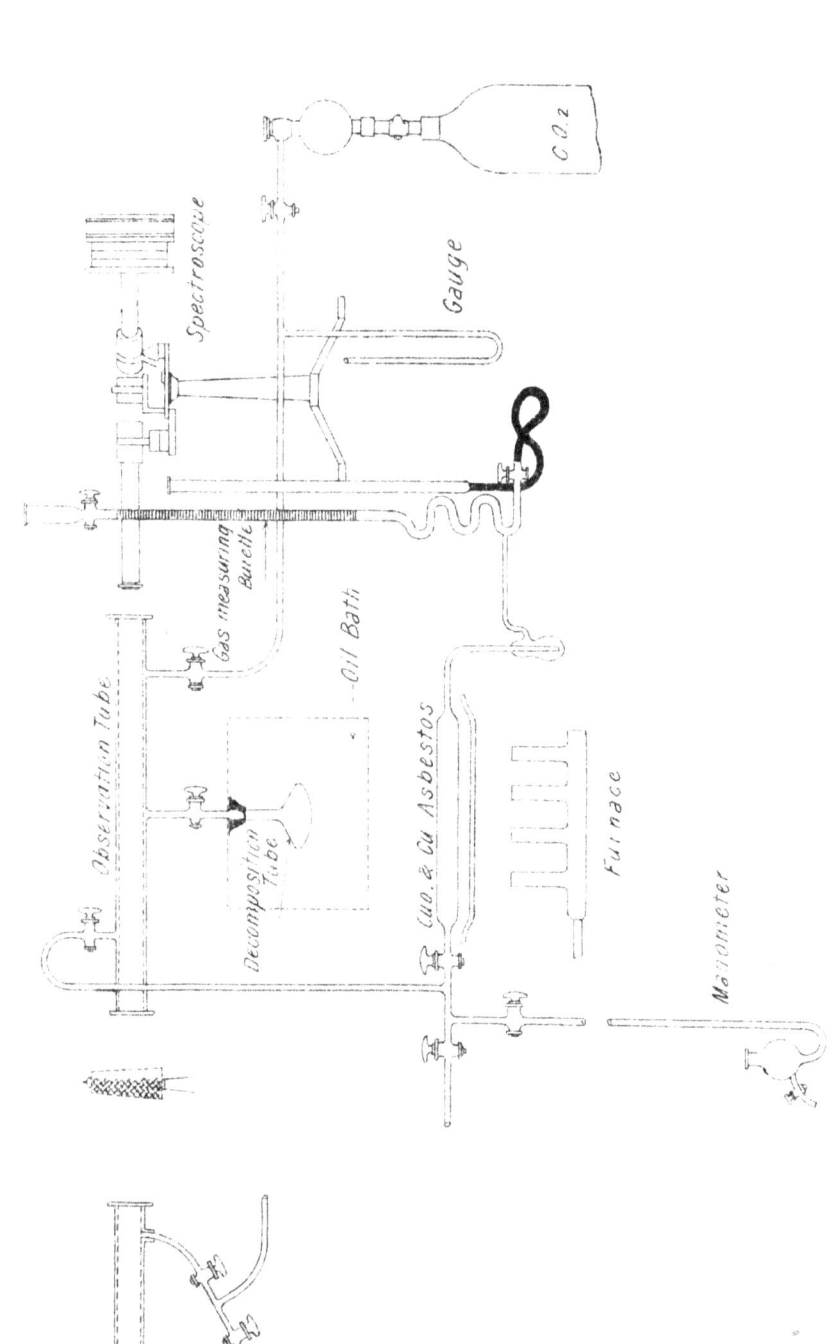

INDEX.

A

	Page.
ABEL, Sir Frederick	58
Acetates, cellulose	61
Acetone	65, 100
Acetylene	115, 117
Acetylides	117
Acid, acetic	61
,, extractor	71
,, nitric	54
Addendum I.—Heat tests	152
,, II.—Silvered vessel test	155
Air	3
Alcohol	55
,, methyl	55
Alder (betula alnus)	8
Aluminium flash light	118
Amino acetic acid	114
,, explosive	114
Amine bases	55
Ammonium hydrazoate	115
,, nitrate	54, 114
,, nitrite	114
,, picrate	112
,, sulphide	65
Analysis of powder	35
Aniline	55
,, nitrate	115
Apparatus, drenching	21

B

BACON, Roger	47
Baptista Porta	52
Bases, amine	55
Bengal fire	112
Benzene	107
Benzenoïd	56
Berthelot	63
Bertholdus Schwartz	47
Bianchi densimeter	33
Bichromate	119
Black service powder	36
Blasting gelatine	92
Blending	26, 28
Boiler explosion	5
Bologna phials	5
Böttger	57
Braconnot	57
Breaking down	21
Brown	59
,, powders	38
Brugére powder	113
Burning, rate of	44

C

CALCIUM acetate	116
,, carbide	117
Caloric	2
Caliche	14

	PAGE.
Cam machine	30
Carbon	3
,, dioxide	2
,, mon	2
Carbolic acid	110
Carbo hydrate	55
Cellulose	4, 60
,, acetate	61
,, decomposition of	8
,, nitrates	61
Chapter I.	7
,, II.—Manufacture of gunpowder	19
,, III.	32
,, IV.	40
,, V.	47
,, VI.	54
,, VII.	69
,, VIII.—Manufacture of glycerine	80
,, IX.	95
Charbon rouge	8
Charcoal, gunpowder, from wood	3, 7, 10
,, mill	11
,, slack, burnt	8
Charring	7
,, speed of	9
,, by superheated steam	11
Charge, green	20
Cheese	20
Chile saltpetre	14
Chlorates	118
Chronograph	35
Classification of powders	36
Coal dust, coal	2, 7
Cocoa	39
Coke	3
Collodion	62
Combustion	1
,, internal	54
Composition of cordite	99
,, powder in different countries	53
Compounds, explosive	54
Congreve, Sir William	51
Cordite	95
,, processes of manufacture of	101
,, for blank	106
Crecy	50
Cresol	113
Crusher gauges	35
Crystallising	15
Cupramine	60
Curb	20
Curve pressure	38
Cut powders	27
Cutting	27

D

Damaged powder, extracting saltpetre from	18
Densimetre, Bianchi	33
,, immersion	33
Density	33
Designolle's powder	113
Detonator	1
Detonating substance	1
Diamond	3
Diazo benzene	115

	PAGE.
Different countries, composition of powders in....	53
Di-glycerine	93
Di-nitrobenzene	108
Displacement process, guncotton making	74
Dog wood (Rhamnus frangula)	8
Doubtful powder	37
Drenching apparatus	21
Drowning	21
,, tank	82
Drying or stoving	25
Dust explosion	2
Dusting	24
Dynamite	78, 91

E

EDER	63
Elizabeth	50
Endothermic	3
,, compounds, naturally occurring	4
Ester	65
Ethyl acetate	101
Examination and proof of gunpowder	32
Expansion of gases	4
Explode	1
Explosion	1
Explosive action	1
,, compounds	54
,, high	1
,, low	1
Exothermic	3
E.X.E. powder	29

F

FERROUS sulphate	65
Figure 1A	89
,, 2A	90
,, of merit	35
Filtering	15, 85
Finishing	26, 28
Firing proof	35
Fired powders, products of	40
Fulminate	115
,, of mercury	116

G

GAS carbon	3
Gauges, crusher	35
Gelignite	93
Glass	4
Glazing	25, 28
Glycerine	78
,, formula of	78
,, manufacture of	80
Glycerol trinitrate	77
Græcus Marcus	48
Gramme, atom	3
,, molecule	3
Granulating	23
,, machine	23
Graphite	3
Greek-fire	48

	PAGE.
Green charge	20
Guncotton	57
" by the displacement process, making	74
" history of	57
" Old process of manufacture	69
" Packing wet	73
" Properties of	57
" Service, water in	67
Gunpowder	1, 7
" manufacture of	19
" history of	47
" examination and proof of	32

H

Heat of combustion	2
High explosives	107
History of gunpowder	47
Hydrogen	2
Hydrazoic acid	115
Hydrolysis	78
Hydroxide nature	78
Hydrometric quality	35
" test	34

I

Immersion densimetre	33–34
Importation of saltpetre	50
Incorporating	20
" machine	102
Indian nitre	14
"Insoluble"	63
Internal combustion	54
" strain	5
Iodine	14
Isomeride	109
Iso purpuric acide	114

K

Kainile	14
Kieselguhr	78, 91
Kissler concentrator	76
Knop	57

L

Lead picrate	112
Lignin	60
Lyddite	111

M

Mannitol	55
Manufacture of glycerine	80
" gunpowder	80
Marcus Græcus	47
Melinite, Turpin	113
Mercury fulminate	66, 116
Methane	8
Methyl nitrate	55

	PAGE.
Microbes	13
Milling	20
Mill cake	21
Mineral jelly	100
Miscellaneous explosives	107
Mixing	19
Moisture	34
Mono-chlor-hydrin	94
Mother liquor	17
Muzzle velocity	35

N

NAPHTOL	114
Nathan and Thompson	74
Nitrate of Ammonium	54
Nitrates, cellulose	61
Nitrating	80
Nitre	13
,, flour of	16
,, Indian	14
,, making of	13
,, washing of	16
Nitric acide	54
Nitro compound	56
,, benzene	108
,, phenol	110
Nitro-glycerine	77
,, crystallising point	77
,, properties of	78, 79
,, newer process	88
Nobel	78, 91

O

OLEFINES	100
Otto	57
Oxygen	2

P

PACKING wet guncotton	73
Pélouze	57
Perchlorates	119
Permanganates	119
Petre	17
Petroleum	2
Phenol-phenol sulphuric acid	110, 111
Picric acid	110
,, properties of	112
,, purification of	112
,, Solubility of	110
Picramic acid	113
Plate 1	10
,, 2	12
,, 3	15
,, 4	20
,, 5	21
,, 6	22
,, 7	23
,, 8	25
,, 9 and 10	28
,, 11	29

	PAGE.
Plate 12	30
,, 13	69
,, 14	69
,, 15.—Beating engine	71
,, 16	72
,, 17	73
,, 18	75
,, 19	80
,, 20.—Nitroglycerine factory	84
,, 21.—Washing tank	85
,, 22 and 23	89-90, 102
,, 24	104
,, 25 and 26	106
Ploughs	20
Poaching	72
Poly-glycerine	93
Potassium nitrate	13
,, nitrite	39
,, picrate	112
Powder analysis	35
,, brown	38
,, class A	19
,, classification of	36
,, doubtful	37
,, E.X.E.	29
,, fired in the bore of a gun	45
,, ,, a confined space	44
,, S.B.C.	29
,, Schultze	59
Pressing	22, 73
Press box	22
Pressure curve	38
Pre-wash tank	83
Primer	59
Primers	73
Processes of manufacture of cordite	101
Products of fired powders	40
Prism brown powder	29
Prismatic powder	29
Proof firing	35
Propane	78
Propellants	1
Properties of nitro-glycerine	78, 79
Pulping	71

Q

Quality, hygrometric   35

R

Rack-a-Rock	108
Rate of burning	44
Reducing agents	65
Reel	11
,, slope	25
Refining coppers	15
Refined sulphur, testing of	13
Retorts.—Plate 1	11
Rhamnus frangula	8
Robins	52
Robertson and Napper	154
Roger Bacon	47
Runners	20
Ruperts' drops	4

S

	Page.
SALTPETRE	4, 13
,, Artificial, production of	50
,, Chile, melting point of	14, 15
,, Flour of	16
,, Importation of	50
,, Refining of	15
,, Specific gravity of	15
,, Testing of	17
S.B.C. powder	29
Schöubein	57
Schultze powder	59
Schwartz, Bertholdus	47
Separating	82
Serpentine	51
Service guncotton, water in	67
,, powder, black	36
Shover	21
Shuter	21
Slabs	73
Slack-burnt charcoal	8
Slips	10
Slope reel	25
Smokeless powders	95
Sodium iodate	14
,, nitrate	14
,, picrate	112
Sobrero	77
"Soluble"	63
Solubility of picric acid	110
Specific heat	2
Speed of charring	9
Stassputt salt	14
Steam	2
Stoving	28, 30
,, or drying	25
Straw	7
Stuff-chest	72
Sugar	7
Sulphur, allotropic modification of	12
,, boiling point of	12
,, dioxide	2
,, flowers of	12
,, grough	12
,, Melting point of	11
,, physical changes of	11
,, refining of	12
,, ,, apparatus	12
Superheated steam, charring by	11
,, water	6

T

TARTAGLIA	52
Test, hygometric	34
Testing of refined sulphur	13
Tetra-nitro benzene	109
Thompson and Nathan	74
Tri-nitro benzene	109
,, toluene	114
Turpin's omelinite	113

U

UREA	55, 114

V

	Page.
VASELINE	100
Velocity, muzzle	35
Vielle	63
Violette	11
Von Lenk	58

W

WALTHAM Abbey charcoal	9
Washing	84
,, tank	84
Water, superheated	6
Willow (salix-alba)	8
Wood	7
,, from charcoal	10
,, spirit	55
Wool	7

X

XYLENOL	114
Xyloïdine	57

www.ingramcontent.com/pod-product-compliance
Lightning Source LLC
Chambersburg PA
CBHW080322170426
43193CB00017B/2878